# OUT OF THE DEPTHS

# OUT OF THE DEPTHS

The Story of a Priest-Patient
in a Mental Hospital
by *William J. Collins, c.s.s.*

1971
*Doubleday & Company, Inc.*
GARDEN CITY, NEW YORK

*Faith plants the seeds of the future,*
*Hope nourishes them,*
*and Love brings them to full growth.*
*These are three things at the very*
*heart of life,*
*three things that last.*

Eugene C. Kennedy
(from *The People Are the Church*)

# CONTENTS

# FOREWORD

THIS is a poignant description of the ordeal of a dedicated young priest who laboriously and painfully worked his way "out of the depths" of a serious emotional illness. The book is written at the urging of friends, coupled with a desire on the part of the writer to share with others the inner workings of a *via dolorosa* and the things he learned about himself in therapy.

For a long time before "the break" came, he, like hundreds of thousands of other people, had been leading a life of "quiet desperation," but he, more fortunate than others and though reluctant, was willing to seek help and accept advice even though it eventuated in an admission to a mental hospital.

The author, obviously an idealistic and zealous man and anxious to do a good job, had sought solace and help from colleagues and friends in his own milieu. Although most were sympathetic it was obvious that the illness was beyond their understanding, and the advice they could give was not of lasting value.

Cotton Mather, in his accounts of early New England clergymen, emphasized the depressive emotional storms through which many of them passed. Although he mentions a few in particular, there must have been a large number around, for he is said to have become more famous for his "wise and fit management of wounded spirits" than for his preaching and ministerial abilities. Some of the men he names were famous indeed, and one of them founded the city in which Father Collins was hospitalized.

Of course, in the spirit of the times, Mather saw in these illnesses the workings of an evil influence. Unfortunately, some of that outlook is still around among the unknowing; to some these illnesses still have moral connotations. Those who think this way apparently have forgotten the outlook of the Pharisees; the philosophy that underlies the belief of these moderns is "Lord,

if he were only like me this would not have happened to him."
Not too strangely, many of those inclined to think this way
have a few ill-concealed problems of their own.

It did take courage to write this book. So many people see a
sharp dividing line between mental illness and mental health—
the person is either one or the other. This line does not exist.
It is in the gray areas, the demilitarized zones, if you will, in
which much of the drama of emotional distress is played. The
author states that he writes for the "emotionally crippled silent
majority," and he wonders about the critical comment that
might follow upon this exposition of the depth of his misery.
Actually he should have no fear. It was brave of him to walk
the path that he followed, and although there will be comment,
of course, some of it will come from people who might themselves
benefit from a little therapy.

There is no doubt about the depth of suffering of this good
man as he stayed on the job and assuaged what he could of his
anxiety with an extra dash of hard work. There are thousands
following the same path as they labor in the workaday world.
Early, as Father Collins sought assistance, he met with varied
reactions. Some superiors were not too understanding, and on
his mission he ran into one or more of the old "knuckle-duster"
type of clergymen who unconsciously were working out their
own problems by means of rudeness to others. Fortunately,
the ranks of this type of clergymen are thinning, and as the
older representatives pass on to their celestial reward one can
only hope that they are not put in charge of anyone.

The details of his learning process as he worked with his
therapist in the hospital are most interesting. They need not be
detailed here. However, in that the events took place several
years ago, one must allow for the necessity of change and perhaps some distortion as the author recalls the conversations with
his doctor—there are probably some wide interpretations in the
way in which he remembers them. None of us has total recall,
and no patient can ever quote his doctor verbatim. Often the
doctor tries to say one thing while the patient sees it as another
thing.

He came to recognize how his life had been an unending

search for approval—a throwback to his childhood, in which he unsuccessfully sought the approval of his father. His father was a good man, but one who like many men today believed that by giving his children material things he was discharging his duty. Mother was in charge of the family, and, apparently, no one recognized what an interested father who can serve as an example means to a boy.

The author learned of the quiet rage that simmers in a man unable to give vent to his anger or express his real feelings. He saw how anger and hostility can boil beneath an ostensibly quiet and polite exterior. Anger is not a bad thing, but it can become bad when one cannot cope with it. Depression, the diagnosis made most frequently today, is inner-directed anger and hostility, according to the tenets of modern dynamic psychiatry.

The details of the hospitalization and treatment, the frustrations, the anger, the small joys, and the interpersonal reactions that take place in an institution all are fairly set forth; even his sojourn in a disturbed unit is described in detail. He had an interesting interlude while on the road to recovery when, as part of his therapy, he was allowed to work in the stock room of a large department store. Here he saw and experienced the joys and sorrows of workers in everyday life. By that experience he says he touched a part of life that he otherwise would not have known or understood. It was a valuable experience and one that every professional man should have, lest in his own little world he forget the problems that beset another segment of life.

As he slowly and painfully made progress in understanding himself, the author's phobic reactions disappeared and his cruel perfectionism came under control. He saw that he could stand failures even in living life as it is and that despite obstacles that might appear he could faithfully perform his priestly tasks. He counted his therapy as a blessing, and in retrospect saw his sojourn in the hospital as "next to Holy Orders the greatest blessing of his life."

Interestingly, as he thinks back over the years he wonders about those among the clergy, the religious, and the married couples, who once made a willing and sincere commitment by which they dutifully lived for many years and who now have abrogated their contracts. They give apparently justifiable reasons for this—they are against structure, restrictions, incompatibility, establishments, systems, authoritarianism, etc. He wonders whether or not the real underlying and unrecognized causes are not unresolved emotional conflicts, and whether too they might have been helped before uncommitting themselves by intensive spiritual and emotional therapy. His interests are genuine, his comments are not snide; he sees in many situations hidden and unresolved inner conflict precipitated by an "unstable society and a restless church."

Throughout his illness and recovery the author remained faithful to his calling—he was a good priest. Like the psalmist he believed "even when he was greatly afflicted." His answer to a lady whom he met in his hospital stay was interesting. She said: "You poor priests; if only you were allowed to marry you would not be in a place like this." He replied (not too kindly): "My good woman, I'm afraid marriage did not keep you out."

I recommend this book highly. It is timely and it is well done. It has a great deal to say to clergymen who, like physicians and others, are presently undergoing identity conflicts in a rapidly changing, disturbed world. Its message just might be of help to others.

Francis J. Braceland, M.D.
*Psychiatrist-in-Chief,*
*Institute of Living, 1951–65*
*Editor,* American Journal of Pyschiatry

# AUTHOR'S PREFACE

THESE pages tell the story of that period of my life while undergoing treatment as an emotionally disturbed person at a mental hospital. The writing of it has been an arduous task and one that I was unwilling to attempt until almost forced to do so by the continual requests of many friends, clients, professional acquaintances, and others who, having learned of and benefited by the many helpful insights that I gained through therapy, have urged me to reach out and offer some sort of help to that multitude of other mental sufferers by recording and publishing these hospital experiences.

The decision to write, finally, was based on the conviction that the curative insights that I had received in therapy were not given to me to retain for myself, alone, but actually were intended for the many others who, somewhere, sometime, might be in desperate need of them. A merely person-to-person help, I decided, was not enough. There was that silent majority of people who were living lives of quiet desperation. They, and others also, had a right to whatever help I might be able to give.

This self-revelation is a risk. It is a far, far greater risk than the one whereby I dared to expose my hidden self to my doctor. All of that exposure, up to this moment, has been a well-kept secret between him and me.

Now, in presenting many of these, my human fears and failings, to the general public, I stand exposed and defenseless before the "slings and arrows" of perhaps a multitude of critical comment. But if only one emotionally disturbed person (and there may be many more than one) is helped, relieved, encouraged, then I am willing to take the risk, and am happy to have had the courage to write of my therapeutic experiences out of a concern for that legion of misunderstood and oft-times despised emotionally crippled silent majority.

The conversations as recorded herein are not always, of course, verbatim. But they do contain essentially the substance of what was said, especially those observations of "Dr. Mack," who has reviewed the transcript. Concerning other conversations, I have had to depend on memory and on the several notes I made during hospitalization.

The first few chapters may appear to contain an over-burdening pessimism, agony, and hopelessness. But that's the way it was; and that's the way it is for many mental patients. "You have to get worse before you get better" is a truism for many of us who have had to go through a therapeutic treatment. In the latter chapters, however, there begins to emerge an ever-increasing hope, confidence, courage, and a solid contentment. Not only have these feelings remained with me during these past several years, but they have grown deeper and wider and will, I feel sure, continue to do so. Every challenge faced, every risk taken despite the danger of adverse results, every failure accepted without loss of equilibrium, is representative of growth in emotional maturity. It is what I had hoped and prayed for. It is what I have received.

Naturally, this book is not meant to be a key for everyone's anxiety conflicts and emotional problems. It is simply the story of one man's agonizing enigma and how he found a solution to it with the help of many others, especially Dr. Mack. In the telling of the story, however, I do trust that it will, at least, offer some sort of "hope for the hopeless" and be an encouragement to seek help for those who suspect that they need assistance.

The names of fellow patients mentioned herein are, of course, fictitious. I owe them not only that privacy but also I am indebted to them for their many kindnesses to me and for the countless invaluable lessons I absorbed through their companionship.

# CHAPTER I

# SPRINGFIELD

## *Phantom Fears*

---

*"But day doth daily draw my sorrows longer,*
*And night doth nightly make grief's length seem stronger."*
—Shakespeare, *Sonnet 28*

EACH day seemed to become a little more difficult and a little less hopeful than its predecessors. The horizon of my future, as I often tried to envision it, contained more threatening clouds than I cared to contemplate. Here I was, over twenty years in the priesthood and at an age when a wide variety of sacerdotal experience should have established a feeling of confidence in my ability to undertake just about any priestly activity. Instead of an easy familiarity, however, I was undergoing a painful and growing tension and an unaccountable distress in the performance of certain simple public functions, activities that I had discharged for years with hardly a second thought. Now I felt intimidated, uncertain, nervous. What was going on?

With a relatively large amount of theoretical knowledge of psychology, gained over the years through readings, lectures, and classes on the human emotions, I strongly suspected that I needed professional help, but dreaded taking that necessary step. Somehow it seemed to be a fearful risk. Besides, it would represent a definite admission of failure, of incompetence, of inadequacy. The fear of making such a decision, however, only added to the gradually mounting tension that now featured my days and nights. But something drastic had to be done. I could not go on like this.

Some few years before, while engaged in preaching retreats and parish missions, I had the very good fortune to live with and, periodically, to sit under Adrian van Kaam, Ph.D., who was engaged as an interim professor of Psychology at Brandeis University in Waltham, Massachusetts. A native of Holland and a victim of Nazi imprisonment during World War II, Father van Kaam had brought to this country a type of Christian existentialism that aroused considerable interest in the fields of philosophy and psychology in America. His personalist approach to the human condition had a profound effect on my spiritual and religious life and on my preaching and counseling activities. Perceptive, incisive, and humorous, he gave to his classes not only an extensive erudition derived from philosophy, psychology, and theology, but he emanated a personal kindliness and concern for the individual and for humanity that could not but evoke a spontaneous and constructive response from his students. By far the most popular course on campus, the original student attendance grew from a normal thirty-five to over 125 before the year ended.

More rewarding than the classes, however, were the informal and informative chats I had with him, the smorgasbord dinners, the trips to Cape Cod, the pizza lunches. In these conversations with Father Adrian, I knew that I was looking for a solution to my own problems that were not inconsiderable even at that time. But, of course, I could not approach him outright. I could not endure the shame and embarrassment of admitting to him that I needed help, that I had problems, that I was one of those unfortunate victims of emotional conflicts. A statement, however, that he had made in class one day and upon which I had often pondered as I paced the parqueted floor of my room, gradually began to undermine my resistance to seeking therapeutic assistance.

"Everyone could use therapy," he said, "everyone in this classroom, including myself. Some people, of course, need it more than others. Some need it in order to be able to function comfortably in life. But even those who are what we call normal and reasonably content could also use therapy. And this is because even the normal person has a rich and untapped potential of creative, productive, and joyful living within him. He simply does not know that it is there, nor how to use it. Therapy would release it for him and for the world in which he lives and influence the lives of others."

On the many occasions when I paced restlessly or stared out of my window at the nearby, broad-flowing Connecticut River, I would often reflect on this thought in particular and on the many other valuable insights he had transmitted to me in and out of class. How I had wanted to speak to him of my own hidden anxieties. Especially, I had wanted to discuss the possible causes of my first breakdown, which had taken place over twenty years before. It had happened just a few months before my class was due to receive Holy Orders. How clearly I could recall now the time and circumstances . . .

*It had happened so suddenly and unexpectedly. Right after the celebration of our director's birthday, in fact. There had been the usual songs and jokes and the especially good food, which always featured the big feast days in our community or the birthday of some member of the faculty. The festivities concluded, I made my way to the chapel, as was the custom in the seminary, in order to say a prayer of thanksgiving or to indulge in private devotion.*

*Then it struck me! Without any apparent cause or warning, I was suddenly seized with an acute anxiety and an indescribable sense of fear as I walked along the polished marble corridor. Everything admirable and beautiful now seemed so strange, almost threatening; the delicately wainscoted walls, the black and white marble slabs that made up the floor of the hallway, the dull-gleaming chandeliers, the shaft of sunshine that drifted through the white-curtained front doors. Confusion became anxiety. I felt isolated and at an extreme distance from the material realities that I had known and admired for three years, and that now appeared so remote and unfriendly, familiar yet strangely alien.*

*What was happening? I knew it was not the banqueting, for*

*we had nothing alcoholic to drink. What was it? In chapel, I tried to shrug off the depressive feeling by concentrating on Him, the True Presence, and by reverting to the consoling little prayer: "Come, Holy Ghost, Creator blest; and in my heart take up Thy rest. . . ." It had always been a source of strength and a definitive answer to me on those few occasions when I had wondered if I were really called to Holy Orders.*

*But now the prayer was useless. It did not dissolve the growing anxiety. I could not help but wonder if this were God's way of telling me that I was not really called to the priestly life . . . even though for ten long years of difficult training and persistent study I had no other desire but to serve Him and His people as a priest in this Congregation. The thought persisted because no other plausible explanation appeared. And with it, my agitation grew apace. I could pray no longer, and hastily left the chapel to walk around the seminary grounds.*

*An early spring had made the lawns a carpet of bright, new greenery; the trees were early-budding and some displayed wispy, virgin leaves; the majestic fir and hemlock were tinged with a bit of indigo; the arbor vitae hedges were neatly trimmed and lined the crushed-stone walks and roadways; a few white clouds drifted errantly against an azure blue sky. All of this beauty, which I had so much enjoyed in the past, should have been delightful and relaxing. It was not. Again, as in the building, everything seemed strange, foreign, ulterior, and pigmented with some sort of secret foreboding. Everything inanimate appeared to be saying something to me . . . something I did not want to hear or to think upon.*

*For a half-hour or so I walked by myself. I dared not join the other seminarians lest they notice my strangeness or distress. Besides, the dreadful, unwanted thought kept occurring: "This could be God's way of telling me to leave the seminary." But I did not want to leave the seminary. It was my deliberate choice, and the priesthood was my life's hope. And yet, this feeling . . . ? Perspiring despite the cool air, I wrestled against the unwanted thought and its myriad attendant feelings. God surely did not act this way. He did not give an ardent desire to serve*

Him for ten years and then suddenly reverse His will. And yet, how could I be sure? Absolutely sure? God is mystery. His will is not always crystal clear. At times, especially in difficulties, He wants us to grow in humility by opening ourselves to others, and by this "opening" to grow in trust and in faith. Others. Yes. I would have to speak to some priest about all this. But here, too, was a difficulty. You were not supposed to have this kind of doubt in the seminary, at least not in the senior class and as a subdeacon wherein, presumably, your doubts and difficulties were all behind you. Perhaps a little more time and thought and prayer would resolve the problem. Yes, I would delay awhile. Perhaps the feeling would leave, or dissolve itself if I applied more faith and trust.

For a week or ten days I grappled with the problem by myself, intensifying prayer and meditation, while trying cautiously to keep others from gaining any suspicion of my gnawing inner conflict. Classes became increasingly difficult to follow, and concentration on study was almost impossible. I could eat but little food and the long, sleepless nights were tortured by a stomach that seemed intent on digesting itself. Prayer life, eventually, was reduced in essence to a repetition of: "I want you, O my God, but do You want me?"; for by now, this seemed to be the real crux of the whole tragic situation: "Do you have a vocation, Bill? If so, how do you really know? And how do you explain this strange and persistent anxiety?"

Finally, exhausted physically and mentally, and perhaps beginning to show the strains of my struggle in various subtle ways to my seminarian companions, I selected one of the younger and more understanding priests on the faculty and haltingly stated my dilemma to him. His answer came readily enough and, for a few minutes as he talked, I felt relief and hope.

"It's only a temptation," he said, flatly and firmly. "Such thoughts are almost bound to happen, especially when you are so close to ordination. Forget the whole thing. Shrug it off!"

But I could not "shrug it off," for the anxiety arose again almost as soon as I left his room, and it remained with me just as strongly for the rest of the day and during the night. Ashamed to return to him again the next day, I sought out another, older priest. He was more interested and concerned, questioning me rather lightly on vows, community life, and so forth. His final judgment, although somewhat helpful, did not dissolve my depression or fears.

"Well, Bill," he said. "The faculty here has a good impression of you, and if, as you say, you really do want to be a priest, I can't think of anything else to say but 'go ahead.' However, it occurs to me that this feeling might be something physical. So why not ask the director for permission to have a complete checkup? Also, I might suggest that you see Father Bernard, who has been your spiritual director for the past three years. He knows you well and you seem to have a lot of confidence in him."

Both of these suggestions made sense and did arouse a sort of hope that the answer to my depressive feelings might be found in some unsuspected physical ailment, although I doubted it. The other suggestion seemed better because I had much confidence in my old spiritual director, who also had been my professor in moral theology. I greatly admired his scholarship and his priestliness. Now, however, he was pastor of a parish some twenty miles distant. I wanted to see him, but a dilemma arose in following either of these suggestions because I would have to see the director and inform him of my emotional depression and vocational doubts. Our relationship was strained, at best. On several occasions he had publicly singled me out and berated me for some real or imagined minor violation of seminary rules and regulations. Two or three times I had gone to his room to explain myself and to attempt to better our relationship, but had been further accused and berated. After that, I lived in fear of him and stayed out of his way as much as possible. I was not the only one who felt and acted this way.

His whole attitude, especially toward our class, was one of demanding and domineering rigidity, intermixed with scorn, ridicule, and lengthy, public chidings that were both repetitious and threatening. He was a child among men, but he had the power to keep us from the cherished goal of the priesthood. Somehow we put up with his puerility and injustice but, as the saying goes, we were "running scared."

As I thought of all this, I wondered what he would do with the necessary revelation of my depression which, as far as I could see, was related to my vocation. He could easily use this information to decide that I should leave the seminary. I feared seeing him, but now I was forced to do so.

Surprisingly, the director showed a remote kindness when I related to him my state of mind the next morning. He was most amenable to the suggestion that I see Father Bernard, and even offered to phone for an evening appointment which, fortunately, he arranged within the next few minutes.

Father Bernard listened intently to my story in detail. I concluded by summing up my feelings in the words that had so often occurred to me in recent days: "It seems to me, Father, that I am continually saying to myself: 'I want You, God, but do You want me?'"

After thinking deeply for some few minutes, Father Bernard began a thorough examination of my motives, desires, and vows, especially chastity and the married life; what I expected to give and to receive from the community; why I really wanted to be a priest; the occasions surrounding the minute doubts that had occasionally appeared during my seminary years. He literally turned me inside out. I felt that there was nothing of importance that he did not know about me. While he thought, rubbing his eyes after he had removed his glasses, I knew that he knew me better than I knew myself. I was content. I had been absolutely honest. And now I was ready to accept his decision as being the mysterious will of God. I had given all of myself to this man and awaited his decision, unafraid of its consequences.

Father Bernard's face reflected nothing, and he assumed a noncommittal silence for some long moments. Possibly he was praying for light and guidance. My own prayer was one of ready acceptance. Finally, putting on his glasses, he looked at me squarely and pronounced himself.

"Billy," he said, "I am not Almighty God, but I do know you. I know you very well. There is no doubt at all in my mind that God wants you for the priesthood. I can find nothing at all that would indicate you should leave the seminary. It is my *considered and prayerful judgment that you should go on to ordination in spite of your feelings."*

*The relief I felt, the suddenly resurgent hope that engulfed me was almost too much to bear. For better or worse, I had disposed myself completely to the will of God. And here, in this unexpectedly joyful decision, it was firmly announced. I was going to have my heart's desire—the priesthood!*

*"Now," he said, anticipating my physical needs, "after what you have been through these past two weeks, you must be a little bit hungry. How about having dinner with me?" I was ravenously hungry and eagerly accepted his invitation. Never had food tasted so good. Never had life seemed so full of promise and rosy with hope.*

*The drive home was sheer delight, for a few miles. Strangely enough, however, the closer I came to the seminary, the old anxiety and fear began to revive. By the time I had entered the driveway and parked the car, I was as emotionally depressed as at any time prior to seeing Father Bernard. I sat there trying to figure out this strange phenomenon, this incomprehensible transition from sunlight and joy to the enveloping darkness of trepidation and depression. What had happened? I could not understand it. Desperately, I recalled the firm and reassuring words of Father Bernard; but now they had little effect on the panicky feelings that seemed to engulf me. Even a prolonged visit to the chapel, and a desperate plea for relief, failed to dispel the feeling of impending disaster. More dispirited than ever, I retired to my room through the dim, silent halls and stairways of the seminary, and tossed restlessly on my bed in a long, sleepless, and tormented night.*

*In the morning, knowing that something else had to be done, if anything possibly could be done, I went reluctantly to the director, telling him of Father Bernard's unconditional approval of me, my happy feelings on the way back from the parish, and then the inexplainable depression that seized me upon my return to the seminary, which feeling, I added, had not dissipated through the night nor had it diminished during meditation and prayer during the morning.*

*The director nodded reflectively, then said that he knew a priest nearby who had been a psychiatrist prior to ordination. Perhaps he might be of some help. If I wished, we could visit him that evening. It was a new approach, although I had little hope that a psychiatrist could help. That science, such as I understood it, dealt with hidden, unexpressed desires and unresolved frustrations. As far as I could understand myself, I had none of these except that major desire to be a priest and which, seemingly and mysteriously, was being denied to me. But I acceded to the suggestion. There was nothing else to do. And it did offer a little bit of hope. Perhaps some emotional frustration was short-circuiting my spiritual aspirations.*

*The pastor listened impassively and evaluated me impersonally, it seemed, from behind heavy, horn-rimmed glasses with his slate-gray eyes, all the while twirling a pencil endlessly between thumb and forefingers of his soft, nicely manicured hands. He seemed unimpressed, remote, unconcerned. Ill-at-ease and perspiring slightly, I sensed a lack of warmth and real human interest in my difficult situation. I had expected someone entirely different, someone who, as a psychiatrist, would try to collect as much information as possible by various forms of questions that would probe into my past, close and distant, a professional who would want to know deeper feelings, who would want to collect and assemble as much as he could of the various fragments of my life, and then attempt to suggest some areas of research on my own part. He did none of these things. He twirled his pencil, swiveled constantly—and stared impassively. Finally, his decision, if it could be called such, came in the form of a disconcerting and jarring question.*

*"Well, son," he boomed out, "you can't solve your problems very well by running away from them, can you?"*

*The confusing question stunned me. It was so unexpected, unsupported, and unprofessional. If I had problems that I didn't know of, I had come to him to indicate and clarify them. His implication of my being a fugitive from the facts of life added to my bewilderment and anxiety. I could only stare at him, speechless. Then everything in the room shimmered and shook while I* blinked my eyes rapidly to regain control of quivering vision. Vainly, I awaited some other observations, comments, suggestions. But nothing more was forthcoming. I arose, stood silently, hopefully for a moment, then thanked him and left the office.

The director was silent on the way home. Vaguely, I wondered if he had sort of "prepped" the pastor and by so doing had precluded any therapeutic process, any human concern for my situation. I was depressed, but I was also angry. If this was psychiatry, then it was for the birds. It would help them more than it could help a distressed human being. Another hope was shattered. What was next? The night was another in a continuing series of tossing, tormented nocturnal anxieties.

The "next" thing was an announcement by the director in the morning that I was to take time off for a while. He had been on the phone with the Provincial and I was to be assigned to Lynn at one of our parish houses some forty miles distant. I could rest up there, he told me, help out with religious instruction of the youngsters, think things over at my leisure, take advantage of the nearby beach, and perhaps get some help from a good spiritual adviser. "This is it," I thought, as I hurriedly packed my few belongings. "The slow beginning of a long end."

My four and more months of Lynn were a quandary of hope and nonhope. The community there, about five priests, was more than kind to me and were happy to have my assistance. But, of course, I could not confide in them. I merely indicated obliquely that I had to take some time off for reasons of health.

Fortunately, on one of my Boston visits to a Passionist monastery, I found a very good spiritual director, a Father Theodore, whom I saw regularly every week. I felt at ease with him and, in a few visits, filled him in on just about every aspect of my life, spiritual and otherwise. As with Father Bernard, his continual advice was that, eventually, I should proceed to the priesthood when my superiors saw fit to advise it. Meanwhile, I busied myself with various parish activities, such as my limited status would allow, and prayed for a clear indication of God's will with regard to ordination. My prayer life became intense and was dominated by the continual refrain: "I want you, O my God, but do You want me?" Just what sort of clear answer I wanted, I do not know, except perhaps the sudden lifting of the anxiety and dread that still followed me, though at a more remote distance than while I was at the seminary.

In early June, my Provincial, who had been traveling considerably and was unable to visit me, arrived at the parish one day and conversed with me at some length about my feelings. He was a kindly man and listened intently to all that I had to say, all that I had already told my various other confessors and spiritual directors. He was also a very brusque individual and, after listening patiently for some time, announced that if I were still willing to be a priest, then I could proceed to ordination the next month. His councilors, he said, were all in favor of me and he had received a very favorable letter from Father Theodore, my Passionist confessor.

In his straightforward manner and blunt honesty, he said: "You're a good lad, Billy, and we are all sure that you will be a good priest. You're just scared, that's all. You need a good push. Once over the hump, you'll feel much better. And you can help so many people. How about it? Do you want to take a chance with the goodness and the love of God?"

Put this way, and with all other priest-consultors urging me on, it seemed as though this was the final possible expression of the divine will, almost the equivalent of a demand from God that I trust in Him with an unconditional trust. With considerable relief, tinged with no little trepidation, I consented, and was told that ordination, with a time dispensation between diaconate and ordination, would take place on the sixteenth of July.

On that feast of Our Lady of Mount Carmel at the Sacred Heart Church, Newton, Massachusetts, I was raised to Holy Orders at the hands of the then Bishop Cushing, Auxiliary to Cardinal O'Connell of Boston, before a church filled with friends and confreres and my family sitting proudly, but self-consciously, in the front pews. The long ceremony of ordination was no easy or gloriously joyful event for me. I knew, as I kept saying to myself during the event, that I was doing the right thing, the thing

*I wanted to do, the thing that God wanted me to do—and I was quietly content with the tremendous and meaningful ceremony that was conferring a magnificent dignity upon me, but the emotional exaltation that I had secretly been hoping for was lacking. Continually, during the lengthy ritual, I reminded myself that I must trust God completely, that He wanted me to make this naked act of trust in His name and for the countless people He would present to me for priestly service in the years to come. To help and serve people in His name! What a supreme privilege! What a sublime gift! And now it was mine! Forever!*

*Once the holy rite was over and I gave my first priestly blessing to the kneeling Bishop Cushing, I did begin to feel something of the emotional joy every priest talks about. Stronger still was the warm glow of fervent gratitude as I passed along the altar rail, blessing family, friends, and relatives. The Provincial was right. I was now "over the hump." I was irretrievably and happily "one with Christ" through the sacrament of Holy Orders.*

*After ordination, things had gone comparatively well. I was assigned to teach at our Juniorate on the high school level. I enjoyed both the challenge of teaching and the pleasant companionship of a community made up of about ten priests, all of whom made life as pleasant as possible for me. But there were two or three things that began to characterize my activities, and would continue to dominate my life attitudes and self-image. I began to delve into the mystics and to read extensively on matters pertaining to the spiritual life. Since God had called me, I must respond by learning as much of Him as I could and therefore become that "ideal" priest that training and retreat masters had reiterated and emphasized. And so I must study and learn how to be that particular kind of priest. Then, too, my assigned work became a "must." I had to be certain to fulfill the various community chores given to me; and I must have well-prepared classes. By the same token, I must not fritter away my time by unnecessary recreation with the other priests, or take time off for relaxation when there was so much work to be done. "To work is to pray," said the monks throughout the ages. This would become my life's attitude. I was supposed to become a holy priest, was I not? This then—work—was one of the necessary means to that end.*

"Everyone could use therapy . . . including myself," said Dr. van Kaam, ". . . even those who are what we call normal . . ." I mused on the words, deeply, frequently. If a professor of psychology could say such a thing about therapy, how much more was I in need of professional help. True, I had been able to function normally for over twenty years. But it was also true that I had experienced often that free-floating anxiety of which psychiatry speaks and which, according to its scientific findings, represents hidden and unresolved conflicts, unrecognized hostilities, and perhaps some fearful traumatic experiences originating in childhood. He had said that "therapy could bring about creative, productive, and joyful living." And right now I knew that I was not joyful, that something fearful and threatening was closing in upon me day after day, encroaching upon my sleep, and subtly but consistently interfering with my work.

On those many restless occasions when I paced the polished oak floor of my room or stared out at the placid Connecticut River, I would envision the embarrassing scene wherein I would be asking my superior if I could see a psychiatrist. I would have to admit that, despite my years of conscientious work and the placid exterior of a normal priest, comfortable and capable in my calling, I was, in reality, a failure. I had an emotional problem and would need professional help. What would he say? What would he think? What would be the eventual consequences? I did not know. But I did know that therapy offered some kind of hope. And there seemed to be no other avenue of escape from the depression, the loneliness, the uncertainty that had grown more unmanageable with the passing years until now it had become *the* major concern of my life—and my future. I felt cornered. The only possible escape was to see a psychiatrist. I would ask permission to do so.

Pride and shame were still strong within me, however, and I can still vividly recall the hot flush of embarrassment that must have suffused my countenance when finally, with a faint and sickly feeling, I muttered the request to my superior, who was also Provincial at the time.

"Father," I said in a hardly audible voice and avoiding his glance, "I think I should see a psychiatrist."

"Sure, Bill," he answered, amiably, almost matter-of-factly. "Go right ahead and make arrangements." There was kindness and understanding here and no questions asked, for which I was most grateful. However, I felt that some sort of explanation was necessary and lamely began to tell him that I didn't feel well and had not for quite some time, and thought a psychiatrist might be able to help. He waved off the explanations, saying: "You know how you feel and what you need. Go right ahead and don't feel ashamed about it."

This reaction on the part of the Provincial was a relief, a great relief, and immediately I began to feel better about seeing a psychiatrist.

It was with mixed feelings of fear and hope that I sought out a local psychiatrist, a Dr. Daniels. I selected him because I thought our similar religious training and culture would make it much easier to discuss various areas of religion if it became necessary to do so. At our first meeting I presented him with my apparent problems and, with his patient and interested listening, I was encouraged to talk with an openness and confidence that I had never experienced before in my life.

It was not long before the doctor began to show an interest in my early life, childhood and adolescent experiences, relationships with parents and other personalities, attitudes toward authoritarian figures, the fearful as well as the happy occasions of the almost forgotten past. It was with great difficulty and reluctance that I would recall and try to verbalize certain anxious and hostile feelings that I thought had been wiped away with the passage of time. In describing my father as distant, scolding, rigid, demanding, and unloving, I experienced feelings of guilt and disloyalty and, therefore, a depression. Dad had died of a long, lingering illness when I was fourteen. And now, in response to the doctor's gentle inquisition, it seemed so evil and malicious to speak ill of the dead, of one who had brought me into the world and worked so hard to feed and educate me, who had labored beyond his strength to provide for his five children during the tragic Depression years of the late twenties and early thirties. Haltingly, and with a deep sense of being ungrateful and selfish, I tried to describe this father-attitude of my childhood and adolescent years. At times I was speechless, although many other hostile thoughts were teeming within me. Again, when the doctor's queries threatened to open up other embarrassing or guilt-producing feelings, I would talk easily and freely about irrelevant topics that were less threatening and fearsome.

As a result of these revelations and several other self-discoveries, certain very strong and negative attitudes came into focus and I began, dimly at least, to perceive some of the troublesome areas that would need considerable attention. Unfortunately and foolishly, I insisted on maintaining all of my various duties without letup. As a Provincial councilor, I had to attend frequent and often exhausting meetings while trying vainly to shelve temporarily the persistent anxiety that therapy had increased rather than diminished. Often I would have to break appointments with the doctor in order to investigate and report on difficult personnel situations, supervise programs of studies in our various houses of training, and record and balance, as Provincial treasurer, the monthly accounts of some thirty or more financial operations.

My "side" jobs were much more demanding, as I had a rather full schedule of preaching missions and retreats. I loved this work and continually was trying to improve upon it. But always there was the thought of the loaded desk back at the office and the subtle, ever-present to some degree, anxiety and depression, the restless nights, the "must" labors of the day, and the "should" works for which I never seemed to have time or energy.

This exhausting workload, although I did not think of it as such at the time (in fact, I often accused myself of not doing enough), was maintained during the many months when I was supposed to be receiving helpful therapy. As a result, I would see the doctor intermittently, squeezing in an appointment between preaching tours and other assignments, all of which I thought I *must* carry on. To use the term of another writer on the subject, I became a "workaholic," addicted to external activity in order to avoid, possibly, the unpleasantness that a session with the doctor might reveal. Understandably, therefore, the irregularity of these sessions resulted in a forgetfulness of material covered in previous interviews and a failure on my part to do any follow-up thinking. Because of this and the lack of immediate beneficial therapeutic results, it was only natural that tension and anxiety grew stronger. Gradually I became more depressed, restless, guilty, and lonely.

To combat these moods, about which I complained to the doctor and which must have been quite evident to him, I received several different prescriptions for pills at various times. Some were for sleep, which was becoming more and more of a problem. Others were to alleviate the morning-after sleeping pill hangover. Some were mood-lifters and were intended for those very trying situations in which I might find myself more than ordinarily disturbed, a condition that began to crop up more frequently during the latter part of our therapy sessions and that intensified considerably when phobic fears threatened to expose me as being inadequate or visibly nervous at certain public and formal events. The pills helped to relax me on these occasions, but I knew that they were not the answer to my condition. They were only treating the symptoms. They were not reaching the roots of my conflicts and fears.

However, except for the sleeping pills, which had become a nightly *must,* I could and often did go for several days at a time without using any of the other tranquilizers and mood-lifters. I kept telling myself that I did not want to become an addict and would use this abstinence method to prove it. It was a deceptive proof, however, because when I would hit the turbulence of an emotional air-pocket I would reach for the pills, and might even increase the recommended dosage. If this did not serve to allay the anxiety sufficiently, I would try certain combinations of the various capsules at hand. This, I knew, was only a superficial and temporary solution. It was not a real solution to my emotional problems and added a sense of guilt to my other conflicts. Fear also entered because I was aware that drug taking was a perilous business.

Oddly enough, on these occasions I would recall frequently a quotation from Hippocrates that had appeared on the frontispiece of *Experiment Perilous*, a mystery story I had read years ago. I had forgotten the story but well remembered the old Greek's wisdom and warning:

*Life is short and art is long;*
*Occasion instant,*
*Decision difficult,*
*Experiment perilous!*

At what particular point I entered the "experiment perilous" phase of drug taking, I do not know. This is a hidden but ever-present trap for the drug-using emotionally disturbed person. Anxiety and fear can subtly distort a clear reasoning mind and artfully prompt an unconscionable action. Rationalization, always helpfully at hand for the fear-ridden, undoubtedly eased the way for me to make the "decision difficult." I would ask myself, without ever wanting the honest answer: "What else but these pills is going to allow me to carry on my work? This is my assigned task. It is expected that I do a good job. Nothing else can control this fearful and inhibiting anxiety that so constantly threatens my good name and productiveness." The neurotic is at his best when deceiving himself.

This rationalizing on my part also promoted the appearance and burden of a new guilt, that of being dishonest, for I was not telling Dr. Daniels about the misuse of his prescriptions. But how could I tell him? He might well cut off the only means that seemed to assure me of continuing to be that willing, working, producing self that I *must* be—at all costs. Eventually, the cost was to be heavy—and agonizing.

Rationalizations, therefore, aside from temporary relief, only added to the over-all strain of daily living, since they were leading to a dead-end and had added the guilt of dishonesty. Increasingly, therefore, I saw myself as a little bit less worthwhile and a little bit more of a failure.

To escape this lowering self-esteem and its pain, I read

extensively of the many books on psychology and psychiatry with which I had attempted for years to fortify myself and to find the hidden door that would suddenly open upon the confidence and joy I so intensely sought. But there were no pat answers, no matter how many books I read or pages I scanned.

Prayer life during this persistently frustrating period of my life became more intense but less and less satisfying. Prayer simply did not give relief from anxiety nor a clue as to the possible solution of my problems. I was spiritually arid and confused; confused because I could not understand why the "good" Lord did not answer me, why He allowed this inhibiting anxiety to hinder the work I wanted to do for Him. Here again, I was looking for that "pat answer," that semimiraculous, mood-lifting grace. "Ask the Father anything in my name and I will give it unto you." "Come to me all you who are burdened . . ." "Knock and it shall be opened to you." How many heartache hours I had spent before the Blessed Sacrament! Or, lest others suspect that "there's something wrong with Bill," I would retreat to the silence of my room and there search, beseech, beg for that sudden uplift of spirit.

Later on, in retrospect, and after many months of hospital therapy, I began to suspect and then became convinced that really I "had it in" for God without ever suspecting it. How else to account for the many times when I entered chapel to pray and then, after a few moments of forced concentration, would compulsively and unaccountably almost rush out and away from the object of my petitions? An unconscious "God hostility" is not uncommon among emotionally disturbed and religiously oriented people. Perhaps this is why I spent most of the little spare time allotted me in my room and among my books searching for the answer. It never came, of course.

Then I would examine my moral life to see what might be wrong in this area. I was conscious of no major offense, for I knew I loved Christ sincerely and the vows of service I had pledged to Him. Then what was wrong? I could only conclude that I did not have enough faith, enough trust. Ah, yes! This must be it! I must struggle on then, and answer a trusting, believing "Yes!" to the question posed to himself by Francis Thompson in *The Hound of Heaven:*

> *"Is my gloom after all,*
> *But shade of His Hand outstretched caressingly?"*

The "Yes" that I was able to utter gave but small and only temporary relief. I wanted neither gloom nor shade, but the sunshine of joy and peace.

Preaching and retreat work I still enjoyed but, of course, the strain of an unknown anxiety soon began to assert itself in this area, also. I was never satisfied with my sermons, counseling, or confessional advice. It seemed, to me at least, that I never really reached people, never touched them deeply with convincing hope and confidence. This feeling persisted despite the fact that many notes of thanks or words of praise would come my way during and after these preaching efforts. The good feeling that honest praise naturally brings would live only briefly and then would be submerged by an unexplainable tidal wave of anxiety, of interior worthlessness, of futility.

Toward the end of this almost two-year therapeutic period, I am sure that others in the community noticed my gradually worsening condition in spite of my best efforts to conceal stress and tension from them. Kindly, they adapted to my moods and needs, I am sure, but this generosity only served to allow me to retreat, unnoticed, I thought, from the company of persons and to wander aimlessly into the shadowy, endless caverns of a searching loneliness. An alienation was taking place here, a gradually increasing sense of isolation from self, from persons, from God. I knew it, but felt helpless to stem its growth. I knew it because regularly in retreat conferences and in sermons, in order to emphasize the great human need for healthy and trusting relationships in these three necessary areas, I would quote and comment at length on the words of Colonel Nicholson from the book *The Bridge on the River Kwai:*

> *"I sought my God, but my God eluded me.*
> *I sought my soul, but my soul I could not see.*
> *I sought my neighbor, and I found all three."*

Subconsciously, I suppose, I was telling myself that I sought all three, but that it was a fruitless and sometimes agonizing search. What I had found of myself in the much-interrupted therapeutic sessions was not only unacceptable but did nothing to clarify my problems. It was too fragmentary to be of any use. It lacked cohesion, sufficiency, continuity, and effective application. Desperately, I wanted to be "at one" with myself, with people, with God. But the "true" self, the acceptable self, if such there was, I could not see. In my fervent, sometimes frantic prayer life, my search for God always seemed to result in His eluding me. Even my best efforts in the service of people were beclouded with a sense of failure, of inadequacy.

An ambivalence, semidormant for many years and controlled only by will-power, began to emerge. The long-unresolved conflict between the hidden but dangerously potent forces of self-love and self-hate grew in intensity. It became more evident, distressingly so, in the form of a free-floating anxiety, and in sudden and inexplicable bouts of depression and frustration. The needle of my spiritual and emotional energy gauge pointed to a perilously low level. The road ahead was dark, unknown, lonely, and did not reflect even that dim, distant illumination that might indicate a service station of hope.

But I *must* keep going. I *must* hurry along. Something, something would turn up. Perhaps beyond the next bend in the road. I hoped—fervently. I trusted—blindly. And worked.

# CHAPTER II

# HALIFAX
## *Catastrophe!*

---

*"I shook the pillaring hours*
*And pulled my life upon me; grimed with smears,*
*I stand amid the dust o' the mounded years."*
    —Francis Thompson, *The Hound of Heaven*

Despite the confusion and interior disturbance produced by conscious and subconscious conflicts, I looked forward to my next retreat commitment, which was to nuns, at Halifax, Nova Scotia. For three summers in a row I had been invited to give the annual retreats to this particular congregation of nuns in other areas of the province. I had enjoyed the previous retreats and the response of the sisters. Now I had some new material, culled chiefly from the writings of Father van Kaam, whose most recent books had posed some warmly human and personalistic viewpoints on the manner and method of living a healthy and fulfilling religious life. I was most anxious to present these challenging ideas using, at times, a blackboard for purposes of illustration.

This anticipatory attitude toward preaching to nuns was a far, far cry from my early and agonizing attempts at sermonizing. In fact, my very first attempt to preach to a congregation, twenty years before, might well have been that traumatic experience that so often conditions a person for a future neurosis and any of its many possible phobic symptoms.

*It was a huge church, seating about fourteen hundred people. The talk I had prepared was comparatively brief but pretty well memorized. It was to be my first formal sermon to any congregation after the painful ordeal of my breakdown as a seminarian some few months previously. A month's vacation after ordination had helped considerably, but areas of uncertainty still existed. This, my first sermon, and to be delivered before an enormous crowd of people, aroused much of my latent anxiety. I should have written it out and simply read it to the people. But pride forbade such a procedure. No good preacher would ever resort to such a tactic. I had, instead, memorized several points after jotting them down. Speaking on them would give listeners a better appreciation of my innate convictions and would allow a spontaneity of expression that a read sermon would preclude.*

*The person of the pastor made matters worse. He was suspicious of his curates and outspokenly critical of his people, which was somewhat mitigated by a ridiculing humor. A kindly observation might sum him up as an old fuddy-duddy, as, for example, when he would usher people into benches usually with the critical remark to those already seated: "Push in! Push in! These people have paid, too, you know!" Under tousled white hair and bushy brows, his thin red nose was continually sniffing at people and things like a beagle trying to pick up a particular scent. All the while, his ill-fitting false teeth clacked away in a most irritating manner.*

*Knowing that I was newly ordained and that this was my first sermon ever, he launched into a lecture on preaching, interlaced with references to his degree from Harvard. Will he never shut up, I kept wondering and hoping, because all of his "do's" and "don'ts" were making me much more nervous and apprehensive than I had been upon arrival. Mercifully, his constant clacking and sniffing were interrupted by my various duties at other Masses, after which I tried to stay out of his sight and to concentrate on my sermon.*

*Finally, it was twelve o'clock and I paraded out with the*

altar boys for Mass and for that huge event, my sermon. For the latter, I had to come down from the altar where, with my back to the people, I had felt some form of safety, pass through the communion rail gates, march down the main aisle past a few benches, and then ascend a steep flight of winding stairs to the pulpit.

Suddenly, there I was! Alone! Spotlighted! The cynosure of thousands of eyes boring in on me from all sides. Eyes! So many of them! Examining, staring, analyzing, critical, demanding. My mouth was full of cotton and my knees trembled as I read the Sunday gospel. Then I began the introduction to my more-or-less memorized sermon. What if I forgot what came next and began to flounder for words! How awful! The rehearsed thoughts kept coming, however, and I began to grow a little more confident. Then it happened!

From somewhere in back of the church a voice began to say something. I dared not look or listen lest I forget the next thought. But the voice kept coming closer. It was coming down the middle aisle! Shaken but resolute, I kept on talking. Then, from the foot of the pulpit, the white-haired old pastor shouted up to me: "Stop! Stop! Stop! We can't hear you at the back of the church! Now, open your mouth and shout so that people can hear you five miles away!"

Confusion, shame, embarrassment, and a horrible sense of failure overwhelmed me. For a few seconds my mind was a sheer blank. I know I began speaking again, but even after I concluded my sermon, I could not recall what I said. Eyes, those thousands of eyes were upon me and witnessing my abject failure. I do remember my shameful and trembling descent from the pulpit and the monumental condemnation of the huge throng of parishioners behind me as I finished the rest of the Mass, mechanically, numbly.

This public disgrace (and I could only see it in this light) must have aroused or originated a variety of deep, subconsciously negative reverberations, especially since the agony of my recent breakdown was still fresh in mind as an unexplained

mystery. Some twenty years later, hospital therapy would indicate what they were and how their power and presence had
motivated a variety of unhealthy self-attitudes, fears, and phobias. The immediate effect of this humiliation, however, was to
cause me to look upon every Sunday sermon effort as a difficult
and sometimes fearsome chore. To a greater or lesser degree,
this attitude was to persist for the many intervening years when
I was confined to teaching, doing graduate work for a master's
degree, acting as chaplain at a state prison and later at an
army hospital, and while editing a monthly periodical for my
Congregation.

But at the same time and during all those difficult years, I had
a strong desire, almost an obsession, to be a good and effective
preacher of the gospel. I wanted intensely to be able to dis-
pense freely, easily, convincingly, all the beauty, truth, and
wisdom of the Scriptures: all the love and inspiration that ema-
nate from the human and divine person of Christ. Preaching
was something I felt I *had* to do, and to do it well. My idealized
self-image was a prominent element in such a motivation, I
now know, but there also was present an honest love for Christ
and His redemptive message, and a deep compassion and concern for His people.

If it meant hard work to be a good or even fair preacher, then
I would work at it. Accordingly, after about twelve years of
performing other priestly activities, I asked for and was allowed
to give, retreats to the laity at our newly established retreat
house. These talks were more or less informal—no great feats of
memory or pulpit dynamics were demanded. It soon became a
work I enjoyed.

Success in this area prompted me to ask for the more arduous
and demanding work of preaching missions wherein I would
have to travel from parish to parish, delivering a compact but
well-organized series of talks before large crowds. It was not
easy work, but I renewed my efforts and eventually was rewarded with a feeling of ease and familiarity in the pulpit.
Crowded churches became a welcome challenge. These people
needed me. Christ had sent me to give Him, as best I could, to

them. This was my vocation and exciting privilege. Though physically exhausting, spiritually it was most consoling and emotionally fulfilling, even exhilarating, at times, when reflection would indicate the power and beauty of grace working in and through the human condition—in and through me!

The next form of preaching was not sought, it was imposed. I was told to prepare a series of conferences for nuns. I did not want to. It meant the struggle of facing a group of listeners much more alert, perceptive, and demanding. It meant leaving the security of a work I enjoyed and facing a new threat to my restored self-image. Besides, most nuns had always intimidated me. During the formative years of my youth in grammar school, they had been the sign, symbol, voice, and fact of learning, correction, devotion, discipline, authority, punishment, obedience, "godliness," and the myriad other specters of fear and reverence that haunt and inhabit worrisome little minds and sensitive little hearts . . .

*The third grade: "Master Collins, you've been talking again. Come up here so that I can measure your mouth for a muzzle." And she did, there before the tittering class.*

*The fifth grade: "You hit that boy in front of you, Master Collins. You're going to get the ruler! Into the cloakroom!" It hurt, but the sting was nothing compared to the embarrassment of returning, shamefacedly, to a grinning class.*

*The eighth grade: "The school supervisor [and my sometime confessor] thinks you do not belong in this school!" But why? "I cannot say anything more." A deep depression set in and remained with me for several weeks thereafter.*

*Fear of failure. To fail meant a severe, chastising look, sometimes a scolding for not having studied, and then a humiliating return to one's seat amidst the deep, accusing silence of the rest of the class. "He failed. He doesn't know his religion," I could hear them all thinking.*

With the order at hand to prepare retreat sermons for nuns, I reflected how odd it was that these long-forgotten incidents and childish fears should have revived. But, I told myself, orders are orders; besides, I have grown up now and have had the experience of success in retreat and mission work for several years. True, spasms of anxiety occasionally afflicted me, but they were not deep-seated, at least as far as I felt them, and they were not by any means a crippling affliction. Besides, preaching to nuns would add another necessary dimension to my priestly role. At this time (a few years before I would find it necessary to seek psychiatric help), I did not have the artificial support of pills. This was the real me, conscientiously preparing the necessary sermons and looking forward with only a natural anxiety as to the results of my efforts.

After three or four excursions in this new area of preaching, I found myself enjoying the work. The nuns, I found, were attentive, responsive, and hungry for the type of preaching topics I gave them. The major theme I had chosen was love. Human love first, its nature and natural expression. I drew heavily from Erich Fromm, Fathers van Kaam, Gleason, and Kennedy, and others in this regard. From this basis, I went on to explain how to "love one another," how to "love thyself," both of which were necessary before one could love God and enjoy the promised fulfillment of community life. Interspersed with the psychology and theology, I included humorous stories that would point up the fallibility as well as the nobility of human nature. To these nuns it was a new and welcome approach and a tremendous relief to be free of the dull, cumbersome and impractical type of retreat to which they had been subjected since their entrance into religious life.

To me, personally, it was a joyful and fulfilling experience. During these retreats, all day and often well into the evening, my door was open to all who wished personal interviews. I learned that there were very few nuns who did not wish to talk, and to talk at great length. Unstintingly, and far beyond prudence and my limitations, I gave. But no matter how much the response, I often felt vaguely uneasy, inadequate, at times guilty or somewhat depressed. I did not know actually what it was that made me feel this way, or what it was that I, myself, wanted to receive. Some years later, in hospital therapy, I would come to understand the genesis of these feelings and why they kept intruding even after a well-done effort.

Now this retreat at the motherhouse. In addition to the approximately 150 teaching nuns in attendance, the mother general and her staff would be there. This was a more challenging retreat than any other I had given. I felt equal to the task, but there was more than a twinge of anxiety. I wished that I could have seen Dr. Daniels prior to leaving Springfield, but other duties kept me busy. In fact, I had not been able to see him for about two months. However, I had the pills. They would see me through, I thought, with an effort to bolster my confidence.

The first two days of the retreat went very well. I felt free and easy, challenging and yet convincing. And—I did not use any pills. It would be a good retreat, I thought to myself, for the nuns and for me.

It was on the evening of the third day that disaster befell me. One of the phobic expressions of my deep-seated anxiety was the fear of giving Benediction, a simple ceremony wherein the priest exposes the Blessed Sacrament on the altar, a few hymns are sung, and then the priest chants a short prayer. It was a function I had performed a thousand times without giving it a second thought. But some few years previously, while still teaching at the major seminary, a sudden fear of chanting the prayer had seized me. I tried again and again to perform the ceremony, but the fear mounted each time. Finally, I avoided the function as often as I could. Strangely enough, though, the same symptoms did not bother me at all when I had to conduct the service before the laity in parishes or in the process of giving retreats. During the past year, however, the nervousness had returned whenever giving retreats to nuns. I could not explain it, nor was Dr. Daniels very helpful in this area. The tranquilizers, however, and now and then a sleeping pill, were sufficient to control the anxiety and its external symptoms.

Thus far, during this retreat, I had no need for narcotic assistance because the convent chaplain was taking care of the Benediction services. But sometime during the morning he had asked me to fill in for him because he had an errand to do and would be late. I was cornered, I felt. But then, there was my little pharmacy at hand.

After lunch I began to experience a depressive feeling. It must be, I immediately concluded, because of the up-coming Benediction service in the evening. At about two o'clock I took a sleeping pill, rather than a tranquilizer, because this barbiturate was more powerful and usually made me drowsy enough to shrug off any kind of anxiety. The first pill didn't work. Apprehension grew. About three-thirty I took another. At five o'clock, with anxiety still present and on the increase, I took a third sleeping pill. It worked. The Benediction service went off without the slightest difficulty. With a long, tired sigh of relief that I had survived the ordeal, I left the altar and began to unvest. With all the Seconal in me, I should have dropped to the sacristy floor and fallen sound asleep regardless of what the one who found me might think. It was to be much worse than that.

The full effect of the pills became disastrously evident at dinner. The convent's regular chaplain and another priest were present. I tried to talk and to eat but could do neither very well. Vision was blurred, food eluded my fork, speech was slurred. Remotely, I thought, they must think I'm drunk. Well, I have never been drunk in my life: but I wished I could lie down and sleep.

Dinner over finally, I made a short visit to the nearly empty chapel. I decided I would have to lie down just for a while before the evening conference at seven-thirty. I went to my room, took off my shoes, and was about to lie down when someone knocked on my door. It was the convent chaplain. He sat down and without preamble asked what had happened at the dinner table. Was I drinking?

"No!" I exclaimed strongly. "I seldom drink and have never been drunk in my life!"

"Well," he said, "mother general saw you in chapel. You

were staggering, apparently. She ordered that you are not to give this evening's conference nor to go on with the retreat."

With these words, the full horror of the situation began to pour all over me. Words of protest, excuse, explanation, pleading, promises tumbled out in what must have been a pitiful display of pathetic incoherency. Confusion, grief, fear, shame, dread, helplessness tore apart my defenses and shredded to bits my dignity.

The chaplain listened intently, and then made an observation, the truth of which I immediately recognized and yet strove desperately to reject.

"Father," he said with absolute finality, "you need a complete rehabilitation!"

He was right! I knew he was right! For years I had felt that I needed to take time out. To get away from all the pressure and tension of work. To be assisted in the study of myself in order to find out what was bugging me, what was disturbing, threatening, and depressing me. But I simply could not ask for such time off. "They" needed me for this work or that. "They" were depending on me to do a good job. "They" asked me to undertake tasks for which I was completely unprepared. "They" planned on me for years ahead. There never appeared to be a hiatus in this planning whereby I could say: "Now for the next six months you don't need me. Let me take time off for this interior sickness of mine." No. I had always to be ready, adaptable, willing, unobjecting.

That's how it was when asked, as a young priest, to be a prison chaplain despite the fact that I had no training, no intimation of what to expect in this work. For the first year of my three-year term at the prison, I was scared stiff every time I walked through the prison gates.

It was that way when assigned to teach subjects in philosophy and theology despite the fact that I had insufficient knowledge and background training in these specialized areas. So, too, when I was made director of a summer boys' camp, a work to which I was a total stranger.

It was that way with many other chores and duties, assigned or implied. I had to be a "yes" man every time "they" asked me to undertake something. "The will of superiors is the will of God," we had been constantly reminded throughout our years of training.

"Total rehabilitation!" My mind shrunk from the words in horror while, at the same time, it admitted the truth of them. I was caught—and helpless. Look to what an inexcusable stupidity had brought me! A shameful, abject failure!

The chaplain sat silent as I buried my face in my hands. Why? Why, at this particular time had anxiety risen so massively as to compel me to take three pills when one or two, at the most, should have sufficed? There was a reason for it. Confusedly I groped for it. Somewhere, sometime I had read about why people do irrational things, things they would never do in other circumstances. Yes, it was coming now; slowly, unwillingly I began to recall what psychiatry had to say about such things.

It is a well-substantiated fact, they said, that in deeply agitated persons, the subconscious mind will often prompt or compel an external, observable disturbance, such as phobias, psychosomatic disorders, odd behavior, and so forth. It does this because it is actually crying out for help! It can and often does precipitate a crisis that will bring about that help.

Such reasoning made sense, even though I felt faint with its implications. It was the real reason, I believe, why I reacted with relief, as well as with dismay, at the words "total rehabilitation." I was crying out for help in taking the pills. The help came and I did not want it—and yet I did want it. "Total rehabilitation." I believe I was saying to myself in a faint but honest whisper: "That is what I need. That is what I really want. That is the help I have longed for all these years."

Perhaps this confused but probable answer to my "Why?" was also the reason why I became less hostile and more submissive when the chaplain suggested that we take a trip downtown to meet a friend of his. Reluctant, but helpless and defeated, I went with him.

His friend was pastor of the cathedral, a Father Hayden, now a bishop. He greeted me warmly and invited me to be seated. The chaplain excused himself and left. We talked for about an hour, during which I explained, as well as I could, just what happened and some of my previous life and work. A kindly and sympathetic priest, he listened with concern and interest, asking a question now and then. It felt good to unload some of my burden to him even though I knew that the horrible fiasco at the motherhouse could not be undone.

"Father," he said, finally, "you are a good man. But you are overworked and tired. And you do have problems. Why don't I make arrangements to have you enter the sisters' hospital tonight. There are good doctors there and an excellent psychiatrist. Perhaps you might want to talk to him."

Without waiting for my acquiescence, he dialed a number and spoke to someone about a room. After hanging up, he said: "O.K. We'll take you over to the hospital now. And don't worry. They'll take good care of you." I could not refuse. There was no other place to go. Depressed and hopeless, I accompanied him. Within a half hour I was admitted to the hospital, given a room, and told by a nursing nun to prepare for bed. The doctor, she smiled, would be in to see me soon.

Later on that evening, a doctor appeared and listened to my story about my seeing a psychiatrist back home, my phobia, and my abuse of the pills I had been given. He made a few notes and said he would have me transferred the next morning and that I would be seeing a Dr. Dunbar. Until I arrived at my new room, I did not realize that this was the psychiatric ward of the hospital. Well, that figured. "Total rehabilitation." This was the beginning.

Dr. Dunbar was big, hearty, blunt, and very perceptive. In the several interviews that took place during the next three weeks, I received intimations, as I had with Dr. Daniels, of several deep-rooted conflicts but which, in my dazed and confused condition, I could not pursue, or did not want to.

Halfway through one session, he sharply criticized me for continually answering his questions with a meek: "Yes, Doctor."

"Yes, Doctor! Yes, Doctor!" he mimicked. "Is that all you can say? Haven't you got enough guts to tell me your real feelings? You sound like Uriah Heep. Remember him? From Dickens?

He was a fawning, obsequious old bastard! He was a hypocrite! Everytime he said 'Yes' he really wanted to say 'No.' Underneath, he was full of hostility. Loaded with it!"

As he glared at me for a response, anger had arisen in me, hot and fiery, but only for a moment. Quickly, I smothered it. You got hurt, lost friends, felt guilt, suffered depression whenever you showed anger toward anyone. Besides, anger was un-Christian, unvirtuous. Banish it. Hide it.

Meekly, I answered his questioning look with: "Yes, Doctor."

On another day, when I tried to tell him the kind of priest I wanted to be, he almost roared at me. "Who do you think you are? Almighty God?"

"But," I protested, "I only want to be a good priest."

"Good! Good!" he snorted. "And tell me. How do you know when you are 'good?' Who sets up the standards? How do you know when you've been 'good?' Haven't you ever heard the phrase 'good and angry?' Don't you think it possible to be 'good' and 'angry' at the same time? What about Christ when He angrily chased the money changers out of the temple with a whip?"

His keen observations nettled me; they were true, and I was angry at him, or at something. But, again, I remained silent. I would have to think about this.

On another occasion, when I tried to tell him in my own psychological terminology what I thought had happened during my life, and what was wrong with my life attitudes, he observed with a wealth of wisdom: "You have the words, but not the music."

Later on, after I had returned home and entered another hospital, unfortunately, in a certain sense, I repeated this remark to my doctor. He seized upon it and repeatedly reminded me of it, especially when I would try to quote from psychology books in order to explain myself.

"Words and music, again," he would say. "If books on psychology could have solved your problems, you wouldn't be here now, would you? All the theories and cases you have read about never showed you effectively your own particular root problems, nor your own defensive attitudes, or unique life patterns. I want to know how you *really* felt about each incident. Not what some book may have told you *how* you should feel."

Another point that Dr. Dunbar made during my short stay at this hospital, but one that needed much thinking on my part to absorb it fully, was the analogy he made between my condition and that of several foreign missionary priests whom he had treated.

"They all felt that they had to conquer the world, the pagan world, for Christ. They saw the vast jungle, a tremendous barrier in itself, and the millions of ignorant, superstitious natives, hundreds of miles apart, without the saving word of the gospel. Their best efforts usually met with failure—and that's how they began to see themselves. Inadequate, incompetent, failures. Their human abilities were far outstripped by their zeal, or 'ego image' in psychiatric language. They simply could not accept their human limitations."

This was easy enough for me to understand in their case, and I could see the apparent solution for them. But I was still too dazed, confused, and humiliated to see an exact parallel with my own situation. A constant and depressing smog of *failure,* like a dim twilight, blurred my interior vision.

Sister Thomasina, the nun in charge of the psychiatric ward, and who had a master's degree in counseling, at one time made a most pertinent observation, although I was horrified when she broached the subject. She had been most kind to me and had spent much time in listening to my life's story.

One day, after listening patiently to me, she asked, in a musing sort of way: "Father, did you ever think that perhaps a year or so away from priestly and religious life would be a good thing for you? Rest, relaxation, good advice, a complete change of atmosphere without work and worries might be very helpful to you."

At first, the suggestion shocked me beyond words. How could

she, a religious herself, dare think that this complete "away-ness" would be a good thing? How could she contemplate as being helpful this suggested separation from my work, my priest-hood, my religious and community life? Surely she must see that there would be more danger, much more danger, than good in such a separation. And yet, I asked myself later on, how much different was this suggestion than the chaplain's observation that I needed a "complete rehabilitation"? Indeed, how much different was it than my years-long desire to drop all work and to enter some form of psychotherapy that would enable me to get to the roots of my problems? Although still too confused to consider all the implications of these two ob-servations, together with my own unuttered feelings in this regard, the germ, the seed of a future decision had been planted.

A Father John, who had considerable experience in our mis-sion work and in retreat work, had responded to an emergency call of the mother general and had arrived the day after my hospitalization. Of all confreres, I most preferred having him to talk with during this ordeal. He knew me well, for we had lived and worked together off and on throughout the years. Kindly, generous, and understanding, he was just the kind of a priest-friend I needed in order to unburden myself of some of the shame and guilt that had occasioned his presence. At our first meeting at the hospital, I acquainted him with some of my problems, although I did this reservedly, for I was still intent on avoiding the full impact of the shameful situation and all that it implied.

Just how emotionally disturbed I was, and how distorted my sense of values had become, is probably best depicted in an event that took place about a week before I left the hospital. Father John, after finishing the nuns' retreat, had stayed on for a few days and had received the doctor's permis-sion to take me for a ride along the shoreline. We had hoped to find some sort of quaint and busy seaside town and relax there for a couple of hours. The further we traveled, however, the more deserted the countryside became.

Finally, we spotted a lane that seemed to lead to the sea-shore. No town being available, we hoped to enjoy the warm sun and trudge for a while along the sandy beach. But the wind was sharp and penetrating, the beach nothing but shattered gray shale, and the shoreline was deserted of people and houses. The only activity was the white-topped, wind-whipped waves smashing relentlessly against the shuffling shale. We watched for a short time and then decided to return to the comparative warmth of the car.

Suddenly, I found myself looking at the twisted, stunted limbs of weather-beaten trees, the ugly rock formations, the stagnant pools of brackish water left by high tides, the colorless, craggy hills, the millions of mottled pebbles slung about in haphazard heaps, the dry, withered, and broken stalks of tall swamp grass. All of this barren scene, etched clearly by bright sunlight, seemed to leap in upon me, screeching a demand for the purpose of its existence, for meaningfulness. With a dread, sinking sensation, I felt completely helpless and hopeless in the face of this frightful onslaught of what I could only describe as the "unreality of the real." In rising horror, I asked myself: "Am I losing my mind? Is this the beginning of insanity?" I stumbled toward the waiting car.

"What a Godforsaken place," observed Father John, as we drove out the winding lane.

"You can say it, John, but I feel it. God, how I feel it! Please take me home, quickly."

Godforsaken! That was it! The place was Godforsaken! It was desolation, barrenness, purposeless. And I, as a human being, as a priest, as an educated person, a quasiphilosopher and theologian, should have been able to see and understand the purpose and reason for the scene. Yet I could not. Godforsaken! But was not that the way I felt? I, too, was barren, fruitless, estranged, purposeless, desolate. "O God," I murmured to myself. "Where are you in this wasteland? Why have you hidden Yourself? Where is Your beauty? Where will I find you . . . ?"

Slowly, as we entered the outskirts of the city and with the reappearance of houses, people, life, the oppression began to lift and the inner turbulence subsided. How I welcomed the security of the hospital, the reason for its being, its humane purposefulness, the friendliness of its personnel, the sense of belongingness that the building and its people offered to me.

"You overdramatize," said Dr. Dunbar of the event. "I'm out there every weekend, fishing. Beautiful spot."

This answered none of the many questions I wanted to ask, but I was afraid to ask them. I wanted to be released as soon as possible and to return to my own home, to friends, and to Dr. Daniels.

Other confreres, I knew, would be wondering and speculating over what had happened despite the fact that Father John assured me that no one except the Provincial was aware of the situation. He, himself, had been told to say nothing, and he assured me that he had not. But I knew it would not be long before some of the details would leak out. My precious reputation! How long would it survive the infiltration of rumor —and fact? At best, it would fare poorly, and I sagged interiorly with the weight of another burden, another anxiety. These others, these confreres whose opinions I valued so very much, would know of my disgrace, enough of it, at least, to cause them to re-evaluate my worthwhileness—downward, I was sure. How could I possibly face them?

Despite this attitude, and the threat I would have to meet on the home front, I was anxious to leave the infirmary. I was more than glad, then, when Dr. Dunbar announced that he would release me in a day or so provided I would report to Dr. Daniels as soon as possible. He had been on the phone with Dr. Daniels, he said, and both were agreed that I should carry on treatment back home. Happily, I consented.

CHAPTER III

# HARTFORD AND WHITE HALL
## *Omen of Things to Come*

---

*"In the noontime of my life I must depart! To the gates of the nether world I shall be consigned for the rest of my years."*
—Isaiah: 38, 10

Homecoming was not as difficult as I had anticipated. My Provincial, newly appointed and a close friend, was both understanding and sympathetic. He assured me that I could have any kind of help that the doctor suggested, and that I should not think of the cost. Good health was the only important thing to consider.

Somewhat heartened, I reported to Dr. Daniels and related the events that led to my collapse and hospitalization at Halifax. It was particularly painful telling him about my miniature pharmacy and how I had been abusing it for several months. The poor man was aghast but humbly admitted that he, as a psychiatrist, should have suspected what was going on, and should have realized, because he was aware of my depressive state, what I might have been doing with all the various prescriptions he had given me.

His assumption of the blame made me feel much worse because I knew that I had deceived him, that he had trusted me as a priest—and I had failed him. Again, *failure!* I did my best to assure him that it was entirely my own fault. That I knew all along that I was doing wrong in not revealing the misuse of the pills. That the guilt of it should have prompted me to tell him.

At this point, I suggested that perhaps it would be best for me to drop all work and for a time enter a hospital where I could be thoroughly examined emotionally. Many years ago, I told him, I suspected that this was what I needed; more than ever I now wanted to "get this monkey off my back."

He was in complete agreement, and asked if I had any preferences. Yes, I assured him. The Institute of Living in nearby Hartford, only a half-hour's drive away. On several occasions, at various seminars on mental health, I had listened to and had met the Institute's psychiatrist-in-chief, Dr. Francis Braceland, and had been very much impressed with him. Dr. Daniels agreed and said he would make an appointment for an interview with the screening staff as soon as possible. From a pamphlet at hand, he described a day program run by the Institute and thought I might qualify for it. Briefly, the day program ran five days a week and from 9:00 A.M. to 4:00 P.M. It featured periodic sessions with a psychiatrist, occupational therapy classes, and other social activities. This was great, I thought. Free every evening, and on the weekends I could help out at a parish. Confreres would have no knowledge of what was going on. My precious reputation, though considerably tarnished because of Halifax, had to be protected from any further smearing.

Better still, I thought, I knew I could get weekend parish work in the Hartford area and thereby have a further covering excuse for the daily trips to the city. It would explain my absence very nicely.

Within the week, Dr. Daniels called to give me the time and date of my interview at the Institute. I found it easily enough, located in the southern part of the city, its thirty or so acres surrounded by a high, red-brick wall. It was with no little apprehension that I drove through the gates on busy Washington Street.

Since there was plenty of time before registration, I decided to see more of this hospital, which was to be my part-time home.

To the left of the gates was a neat, 2½-story building identified as White Hall. Directly before me was a parking oval before the sprawling Administration building. It was winged on the left by a kitchen and dining room, and on the right by what appeared to be a library. Next to it was a small, Victorian-Gothic chapel. I wondered if I would be saying Mass there. Immediately beyond this chapel was a three-story building that contained an auditorium and occupational therapy classrooms. Attached to it was a huge, high-windowed structure that could only be a gymnasium.

The left-curving macadam road revealed two or three large colonial-style houses that appeared to be offices of some sort, or private dwellings for patients, plus a greenhouse and neatly rowed flower beds. Opposite these, recessed behind a trim green lawn, was the Social Hall, behind the full-glassed windows of which I could see some patients moving around. To it was attached a much larger building, a women's dormitory, I gathered. The road dipped and I came upon two or three modern red-brick houses. Very nice, I thought: not at all what I had envisioned a mental hospital to be. Opposite these buildings were three or four white, clapboard houses, one of which bore the sign "Day Patients." I paused momentarily. So this was to be the base of my daily operations, I mused. Not very attractive, but then, according to the day program leaflet, I would not be spending much time there.

Then came the huge campus, ringed about by a variety of buildings. I liked it. A softball field upon which I could see myself making long hits and fine defensive plays; four tennis courts, which would help me to get into good physical shape; plenty of soft green grass with several benches and chairs for undisturbed meditation; an outdoor swimming pool, which would allow me to regain some of those diving techniques I so much enjoyed as a student at our summer camp. It all seemed to be so peaceful and well-equipped to assist the patient with physical activity and mental relaxation.

Further on, the road gave gateless access to Retreat Avenue, which formed a juncture with the bustling activity of Washington Street. Freedom, I thought. You could walk out of here if you wished. More importantly, it meant that *they* trusted you. It was a heartening thought.

The road veered back to the left, and the ten-story Burlingame Building loomed before me. According to another pamphlet I had, this structure contained doctors' offices, government-sponsored experimental laboratories, and several patients' wards, including one for difficult patients.

To the left of Burlingame and a continuation of the Administration building was a grim-looking brick structure labeled "North One," and above it "North Two." I wondered what sort of patients it contained. Just beyond it, and at a curve in the road, stood the single-story hospital store, quaintly named: "Here It Is." Opposite the store was another old wooden building which, I learned later, was used mostly for psychological testings.

Then I found myself passing between "White Hall" and the high brick wall that separated it from the noisy, teeming traffic on Washington Street.

Registration time came, and I found myself in a small visitors' parlor with a secretary. My palms were damp with apprehension and nervousness. Perhaps it was because of the latter that I signed papers quickly and without reading them closely. One, I learned much later on, committed me to a stay of no less than four months! This meant, of course, that I was not a day patient but a full-time patient!

There would be many days in the near future when I would damn myself for being so stupid as not to have read what I signed. That I be admitted as a "full-time patient" must have been decided upon, I am sure, when Dr. Daniels gave his report to the hospital staff. At the actual signing, however, I was sure that I was being entered as a day patient, and a type of treatment which, after being officially assigned as an assistant curate at a nearby parish, would be a face-saving device and allay the natural curiosity of fellow priests, who would want to know just what I was doing in the Hartford area. Being a day patient, at this time, meant everything to me. I was, therefore, more than a little bit surprised when told that I should bring in my luggage and leave it in the office and that I would be assigned to a nearby building. Why, I wondered, did they want my luggage since I was a day patient? And why was I given a room? I should have asked, but concluded that this was the way it was done, that I would have to go through a few tests and interviews before being allowed the liberty of a day patient.

A male aide escorted me to my new residence, White Hall, which, he informed me, also contained a physical therapy unit and an indoor swimming pool in one wing, plus an unused handball court. White Hall, one of the better units in the hospital, was primarily used for the apparently well-disposed patients, although, after a few weeks of examination, they were usually moved to other quarters. In general, the hospital separated patients into two different categories. "Group Nine" was the elite classification and allowed several different gradations of liberty. "Group Four," again with varying degrees of limitations, was for the more disturbed patients.

The two nurses who greeted me at White Hall, one evidently the nurse in charge, the other a young student nurse, were most pleasant and helpful, as were the other ten or twelve patients who were to become my family for the next several days.

The bedroom on the second floor was small but well-appointed, having a bureau, closet, washbowl, easy chair, and reading lamp. The heavy-leaded windows opened out, but only about six inches, I noticed. Even a child could not squeeze through them. Heavy traffic noises along Washington Street poured in through the open windows, along with the warm midafternoon sun. This street noise did not bother me at the time: rather it was reassuring, because it gave some sense of freedom and belonging to the outside world. Soon enough, however, the roar of traffic would become an increasing torment.

On the first floor, just off the small lobby, was a glass-enclosed nurses' office, the door of which was always locked except when a nurse was present. Next to it was a small kitchen where food from the main kitchen was kept warm before serving. Beyond was a neat dining room, which comfortably sat the twelve or fourteen patients that was capacity for White Hall. This room also served as late-evening snack bar. To the right of the dining room was a large and comfortable combination sitting-and-recreation room with upholstered chairs, a lounge, card tables, and a TV set.

All things considered, the atmosphere of White Hall, and the Institute as a whole, appeared congenial and peaceful. I would soon learn that this unit and the hospital contained more than a small amount of the world's anguish.

With the strange feeling of putting something very valuable aside, I hung my black suit and Roman collar in the closet and donned the "civvies" that hospital authorities said I must wear, since uniforms of any kind were prohibited. While registering I had been asked if I wanted to be known as "Father" Collins or to remain completely incognito. Surprised, I answered that I certainly did want to be known as a priest and felt a slight resentment at the implied suggestion that I might want to conceal the fact. Here I was now, dressed in some old sports clothes, but already beginning to feel the embarrassment of being called "Father" without the dignity and defensive decorum of clerical clothing.

At this point in my reflections, a nurse knocked and informed me that my psychiatrist would be Dr. MacGillvary and that I would see him in about an hour for a physical checkup. An aide would escort me to his office.

While waiting in the sitting room, I leafed through the Institute's monthly magazine, the *Chatterbox*, in which were listed news events, upcoming movies, schedules for occupational therapy, etc. Also shown were pictures of several newly arrived doctors who would be starting their three-year residency. I was more than a bit startled when I saw that Dr. MacGillvary had on a Roman collar, one of those broad, high ones used chiefly by the Episcopalian clergy. The more I thought about it, the less I liked the idea. How could I relate to a Protestant clergyman? How could I talk about some of the embarrassing things that I would have to mention in connection with my background, nuns, priests, seminary training, Catholicism, etc.? Doubt about having Dr. John J. MacGillvary as a psychiatrist turned into resentment. Why hadn't the Administration consulted me on the matter? Oh, well, I was here now, and stuck with this clergyman. I'd have to make the best of it.

Soon, the student nurse appeared and escorted me to the examination room, located in the Administration building. After a short wait, the doctor appeared and introduced himself, inviting me to sit on the edge of the high, paper-covered examining bed. Here was the man who, in the next twenty months, would come to know me better than I would ever know myself; who would listen patiently, observe acutely, probe gently, and dissect carefully. He would uncover hidden fears and expose secret hostilities, touch the raw nerves of anguish, help remove the burden of guilt, unmask false pride, and be witness to shameful tears.

He would be my sole companion down the fearsome and labyrinthine caves of my unconscious, my only support in the chaos of hopelessness, a trusted guest in the sacred precincts of my troubled soul; the object of my admiration and the target of my anger, the cause of silent invective and the source of confidence. My judge and arbiter, my lawyer and jury.

He stood before me now in civilian clothes, tall and slim, an easy smile creasing his clean-shaven, rather sallow cheeks, a high forehead above warm gray-green eyes, hair rather close-cropped and beginning to recede. I began to like the man. There was a kindness and concern that emanated from him. Resentment had just about vanished. I felt I could talk to him openly.

As I answered routine questions about my health and let him probe wherever he wished, I pondered how best to approach the subject of his religious affiliation. It was still a matter of concern.

Finally, when he seemed about finished with the examination, I mustered the courage to ask him: "Doctor, are you a clergyman?"

"Yes," he answered, and added with a smile, "I'm a priest. A Jesuit."

At these words, my body almost shook with a spasm of joy. Never, never had I dreamed of having such a happy combination. A psychiatrist, a priest, a religious like myself. All in one—and all for me.

A warm feeling of relaxation and optimism displaced the tension and nervousness that had begun with my entrance into the hospital. Now, I felt, all would be well. God was so good, good beyond words, by answering my years-long prayers in such a marvelous fashion.

There was much more to his background that I did not learn until many months later. He had been an actor and then a Navy pilot prior to entering the seminary; had earned a master's degree and was chaplain to prisoners at Alcatraz before entering a medical school.

As I prepared to leave the office, it occurred to me to ask a question. "They have given me a room. I didn't expect one since I want to go on the day program. When will I start on it?"

"We'll talk about that later," smiled the doctor. "First we will need some background information, which might take a few days."

In better than good spirits I returned to White Hall, fairly certain that I would be transferred to the day program very soon.

Other patients from White Hall had by now returned from their various classes and I had more time to become better acquainted with them. All were pleasant and informal, although I was quite conscious of being in civvies when continually referred to as "Father."

Of the three women patients in White Hall, Mary Ellen was by far the most prominent, in many ways. Stylish, ash-blonde, fortyish, and wealthy, she was annoyingly loud and irksome in her overfriendliness. Other patients continually complained about her, but later on, when she confided to me her various domestic difficulties, I was aroused to pity and compassion for her and could not maintain my initial impression about her.

Of the male patients, Arnold was the most extroverted, with a rather raucous sense of humor, but most friendly at our first encounter and quite eager to give me the "lowdown" on the whole Institute. He was an obstetrician from New York and was gifted with a brilliant mind.

Ferdinand, a South American with an engineer's degree from M.I.T., arrived more than a week after my own entrance and at a time when anxiety had become an excruciating burden to me. What remains most sharply in memory about him was the evening in White Hall when Dr. Mack, after a visit to Ferdinand, dropped in to see me. Commenting on his new patient, he said with assurance: "He needs help badly but I think we can do a lot for him."

Desperately, I wanted to ask him if he felt the same way about me. Can you do *anything* for me? Is there any *hope* at all? But I did not dare to utter such thoughts. I was terribly fearful of an evasive answer which, to me at that time of severe depression, would have made me feel absolutely hopeless. Somehow, there was a shred of hope in hiding such questions from him, for, if I revealed my real desperation feelings I might be "sent down" to Group Four, to a locked unit, to the horrible disgrace of complete failure.

What else took place during this unusual evening visit by the doctor, I do not recall. I can only remember the feeling of a deepening twilight preceding the inevitable night.

After our first meeting Arnold became my best friend and confidant. Slim, dark-complexioned, blue-eyed behind thick-lensed glasses, he seemed to exude an air of enthusiastic warmth for people. Our relationship was all the more unique because of our differing backgrounds. He was a strict Orthodox Jew and had studied for years to become a rabbi before turning to medicine.

Just what it was that attracted us, I do not know. Perhaps it was his readiness to talk, to talk about anything, and finding in me a good listener. Perhaps, too, it was because our cases were somewhat similar and he had a good insight as to my feelings. Perhaps, also, it was because he was a doctor and by nature and training a sympathizer of suffering humanity. Despite his medical knowledge he, too, had succumbed to the "fear of the unknown." We had this much in common, and it was always a good subject for discussion.

He had gone through the "hell of fear," as he put it, for years, but now, thanks to this hospital, he had recovered his mental equilibrium and could speak with praise and enthusiasm about how he had found his "real self." In our common affliction we found many similarities in its origins and development. He, too, had had recourse to barbiturates in an attempt to overcome anxiety, depression, fear, and sleeplessness. He, too, knew the mounting tension that so subtly robs one of energy, concentration, appetite, and zest for life. On the human level, therefore, and in our pathetic, useless, and potentially harmful defenses, we were very much alike, even though our creeds were far apart.

It was this bond of common suffering, I think, more than other factors, that attracted us. Medical training, certainly, had increased his interest and concern for the afflicted human body, but more than that, I feel that his own mental anguish, now so greatly reduced, freed him and prompted him to respond to the pathos of another suffering human being. It was the free and frank admission of his own problems, at least in general, his various distorted attitudes and unhealthy reactions, plus, of course, the subsequent and revealing insights acquired at the Institute, that prompted me to respond, slowly and cautiously, with some of my own difficulties and fears in the hope that I, too, could gain similar solutions and relief.

It was a vain hope, of course, since no two cases are ever exactly alike in therapy; there are too many variations to life's theme, too many subtle shades of meaning in one's experience, too many different ideals, cultural influences, hopes, hurts, attitudes, and interpretations. As with fingerprints, so with personalities. Each is unique and cannot be duplicated. There are certain generally valid principles in psychotherapy, of course, but these are ultimately effective only when expertly applied by the trained therapist and convincingly accepted by the patient. This latter process is usually lengthy and requires much "thinking through" before the principle becomes a solution, and before the solution becomes an insight. It is the insights that bring about the new and healing attitudes. A learning and unlearning process has to take place.

These conversations with Arnold, however, became a much more sought-after relief from the growing anxiety that began to dominate my days and nights. Talks with Dr. Mack were, for the most part, concerned with my past history, family and personality relationships, education, and so forth. Nothing was of less interest to me than my past. Much of it I wanted to forget. I was primarily concerned with my present and future, with the fist of fear jabbing at my stomach, with slowly diminishing self-confidence, and with the increasing threat of the time element necessary for a cure. Day after day, however, he persisted in reading question after question from a thick sheaf of stapled papers, jotting down the answers, recording observations, slowly compiling a detailed account of the fifty years that made up my life. I became impatient with him, and then resentful and, I am sure, hostile, especially when I felt the tapeworm of fear gnawing away under my ribs.

One day, sick and angry, I demanded to know how long this questioning was going on, how long before I would begin to feel better.

"How long," he asked, "did it take you to get this way?"

To myself, I groaned in dismay. How long does it take to understand and to *undo* fifty years of anxiety-motivated living? The worm in the pit of my stomach gnawed away more viciously.

Talks with Arnold now became more a desperation measure of escape than a hope-giving promise of relief. When I did not seek him out because I did not wish to impose upon him, he seemed to know intuitively my need for companionship and would invite me to go out for a walk or to sit in the warm October sunshine. Each time, he would tell me a bit more about his life, how he had become steadily more depressed despite a busy medical practice, more anxious, more dependent on drugs to get through each day's hospital and office work.

How very much like myself, I thought. Finally, upon the adamant advice of his local psychiatrist and despite his vehement protests, he was committed to this hospital. Because of his violent condition (he, too, had become indiscriminate in the use of drugs) he had to be confined to a small room in the Burlingame Building on the fourth floor. "BB-4," it was called. I came to dread mention of the name because of various stories I had heard of the type of patient who was confined there, under constant watch and under lock and key. It became a symbol of the worst that could happen to me. I was determined, but it was a sickening determination, that I would never allow myself to fall into such a horrible mental condition.

Arnold would contrast his two weeks of panic and terror on BB-4 while recovering from the effects of drugs and shame with his present ability to relax and to enjoy the gradual return of good health and sanity. Sitting out on the campus, he would tell me how wonderful it was to absorb that "good-all-over" feeling in the sun's warmth, and to be relieved through an understanding of his basic problems, of the horrible days and fearful nights that had made up his life some four months before.

Avidly and enviously, I would listen and try to refurbish my diminishing hope. It was useless. His key would not fit my lock. Each patient, I realized much later on, must laboriously fashion his own key, two keys, in fact. The first would unlock the door to that dark and mysterious room wherein all the fearsome emotions of life, real or imaginary, threatening and shameful, had been hidden away from the view of others and from one's own recognition of them.

The second key would open the door to the room to where one's real self, the acceptable self, the approvable self, lived —a room wherein one would feel at home and quite comfortable with his past self, no matter what its history of failures, shames, embarrassments, fears, depressions. It was a room where one could confess and feel the joy of absolution; of realistic comfort, relaxation, and contentment. It was this kind of room in which Arnold now found himself after four months.

Four months! That was an eternity to me! I could not stand it! There must be a quicker way to unlock these doors.

It would take me much, much longer to forge the keys necessary to open the doors to my locked rooms.

In retrospect, I realize that many significant events were taking place in my relationships with the various patients at White Hall and other units. With Arnold it was more pronounced and meaningful. In a growing isolation, away from all that was familiar, friendly, reassuring, and protective, I was gradually losing that identity that had been mine for many long years, years of knowing *who* I was and *what* I was, and *how* to produce effectively. As this form of identity began to disappear, there gradually emerged a sense of disorientation, a loss of self-confidence, a feeling of unreality, a growing revulsion at my apparent failure, the uselessness of trying to be useful and productive, the onset of loneliness, plus the psychosomatic result of all this—the painfully leaden stomach ache of fear.

Hope, however, is difficult to extinguish completely and so, despite the continuing onslaught of such powerful and threatening forces, it will develop many groping, searching hands in its attempt to cling to anything that might give the slightest promise of survival. Of its very nature, it wants to make contact. And because it is a human need, it will seek out the human contact.

Hope comes from without, outside the self, and usually in the form of a person. "Human needs want human comforting," I remembered reading somewhere. How true! And how desperately true that is for the priest, for one whose whole orientation and sense of worthwhileness had been based on and geared to the *amount* of his activity, the *frequency* of his productivity, and the *availability* of his service to others. Even though he believes and knows that he has been "called" by Christ ("I have chosen you; you have not chosen me!"), nonetheless he needs a conviction of *human* worthwhileness, and this, for the most part, has been derived from the *human* response, the *human* concern, interest, care, and love that his efforts have evoked from the humanity to which he has so wholeheartedly given himself. Though cut off and subtracted from this healthy and necessary support, he will, from sheer force of habit, still continue to look for some vestige of it from among those with whom he finds himself. "No man is an island" is truer of the priest, the now lonely, segregated priest, than it is for all other types of personalities. More than ever will he feel compelled to look for hope and the promise of hope, for security and acceptance, for belongingness and for a sense of being really worthwhile and loved "as he is," in *human* kindness, understanding, and compassion.

This, I believe, is what I sought and hoped for in companionship with Arnold. Although his best efforts in my behalf could never have brought about a "cure" to my many and deep emotional conflicts, nevertheless, he had responded to a human need as best he could, and the human contact he generously offered was a greatly needed lesson, the full import of which I was to appreciate and apply as I looked back from the vantage point of several months of intensive therapy and self-understanding.

Alongside this relationship with Arnold, which emphasized the need and value of human contact and understanding, I must describe a similar situation in which, sadly, I failed to respond to a human need.

Mary Ellen continually irked me and other patients, chiefly because of her loudly aired grievances, her domestic problems, and her petty objections to various hospital regulations. Much later on I understood that this was her way of crying for help, just as I had developed my own particular manner of seeking assistance. I was always uneasy in her presence because I never knew what embarrassing subject she might present publicly to the group at large.

One evening, at a movie in the auditorium, I noted thankfully that she was seated at the far side of the hall. She spotted me, however, and hailed me from that distance in her loud, attention-seeking voice. I waved weakly and turned to talk to Arnold and others sitting behind me in order to cover my embarrassment at being singled out by name among the large gathering of patients. Having been "spotlighted" in such a manner, however, was only the beginning of my discomfort. Out of the corner of my eye, I could see Mary Ellen making her way toward me. With a noisy exclamation, amidst an invisible cloud of various perfumes, she plunked herself down in the seat next to mine which, unfortunately, was empty. She prattled away with customary loudness while I prayed desperately for the house lights to go down and the movie to begin.

But even when this happened, she chattered on. Again, I was beset with the fear that she would bring up some embarrassing domestic problem. In order to forestall this, I showed her my corduroy jacket and the shoulder pad that had slipped out of place. Immediately, she demanded that I take it off, that she had repaired such things many times for her husband. With a silent curse, I shrugged off the jacket and gave it to her. After a brief examination, she assured me and everyone else in the immediate vicinity that she would have it repaired in a day or two.

Meanwhile, she had edged closer to me, innocently I am sure, but I had to keep pulling away so that eventually I was half-hanging over the edge of my seat. Had it not been for the armrest, I would have fallen out into the aisle. I resented her more than I can say; I wasn't even grateful for her generous offer to mend the jacket. It had been a diversionary ploy on my part, and it had failed. More than ever, I was shamefully conscious of her unwanted presence and the intense embarrassment it had occasioned. After all, I was a priest! What were people going to think and say about this chummy episode?

During the next day's interview with Dr. Mack, I mentioned the incident. Perhaps this was a defensive maneuver on my part. I certainly didn't want him to suspect that I was becoming overly familiar with any woman. So I related the event with no little resentment at Mary Ellen.

Dr. Mack was more than slightly interested in the story.

"What do you think she was attempting to do in all this?" he asked.

"Looking for attention!" I answered accusingly. This was the phrase used by all the other patients in their description of Mary Ellen. I was on safe ground here because this was the consensus of opinion.

"Attention-seeking," he observed, "is not at all an unnatural thing for human beings to do. We all need attention, favorable attention from others, although the means we use might be somewhat objectionable. Sometimes we need attention quite intensely, especially when we have been deprived of normal and healthy love-giving attention. Human contact might be a kinder, more explanatory word. It would appear that Mary Ellen, with her many and deep problems, was seeking merely to make 'contact' with you—contact with a kind, understanding, compassionate person whom she thought you, as a priest, would be. How does this different interpretation of her activities strike you?"

Shame and guilt arrived at about the same time and began to fill me with an uncomfortable self-dislike.

The human contact! Was this not what I had been striving to establish in my talks with Arnold? It certainly was and, in the light of this, I began to see Mary Ellen in a much different, kindlier, and sympathetic way. She, too, was a fellow sufferer and aching, perhaps, with the same desperate needs that afflicted me. Rather than enlightening me as to the same tragic plight of others, my own self-centeredness had deafened me to their cries for help. Then, too, my repulsive egocentricity was displayed to Dr. Mack.

All of this could have been a revealing and helpful insight, but I was not old enough in therapy to see the positive and useful aspects of such shattering self-knowledge. Rather, I was ashamed and depressed for having been "found out."

*Insight*, therapeutically understood, enables the patient not only to see and admit unhealthy and anxiety-producing actions and patterns of action, it also enables him to correct such debilitating attitudes and to substitute positive and healthier ones. True insight gives one the freedom to accept the past, no matter how failure-ridden and mistakeful it might be.

For me, this necessary attitude would be a long time in coming since there were so many years of deeply ingrained and unhealthy inhibitions and rigidities to dissolve and to replace with happier and constructive outlooks.

At this moment of guilty self-discovery with regard to another human being, Mary Ellen, I could only slip a bit deeper into the gray despondency that now seemed to be closing in on me from all sides.

Anxiety, squirming and sharp-toothed, gnawed away more voraciously.

# CHAPTER IV

# DEEPENING TWILIGHT
## *Futile Search*

---

*"In the middle of the journey of our life I came to
my senses in a dark forest, for I had lost the straight
path."*

—Dante: *Inferno*

P ERHAPS the most salient point Arnold made in conversation
with me was that he and I really belonged in this hospital.

"We couldn't manage our lives on the outside, no matter
what we did," he observed pointedly. "In fact, we came pretty
close to ruining ourselves completely, tragically. If any patient
says he doesn't belong here he is only fighting the real truth
about himself. He's not honest, and he will never get better
until he makes that admission. The chances are that he will
get a lot worse. It took me two weeks in BB-4 before I
would admit this about myself. But, when I finally did, things
began to improve. Honesty about oneself is such a healthy
and necessary thing."

"These men here are professionals," he said about the doctors.
"They would not have accepted us if they were not convinced
that we absolutely needed this kind of specialized and supervised help. Besides, they don't need us. There must be a
waiting list of over two hundred waiting to get in. I thank
God they caught up with me in time."

This kind of advice was more than a little helpful, even
hopeful, and I did not hesitate to admit to him my need for

the hospital. But it would be a long time before I could say that I was glad to be a patient. I had expected some sort of immediate improvement, a lessening of depression, a beginning of contentment. But I was not content. In fact, I was feeling worse every day.

Nonetheless, intellectually at least, I maintained the conviction that I did belong in this hospital as a mental patient. I could not and did not manage my life on the outside. I had to come here for the necessary help and the "know-how" of these specialists. Many times, later on, I was to use this argument on new patients whose initial reaction was one of extreme hostility toward the Institute. It had surprisingly good results, for them and for me.

In all meetings with other patients and personnel, and in trying to adapt to hospital techniques and rules, I became aware of one common denominator in myself with regard to these relationships. It was my severely negative *self-attitude*, one that I projected into the minds of others, especially when introduced to others or referred to as "Father" Collins. I could hear others thinking: "A priest! He has presumed to advise and direct others in life and yet, here he is, a mental patient, unable to direct himself. A failure! There must be something terribly wrong with his faith and trust in God. I wonder what sort of trouble he got himself into."

That I was a *failure*, there could be no doubt, I reasoned, because I could still see myself as *the priest I should have been!* Yet, here I was, a *priest-mental patient!*

At this moment, therefore, some several days after entrance into the hospital, a growing misery and vague foreboding prompted me to seek some sort of help and hope from patients other than Arnold. I sought out two other priest-patients whom I had not yet met.

The first was Father Albert, a priest who already had been in the Institute for over ten months. He preferred not to be called "Father," he informed me at our first meeting. I felt shocked and grieved that he had succumbed to the temptation to "step down," as I saw it at the time, from the dignity of the priesthood and had assumed the anonymity of his first name. Though pleasant enough to me as a fellow patient, his lugubrious countenance was given to deep sighing and continual head-shaking as he described his hospital experiences. Studiously he avoided talking about the priesthood. I could only gather that he had had continuous difficulties with various pastors and priests along the way. He was no help to me at all. The fact that he had ten months of treatment and perhaps several more to go depressed and discouraged me. I avoided him as much as possible thereafter, but felt a deep sorrow for the "I-am-a-failure" attitude that must also be afflicting him.

Father Tom was entirely different. He was a university professor with a phenomenal memory of the Greek and Latin classics, an extrovert with a droll humor and a fund of comical stories for any occasion. Despite his fifty or more years and white hair, he had a disarmingly cherubic face featured by bushy eyebrows surmounting innocent brown eyes. It was always, or rather usually, good to talk to Father Tom, since we both came from metropolitan Boston and had much in common.

My enjoyment of his company, however, at least during the first two weeks of my stay at White Hall, was always undermined by his outspoken dislike for the Institute and his disbelief that it could do anything for him. "Psychiatry," he would often state with rather extreme hostility, "is strictly for the birds. They need it more than I do. Just let me get back to work. That's all I need, and that's all I ask."

Such an attitude merely served to increase my own anxiety because I had entered the hospital with considerable respect for the profession and agreed, with Arnold, that it was an absolute "must" for anyone whose psychiatrist had seen fit to send here. Yet, in Father Tom, I found an apparently rational individual for whom six months of treatment had considerably embittered rather than helped. I had approached him hoping to receive some sort of encouragement, something to the effect that I would soon become adjusted, that with patience I would begin to see through and be relieved of my anxiety. Such helpful remarks coming from a fellow priest would, I felt, sustain me during the most difficult period of growing estrangement and pervasive discouragement. My heart grew a bit heavier each time I talked with him, although I am sure that he had not the slightest intimation of how much harder he had made my task of trying to adjust.

In Albert and Tom, I was once again seeking to make contact, an encouraging human contact, one that would reassure me and support me in trying to find my "real self," the "truth about myself," as Arnold had put it.

Names and faces of other patients occur to me now, as I look back to that several-years-ago experience in the hospital. Sometimes it is just the faces I can see; their names have wandered to the outskirts of memory. Undoubtedly, this is because I did not really meet them as persons at that time. By projecting the negative image of myself into their minds and rejecting it, I could not become interested in them as human beings and retain them in memory. For, while I was going through the formalities of greeting them or chatting with them, my fearful anxiety was rejecting them, hiding them away along with my unwanted and unpleasant experiences. The neurotic self will automatically set up defenses to repel the unwelcome intruder lest he see the shameful interior. This exclusion results in an isolation that is at once sought for because of its apparent security, and yet unwanted because of its terrifying loneliness.

It discourages a friendly openness while encouraging a destructive brooding.

It was toward this wasteland of human aloneness that my destitute thoughts and feelings were leading me. While I could sense this fatal course, I did not know what actually was taking place, nor did I know what to do about it.

Many times, in the attractive and comfortable social area where I had forced myself to go in order to escape the panic of loneliness, amid the convivial hum of conversation, the slap of cards at bridge tables, the tinkle of the piano, the sudden and welcome burst of laughter, I would feel the real impact of the modern phrase that so well sums up the plight of many people today: "alone in the crowd."

Alone! It was a dying without death. I would gladly choose cancer or some other easy way out. Cancer was understandable. People would accept this as a reasonable cause for sickness and incapacity to work. They would not accuse but rather sympathize and try to ease the pain of suffering. Why couldn't I have been so afflicted instead of becoming a mental patient?

To have phobic fears! What a shameful thing! How unmanly! How unpriestly! Worse still, how inescapable the trap into which unreasonable anxiety had led me.

My stomach writhed in protest at the suddenly renewed activity of the animal therein.

Many months later, and with the enlightened objectivity that comes with therapeutic insight, I would sit in this same social area and, while enjoying myself and fellow patients, I would look out over the various groups of people under psychiatric treatment. Often, it would occur to me that an emotional cross-section of this or that particular group would reveal a wide scale of human feelings, ranging from barely concealed depression and isolation, such as I had experienced, to that "good feeling" of genuine joy and self-contentment that is the goal and frequently the happy result of successful therapy. This latter type of patient would be merely marking time preparatory to leaving the hospital and putting to the test all that he had learned about his particular emotional hangups at the Institute.

In between these two extremes would be a mixture of other patients in various stages of therapy. Some would be having their "up" and "down" days: comparative comfort when having found a new and encouraging insight; distress and depression when in the throes of struggling with unexpected exposures through therapy. Other patients who had made considerable progress through honest and arduous self-examination often, and with surprising accuracy, could spot signs of improvement or retrogression in other patients. Such evaluations among those who have worked successfully with their own conflicts is bound to happen because mental illness, of its very nature, will, in its improving stages and in its continuing search for health, generate a deep concern for others similarly afflicted. As happens among Alcoholics Anonymous, so will mental patients begin to realize that they can help themselves by helping others. Besides my good friend Arnold, there were many other patients who unknowingly assisted me.

Another valuable assistance to the banishment of loneliness was the occupational therapy classes, of which there are a goodly number and variety at the Institute. Man is by nature creative and, given the opportunity and encouragement, he can find and develop many hidden talents which, in turn, cannot but result in genuine pride and in a welcome sense of utility and worthwhileness. The consequent self-approval often acts as an effective counterbalance to the feeling of uselessness, the gaunt shadow-companion of depression.

When first presented with a list of classes and told to make a selection that would fill up my days and the time between doctor's appointments, I thought I would rather like these diversions. Ceramics, leather work, metal work, volley ball, tennis, and many others appealed to me, especially since I liked to work with my hands and was eager to take part in sports. The day program, however, was uppermost in my mind at this time, and so I thought it was really a waste of time to start anything. But the doctor had insisted on seeing and approving whatever selection I should make. I submitted the list but definitely felt uneasy about it. Something was wrong. I did not know what it was.

The occupational therapy building was comparatively new and very well equipped. Ed, a kindly old gentleman, one of my fellow patients at White Hall, took me to the leather class first of all and introduced me to the woman instructor, whom everyone called by her first name, Diane. She smiled a welcome and then showed me around the room and what it had to offer. I was being introduced to the several other occupants as "Father"

Collins. I felt embarrassed at this and a faint perspiration appeared as I felt their eyes upon me and sensed their unasked questions. Diane said that most new patients started by making belts, since this was comparatively simple and was a good introduction to the use of the various tools.

The other patients knew each other and kept up a constant stream of conversation and light-hearted banter. My uneasy feeling became one of loneliness. I was a stranger and now known to all as a priest-patient. I seemed not to be able to speak their language and they, I am sure, would not understand mine. Silent and alone, I worked away at the far end of the room, apparently industriously intent on my work, but my mind was becoming more distraught with a sense of futility. My stomach ached and protested at the pain. Alone. Anxious. Analyzed. Embarrassed. Memory dredged up similar feelings . . .

*In grammar school I dreaded being late. It meant I was the center of everyone's critical attention. New clothing, especially shiny, polished shoes singled me out for unwanted attention. I could recall smudging up the shoes so that no one would stare at them, or me. The new suit, my first long-trousered suit, how I had longed for it and yet hated the experience of trying it on. Mother had taken me into Filene's Bargain Basement. The salesman had me stand before a large, three-way mirror. The suit I liked, but how I disliked the face above it. From three sides I could see the face and then deliberately lowered my eyes so that I would not have to look at it again. "Walter," Mother said, "it looks fine. We'll take it." The suit I treasured but shuddered at the mysterious depression that came over me when I looked at my own face. I was twelve years old then, and still the haunting memory remained.*

Deep, indeed! Old, and yet young, were the roots of my self-consciousness.

Despite these distracting feelings and unwanted memories, I worked away on the leather with careful energy, with elaborate planning, with precision and exactitude. Diane passed by and paused approvingly. "You must have done this kind of work before," she said, admiringly. I shook my head. "My very first attempt," I answered. I wanted to do a good job and knew I could. After all, my work was me. And approval of my efforts meant approval of me, the person.

Although my work had been approved, my stomach disapproved. Despite the cool breeze drifting through the open windows, I was still perspiring when the class ended.

And so it went with the various other classes. Embarrassment over the "Father" Collins introductions, the perspiration, the hollow, empty feeling of futility persisted. It all seemed so useless, I protested. I was not ordained to carve leather, to paint ashtrays, to bang away at a piece of metal. Others might be able to enjoy doing these things, but I could not. More and more, I felt alienated from those around me. I tried harder to concentrate on whatever I was doing, but it was no use. My work is in the priesthood, I stormed at myself, not here wasting time in these futile attempts that had nothing whatsoever to do with my emotional problems.

The growing uneasiness, restlessness, and anxiety that afflicted me more acutely each day during these first two weeks at the Institute of Living and White Hall, was not unrelated to that major depression that was soon to assault me. Sensing its threatening imminence, my unconscious mind must have been seeking ways and means to forestall, and perhaps prevent, it. On the conscious level I chose one means which, although unequal to the task, became most revealing and enlightening later on in therapy when understanding and objectivity would indicate and analyze its various layers of defensive motivation.

My good friend and "patient-therapist," Arnold, had insisted, upon our introduction, that he not be called "doctor" or even "doc." He wanted to be known as just plain "Arnold." This first-name-calling and greeting was characteristic of the majority of other patients, I noticed. Many of these were in professional fields of work—doctors, lawyers, judges, clerics, politics, and so forth. Most of them did not even want to be addressed as "Mr." or "Mrs." I, however, kept reminding myself that I was a *priest* and that I must uphold the dignity of the priesthood. I felt that somehow or other I would betray and undignify that supreme calling by being addressed as just plain "Bill."

This set up an ambivalence within me. I wanted to be one of the crowd, anonymous for the most part, just another patient at ease and friendly with other patients. Yet the term "Father" continually recalled the role, the status, and the dignity that it was my duty to maintain. True, I had lowered this dignity by becoming a mental patient but, I felt, I would betray it again by relinquishing the title "Father."

Despite this conflict, however, I told Arnold one day that I wanted to be called "Bill," and no longer referred to as "Father." Immediately, he broke out into a smile and shook my hand. "Congratulations!" he said. "Finally you have come to admit that you are a *person* first and a priest after that." I am sure he saw some of my deeper conflicts better than I did, but he recognized this as some sort of breakthrough.

In making this change of names I am sure that there was an element of flight. I wanted to flee, to some extent at least, the burden and imagined accusation of not being the healthy and normal priest that I thought other patients thought I should be. Then, too, I wanted to be relieved of the difficulty of one identity for the comparative freedom a quasi-anonymity might offer. I felt as though I were assuming an alias; but this was too late, since most patients knew me as a priest, anyhow.

Deeper than these motives, however, was the root-dissatisfaction with my identity. I had been baptized "Walter," or at least this was my parents' intention. I was named after an uncle of whom I became very fond, later on when I came to know him, because of his kindness and amiability, but especially, I think, because of his baseball prowess. For many years he had been a top-notch infielder and excellent hitter for many semi-professional teams in and around my home town.

Nonetheless, as far back as I can remember, I had never liked my own name. "Walter," to me, had seemed odd, uncommon, unwanted. It singled me out, usually, I felt, in my worst light. I was proud of my last name (I don't know just why) but can recall so many times in my youth when "Walter" filled me with dismay and a dislike for the utterance of it. Yes, it was dismally verified when I had tried on that first long-trousered suit at Filene's. "Walter, it looks fine. We'll take it." But I had disliked the name and could not look at the face of "Walter" in the three-way mirror.

Of course, it was my*self*, and the "Walter" that identified it, that I did not like on these occasions. I was attempting to reject my *selfness* at this early age—and still was attempting to do so these many years later.

"William" was a name I acquired upon entering the seminary. In securing my baptismal certificate, the priest could not find a "Walter"; he could only find a "William" for the date of my birth. The relief I felt upon this discovery was beyond describing. I felt like a completely new person. It was not only the thrill of entering the exciting and challenging seminary life, but I felt that the past had been wiped away. The "Walter" of unhappy days was a nonentity! What an unexpected and blessed event!

Although I brought a new name with me into the seminary, I did not bring a new person with me or a new and different identity. My attempt to escape the past and its implications, both while entering the seminary and at the Institute of Living by substituting "Bill" for "Father," was purely defensive. Whether I was addressed or thought of myself as "Walter," "William," "Father," or just plain "Bill," I was, in reality, one and the same person, the same *self*, with roots originating in the far past, dwelling and growing in the "now" moment of life, and reaching out into the future as I envisioned it. Any attempt to obviate the past simply by assuming a new name is very much like a cancer-ridden man rising from his sickbed, donning a new suit, and telling himself that he is now cured.

Being given the name "William" upon entrance to the seminary and thereby being able to discard the unlikable "Walter" was accidental and unplanned. Choosing to drop "Father" and taking on "Bill" was pathetic. What was worse, I knew it. I knew that a change of names would not cure me, even though it indicated a hopeful change of attitudes.

What I did not know at the time was that this name-changing, as with so many other neurotic gambits I had employed in the past and would continue to use until well into therapy, was a flight *to*, as well as a flight *from*. It was a search for something, a *someone*, a *selfness*, and an *identity* that could be approvable from *within* and, to a greater or lesser extent, acceptable from *without*.

Because the mental patient is so emotionally disturbed, he will search continually and hope endlessly for the *good* feeling that will banish, at once, the painful anguish of depression and will lift his spirits. By its very nature, his afflicted human organism will struggle ceaselessly to avoid the haunting fear that now pervades his emotions, and he will almost frantically seek the thought, the word, the thing, the person, the occupation, the atmosphere that promises to give him that so desperately desired feeling of peace, comfort, contentment.

In his legitimate quest for this *good* feeling, and in presenting himself to a psychiatrist for help, the mental patient will have to utilize patiently and perseveringly the two basic features and faculties of human nature: his intellect and his will.

"Honesty and effort." These were the two words that Dr. Mack had presented for my consideration when, after about a week at White Hall and feeling increasingly depressed, I had asked him just what I had to do to get better, to solve my problems, to acquire that *good* feeling that I so desperately wanted. He asked me to think about his answer for a few moments, and I found myself reflecting, despite my distress, on how truly basic and philosophically apposite, how necessary were these two words and their implications in the hoped-for solution to my problems.

"Truth" was the object of the intellect. "Good," or good effort, was the object of the will. Therefore, "honesty" had to motivate one's answers, probings, and eventual findings, in spite of the pain of discovery. "Effort" would have to come from the will in its reaching and grasping for what was "good" for the person as a whole.

These few moments of enforced reflection were illuminating

because they so well coincided with my training in philosophy and my understanding about the activity of the human mind.

This brief glimpse of what was meant by "honesty and effort," in the search for a way out of my distress, was much like the fleeting and limited vision afforded a person, lost and night-bound in a strange forest, when the flickering light of his last match dies out, having revealed nothing more than fearsome shadows and no clear trail to follow. This lost feeling was depressingly underlined by the next comment of Dr. Mack.

"You had better forget the idea of the day program, Father," he said. "It should be quite clear to you by now that you have some very deep problems that will need extensive exploration. You came here because you knew you needed help. It is the kind of help we are prepared to give you, but it will take time. I think you should make up your mind to the fact that you are going to be here for a long time. Just how long depends on many things."

So this was the sentence, finally pronounced. It was not entirely unexpected, for with the daily increase of apprehension and anxiety, which must have been clearly evident to the doctor, I had steadily lost hope of being allowed the comparative freedom of the day program. But I did not expect the dire pronouncement that I would be an incarcerated patient, and a "prisoner" of the hospital for a "long" time. This was incredible! Intolerable! It meant that my precious priesthood would be that much longer exposed to this unbearable indignity. It meant that I was, once again, a failure! A failure as a priest! A failure as a patient! I was, in essence, one great big sad-sack Failure!

At this moment I thoroughly despised myself. I despised that "self in the past" which, through abysmal stupidity, had brought about the shattering defeat of this "self in the present."

Amid the shambles of hopes and ideals, I sat there before the doctor, mute and abject. But there were still other depths of misery awaiting me.

On the first day of entrance and upon meeting Dr. Mack, I had asked about saying Mass daily. He said it was not customary but that he would refer it to the staff and let me know when they had come to a decision. After four or five days, permission was given me to leave the grounds from 6:00 to 9:00 A.M. for purposes of saying Mass at St. Augustine's, some four or five blocks away. I used the three hours not only to say Mass, but to breakfast at the rectory and chat with the four or five priests stationed there.

Mass, to me, was everything. I felt I had to say it as often as possible. Now, as a mental patient, I needed it more than ever for the strength and consolation it would afford. Besides, I had always been convinced that a priest should say his daily Mass, even with the expense of some effort. If sacrifice was the essence of the Mass, and if sacrifice was the proof of love, then it was my duty to sacrifice bodily comfort to prove that love.

The priests at St. Augustine's were all wonderful men. The pastor, a monsignor, and his curates were accustomed to having priest-patients from the Institute. Their easy informality, featured by clerical "shop talk," was a welcome oasis of friendly familiarity as compared to the rather alienating atmosphere of the hospital, an alienation that grew gradually more depressive during my first two weeks at the Institute of Living.

It was good, so very good, to be among priests for even a short time each day. This was the world I knew and loved and the work that I wanted more than anything else. Here, among cassocks and Roman collars, black suits and white surplices, candle smoke and altar boys, breviaries and bibles, I was at home. I was in familiar surroundings, and my identity was not threatened. I knew *who* I was and *what* I was.

Upon returning to the hospital, however, a strange feeling of doubt, depression, and isolation would seize me and confiscate the identity I had felt at the church. I seemed to be two different people. The actions of one person I loved and wanted and could not have. The attitudes and anxieties of the other person, I feared and detested, but could not free myself of them.

# CHAPTER V

# RELIGION AND THE EMOTIONS
## *"O Lord, Make Haste to Help Me!"*

---

*"Have pity on me, O Lord, for I am languishing;*
*heal me, O Lord, for my body is in terror;*
*My soul, too, is utterly terrified;*
*But you, O Lord, how long . . . ?*

—Psalm 6

As spiritual training and habit had formed me, I would start off the day with the Morning Offering: "O Jesus, through the Immaculate Heart of Mary . . ." It had often been said mechanically, sleepily. Now I uttered it fervently, imploringly. "I offer You all my prayers, works, joys, and sufferings of this day." At the word "sufferings" would come pangs of anxiety. They were increasing daily, and I shrank from them. And yet, I reasoned prayerfully, pain was also a part of my life, and seminary training always had emphasized the offering up of all suffering. And so I would. After all, pain was meritorious for other members of Christ's Mystical Body as well as for the one offering. There were many who could profit from the merit of my anguish. Fleetingly, I thought of some of these. The dull throbbings continued. "But only," I murmured in guilty protest, "if only there would be some 'joy' to offer up with the pain."

Downstairs, I asked the aide to heat some milk. This, together with a little sugar, seemed to be the only food that would ease the aching in my stomach to some degree. Sipping the warm fluid while sitting in an easy chair, I would spend a few minutes attempting to organize my thoughts, to arouse a bit of courage, to summon up some hope before starting off to say Mass.

My body was tired and seemed, at times, to ache all over. My eyes were burning and I desperately wanted to close them— and to close out everything else. But the probing fingers of anxiety would pry them open and I would stare unseeingly at the walls, ceiling, and furniture. My mind was dull and then suddenly overactive, in turn. Wearily, I would arise and set off for church.

These were clear, cool October days with brilliant sun, deep blue skies, and leaves not yet fallen. In the past, this kind and time of day always had been a delight to me because the early morning hours seemed to hold a bright promise, an invitation, and an encouragement to meet the challenges of the day. Each hour, I would reflect, and every moment it contains, is grace-full because it offers countless opportunities for personal enrichment and spiritual growth. What a thrilling experience to gaze more knowingly and rewardingly at the splendid treasures contained in the vault of each day!

Such thoughts as these always were supportive and fruitful. But now, despite concentrated effort, I felt barren. As I walked the five blocks to St. Augustine's on the last few days of my stay at White Hall, neither these thoughts nor any others could evoke the quiet joy I had so often known at early morn.

Everything, in fact, seemed to be a reproach or an accusation. The brisk air and bright skies should have lifted my spirits, but I felt myself slipping deeper into the morass of depression. The hustling stream of traffic should have assured me that human activity had orderliness, purpose, destination. I felt disordered, confused in purpose, uncertain of destination. People, waiting for buses, walking to work, chatting, eating at the corner coffee shop, should have convinced me and consoled me that life and work could be interesting, enjoyable, rewarding. My existence now, it seemed, had become a pervading drabness shot through with constant stabbings of sudden fear. A return to the work I had known and loved became an increasingly anxious concern each day, and more difficult to envision amid the encircling shadows of each long night.

On these mornings, when possible, I would say Mass at a side altar of the Blessed Virgin. To her, as "Queen of the Clergy," I had consecrated my priesthood. She must, I fervently urged her, present me to her Divine Son as His needy priest, His ailing priest. She must vouch for my sincerity in wishing only to be that "holy" priest, that "good" priest and to ask Him to relieve me of that depressing anxiety that was so debilitating, so frightening. I would people the altar with the Apostles, Saints and all those other intimates of Christ, those who knew Him, who loved Him, and who suffered for Him. I wanted to feel the intimacy of their companionship, their understanding and sympathy for my weakness, their encouragement and strength, their solid faith and sustaining hope. I tried to imagine them as so many stanch friends standing around me, offering with me, and bearing witness to the authenticity of my priestly desires.

At the consecration, I would silently beg Christ, now present to me as He was to His apostles, for that "peace I give unto you." Then, peering intently into the chalice as though I could see Him, I would try to deepen belief by visualizing His Body welling up from the depths of the wine into that stupendous and miraculous Presence which, as divine revelation testifies, continually encompassed me in Its all-embracing Love. Present now in humble obedience to my human utterance through a power that He Himself had gratuitously given me, would He not now respond to the cry of my anguished heart?

At the Communion, I pleaded for that "oneness" with Him that would give me an unshakable trust and confidence despite the burdens of the fearful day. This "oneness" with Christ, as far as I could determine, was an unalterable fact of my existence. I was not hiding or fleeing from Christ. I was searching for Him. I was completely open to Him, and so this oneness was not merely a physical union, but a desperately intended spiritual, moral, and mental union. Yet the *feeling* of this communion with Christ was dolefully absent.

The fact that faith and the feeling of faith are not necessarily synonymous or concomitant was not obscured in my feverish search for relief, but how, my mind asked with increasing panic, how escape the rising tide of engulfing fear without the bouyant feeling of hope? Why did He not come, He Who alone, it seemed, could calm the turbulent waters that threatened to capsize the frail bark of sanity? For, I had come to feel, this was really at stake.

This thought alone was frightening. Resolutely, I tried to push it aside but succeeded only in adding to the despondency that seemed to grow heavier with every attempt to dispel it. When, and from what source, would relief come? A miracle? I did not ask for such, nor expect it. Indeed, I knew only too well my unworthiness. I merely wanted to feel the first faint stirrings of hope, the reassuring promise of peace: "My peace I leave you," He said, "My peace I give unto you." Do, O Lord, please do give this peace!

Perhaps, perhaps He wanted to try my faith, my trust, as He did the Apostles in the sinking boat. Perhaps this feeling of abandonment was the only way I could learn of my absolute need for Him. Perhaps He would come unexpectedly, consolingly, during the day. I would therefore trust more expansively, more patiently. I would await His coming.

As days passed, however, and brought no alleviating hope, Mass and prayer became more intense, almost demanding. This overemphasis, instead of cultivating hope, served only to proliferate the noxious weed of anxiety that had crept massively and stealthily from the subconscious and that now clung to almost every conscious thought with a smothering embrace.

The spiritual life, of course, was not designed to bestow automatic peace on all turbulent emotional crises, much less was it intended to cure a neurosis. It can, in fact, intensify the latter because it is usually the wrong medicine for this illness.

But the neurotic, desperately seeking some kind of hope to relieve his agonizing depression, will seize avidly upon that which, as he recalls, has always promised hope in any difficult situation, and he will try therefore to wring from religion a cure it does not presume to possess.

"Grace supposes nature," says St. Thomas. But this principle supposes a healthy nature, a comparatively calm and receptive mind in which grace can operate effectively.

The anxieties and guilts that are the causes of a neurosis are so deep and well-hidden that they can be found, recognized as causes, and eventually liquidated only after lengthy and usually involved therapy.

Religion has the proper and helpful answers, thank God, to many of humanity's ills but, as is evident, it was not intended to be a cure for all of them. So closely intertwined are the spiritual and emotional states of man, however, that the causes and effects of the one are easily confused with those of the other. In my prayer life at this time I was demanding the impossible of my spiritual resources and also looking in the wrong direction for the kind of hope that I really needed.

It was a mistake of this nature, also, that prompted me to insist on saying Mass during this initial stage of therapy, although I doubt if anyone could have convinced me of this at the time.

In having the exceptional privilege of leaving the hospital to function as a normal priest in good health, I was refusing to admit that I actually was a mental patient. Because of this dual attitude an ambivalence arose, for I was attempting, unsuccessfully, to reject the stigma of the latter status, while struggling just as vainly to maintain the dignity and self-esteem of the former. My identity, I insisted, was a priest, or that which I thought a priest should be. At the other extreme, "nonentity" I suppose I would have termed it, was the utter humiliation of being a person badly in need of psychiatric attention.

In this losing struggle for identity that went on day and night, there was bound to arise the gnawing suspicion that I was really much worse off than I would dare admit, or wanted others to know.

This new and sickening possibility as to the extent of my illness served but to increase the over-all anxiety that pervaded my thinking at all times, but especially when I retreated into the comparative obscurity of my room and there pondered broodingly over the unreality of the present and the impossibility of the future.

Here, often while saying the Breviary, I would try searchingly to determine what actually was taking place in my life. Where and how, in God's plan for me, did this long and agonizing trial fit in? What was it all about? It must have a reason, but what was that reason? My position was precarious, and it threatened to become disastrous.

In the Psalms, I felt that I was meeting a kindred soul, for the writer well knew my oppressive moods and reflected them in poignant language.

> *Why are you so downcast, O my soul?*
> *Why do you sigh within me?*

This sighing was a continual companion to me. It was, I am sure, the built-up tension arising from anxiety and that would suddenly seek relief in this form.

But why, O Lord, why was I so downcast? What was it, really, that I feared so greatly?

> *I am numbed and severely crushed;*
> *O Lord, all my desire is before you;*
> *From you my groaning is not hid.*

But if you see my desires, Lord, and know them to be truly representative of my love for Your service, then why are they crushed along with my abilities, such as they are?

> *I am very near to falling*
> *And my grief is with me always.*

It was most difficult to enter the hospital, Lord, but I did so because I wanted to regain my health and return to Your work. But, now, time is running out and I seem far worse off than when I entered. Grief is constant and confuses my thinking; it blinds me so that I stumble. How can grief exhilarate? How can it serve Your cause?

> *Have pity on me, O Lord, for I am languishing;*
> *Heal me, O Lord, for my body is in terror.*

Physical suffering, Lord, never really frightened me because I could see and understand the causes and always I tried to

offer it up, but this interior terror that rises and swells and stabs,
what is it? Why should it be? What is its cause? How will it end?
When, O when will it end?

Many were the long pauses in the saying of the Psalms during
these difficult and depressing days as I sought the sacred author's
consoling relationship with his God. Here was a soul that had
suffered deeply, agonizingly at times. Yet, from the depths of
depression he could rise to joyful exaltation. I knew, of course,
that the Psalmist's ascent to delight and serenity had not taken
place overnight. But feeling as I did, that I could bear but little
more of my continual agony, I could only groan inwardly: How
long, O Lord, how much longer before I can say to my soul:

> *Hope in God! for I shall again be thanking him.*
> *Look to him, that you may be radiant with joy.*

This agonizing inquiry as to the *reason* for all this pain was
fruitless, of course. The search, in fact, only emphasized its
absence and prompted a further probing. The very hiddenness
of things is a sufficient motive for human probing. If only I knew
the real reason, then the suffering would become at least
tolerable, for it is no small consolation to be convinced that there
is a good and worthy cause for one's unavoidable pain.

Fleetingly, I wondered: Could this by any chance be the "dark
night" of the soul? That trek through a spiritual wasteland
experienced and described by not a few intrepid individuals in
the ascetical history of the Church? For a brief time, the consideration of this possibility shed a ray of hope, a promise of
peace, for if this experience really were the dark night, then it
would also mean that God had *chosen* me for this particular
mysterious purpose, and my pain would, gloriously, be the
means to His holy end. I did so desperately want to feel *chosen,*
for this would mean that I was, after all, worthwhile, not really
a failure, that my pain was acceptable, useful, purposeful.
"Failure" in this sense, I could accept as part of my identity,
indeed, its most significant aspect.

But further reflection convinced me that it simply could not
be. The dark night was only for those select souls who had

proved their fitness for this privilege by heroic virtue, unflagging zeal, magnificent fortitude, and constant trust. A passing glance at my spiritual life showed beyond doubt that I did not qualify. There was very little accomplished here, and certainly nothing of heroism.

Yet, I wondered, how could the pain of their "dark night" be any worse than that which I was presently experiencing? How could their barrenness and desolation be more oppressive? To what lower depths of destitution and aridity could the human soul descend?

Despite the intensity and constancy of my own particular agony, however, I could not but conclude that I did not belong among those valiant individuals who were especially called to bear witness through the "dark night" of the soul. Their trust in the apparently absent God was without limit or qualification. My trust was weak and whining. How subtly pride prompts to the usurpation of others' glory!

With a heavier burden of oppression, therefore, I was left wandering in a no-man's-land between that chosen group for whose company I was inadequate and a former way of life for which I was incompetent.

As is evident, such laborious searchings and somber reflections were not only fruitless but harmful, and undoubtedly precipitated that distressing event that was to catapult me into the most disastrous phase of my life.

During these last three or four days of my stay at White Hall, I could no longer conceal the external manifestations of depression, if indeed I had been able to do so prior to that time. Miss Amadon, the young student nurse, frequently invited me to play cards or Scrabble, but I could not concentrate. I was too much aware of the leaden ball of fear in my stomach. One day, sensing my distress and extreme discomfort, she suggested a walk in the warm afternoon sun and offered to listen if I wished to talk. Sitting on a shaded bench on the campus, I tried to describe my feelings of "failure" in the priesthood, my lack of efficiency, of productiveness, of usefulness, and that here and now being a mental patient was the final, conclusive proof of abject failure in one who had been given so much.

Calmly, reasonably, she responded by defending failure in human nature. After all, she asked, who is perfect? We are imperfect and have to accept the state of our imperfection. What batter, she observed, makes a hit every time at the plate? What businessman does not make mistakes? Isn't every success in life really built on the profitable lessons that mistakes and failures have provided? She herself was only an 85 percent student and had never been any better, although she had always tried to improve. She wanted the 100 percent as much as anyone, but was not defeated when the old familiar 85 percent turned up again.

This 85 percent was also familiar to me, I observed silently, for it was my average grade in college, seminary, and postgraduate studies.

Her logic was unassailable, of course, But it was also unavailing because, I asserted, my case was different. I expected to fail in certain efforts, but there was no excuse for me failing in those very areas where I should have succeeded. My case didn't deserve a sympathetic explanation. I was a mental patient, was I not? So, I was a failure! I was not just a human failure, I was the *priest* who failed!

In this worsening condition, it seems as though the mental patient will purposely select the thoughts and scenes that have an unpleasant content. Every impression appears to be heavily slanted with the propaganda of mental agony, of accusation, of foreboding. Returning to White Hall after my conversation with the student nurse, I paused to watch two workmen gathering goldfish from a large cement pool before cold weather set in. A small bridge spanned the pool and this, together with fallen leaves from a maple tree, formed shaded and protected areas in the water for the frantically darting, brilliantly colored little fish.

Patiently, methodically, the men swept the pool with their nets, catching several of the finny little creatures with every cast and depositing them carefully into a large water-filled can.

The remaining copper-gold streaks, still free, had shot into the temporary shelter of the bridge and leaves.

Try as they might to escape, though, the goldfish were trapped. There was no escape. It was only a matter of time. I shuddered. I, too, felt trapped. How much time did I have left? Again the pang of fear as I thought of BB-4.

What did I know of BB-4, actually? I had learned of it mostly from Arnold, who had described it graphically in telling of his terror when he awoke to find himself tied in bed and in a locked room. It was painful for me just to listen to him relate the agony and disorder of the subsequent two weeks. Factually, BB-4 was the fourth floor of the ten-story Burlingame Building and was used mostly for patients needing temporary medical attention. As a patient unit, it was included in Group Four, and that meant many restrictions and supervised confinement.

Although at the time, I thought that it was this severe curtailment of freedom that I feared when thinking of BB-4, I came to realize that there were other undercurrents of fear more strongly present. Because mental patients are human, they will automatically seek to maintain such status symbols as are available. Group Nine indicated that a patient was in fairly good condition and could be trusted with a certain amount of unsupervised liberty, plus being allowed visits home and to the city. To be "sent down" to Group Four meant that a patient had worsened, that he needed the protection and discipline of a supervised unit. A constant topic of conversation and observation by other patients were those unfortunate ones who were "sent down."

To me, this demotion to Group Four would mean the ultimate defeat, because it would clearly indicate that I was a failure even as a patient! Also, whatever small dignity I had preserved for the priesthood would go down with me. To what further disgrace could I descend? There *were* lower depths—and I would experience them.

Besides this evident and admitted fear of losing status, there was a still deeper dread occasioned by the thought of being "sent down" to Group Four. It was a horrible thought, and I desperately strove to keep it in abeyance whenever it threat-

ened to burst in upon my consciousness. On many occasions at
other hospitals, I had seen people with deranged minds. Now, I
fled in terror at the memory.

Everything, it seemed, during these last few desperate days,
was tinged with the dull gray of my pessimism and the hopeless
longing for escape. With sad envy I watched the hired help,
mostly black, as they went about their work in an apparently
carefree and lighthearted way. In comparison, I had so many
more advantages in life than they. I was white and therefore
accepted everywhere; well-educated and deferred to because
of it; a Catholic priest and accorded respect, privilege, and
even reverence by virtue of this calling.

They, on the contrary, were the unwitting victims of dis-
crimination, limited in educational opportunities, shunted into
ghettos and often deprived of the barest civilities. How could
they stand such demeaning treatment and so much injustice, I
wondered? Yet, here they were, the happy ones, laughing, joking,
singing as they went from chore to chore. And I, with all my
accumulated abilities, gifts, assets, advantages, and position, I
was the miserably unhappy and fearfully depressed one. What
I would have given to enjoy their peace of mind for a day, for
just a few hours!

Animals, too, were the object of my envy. Squirrels, friendly,
inquisitive, and always hungry, would squat expectantly as I
walked by. They were not concerned about the past or the
future, their reputations or abilities, anxieties or phobias. They
were alert to the present moment only and to the pleasant task
of filling their plump little stomachs. If I didn't feed them,
someone else would, or a bountiful mother nature would care
for them. They were "themselves," content to be what nature
intended them to be, nothing more. Much later on, we would
become the best of friends. They would teach me much about
myself. Now, however, in the dull gray of their fur I saw only
the color of a vast loneliness.

Pigeons often attracted my attention as they drifted effortlessly
over trees and roofs or as they clustered in friendly gatherings
round the gables of the Administration building. As I watched

them now, their graceful, carefree soaring and contented cooing made me ache longingly to escape the creeping dread that paralyzed energy and smothered hope. A verse from Terse of Thursday, which I had read that morning, occurred to me:

> *Had I but wings like a dove,*
> *I would fly away and be at rest. . . .*
> *Far away would I flee*
> *From the violent storm and the tempest.*

How blessed it would be to escape the menacing present! To take wings by wishing, and to soar far above the gathering storm! To alight, finally, in some far-distant pleasant surroundings, and there to experience peace, to luxuriate in rest, to relish sleep.

But, I thought bitterly, one cannot flee from one's own mind. Its dread and vociferous content was always at hand, a malignant prosecutor of guilt, a malicious "Big Brother," as constant a companion as one's shadow in the noonday sun.

Flight through fantasy, I argued scornfully against myself, was dishonest and unrealistic. Honesty and effort were what I had promised Dr. Mack. So far, it seemed, this was the only morsel of hope our sessions had produced. In view of a mounting hunger for the food of solid encouragement, it was slim fare, indeed.

"The patient must face reality," all books on therapy had advised. Sincerely, desperately, I wanted to do so. But what was this "reality" whose threatening grasp was chasing me into the unrealistic escape of fantasy? I did not know. I knew only the heavy despondency of life—of life in a hospital that had promised much, and that it now seemed, was giving less than nothing. Others might profit from this hospital, but for me, at least, it seemed to be the Institute of the Dying!

"Look at the birds of the air," He had said encouragingly to all who would grow faint on the way and cringe from the burdens of life. "They neither sow, nor do they reap, or store up provisions in barns, and yet your heavenly Father feeds them! Are not you more precious than they? . . . Why do you fear, O you of little faith?"

These pigeons, strutting, preening, cooing, eating. Life was good to them, and they enjoyed it. They were cared for. What was wrong with me? If I were more precious than they, then why was I not fed with some sort of peace of mind? Was it too much to ask?

"O you of little faith!" Yes, I was of little faith, and woefully inadequate in trust. But I had tried, desperately, intensely, to acquire this supportive faith, this dauntless trust, this invincible confidence. I had tried—endlessly, it seemed.

Now I was tired of trying, very tired. My cup was running over—with grief.

> *I am very near to falling,*
> *And my grief is always with me.*

# CHAPTER VI

# THREE DAYS IN A
# LABYRINTH
## *No Exit to Hope*

---

*"Return, O Lord, save my life;*
*rescue me because of your kindness,*
*For among the dead no one remembers you;*
*in the nether world who gives you thanks?"*
—Psalm 6

T HIS last Thursday of my two-week residence at White Hall was marked by a harrowing incident that almost brought about a complete collapse. It was the dire consequence of continual brooding, and it presaged the immediacy of chaos.

On the preceding Tuesday, Dr. Mack had rendered the dismal decision that I would have to spend a "long" time in the hospital. After the first harsh impact of this sad news, I had rallied somewhat with the consoling thought that I would, at least, be a Group Nine patient and would be able to enjoy such privileges that came with this rating. It was not long, however, before many of the more distressing aspects and implications of this "sentence" began to infiltrate my thinking. Soon they became distressingly predominant.

My family, for instance, would have to be informed of this hospitalization. Shame, embarrassment, worry would be added to their daily problems. We had always been close and very much concerned about one another, sharing in problems, trials, vacations, and good times.

We were not emotional in expressions of love and concern, but there was no doubt that we felt deeply for each other. It was a sort of silent loyalty that could be depended upon when need arose.

Now, because of my shameful plight, they would all be greatly upset, and I was at fault for causing them this added worry. Then too, I would have to face them eventually—as a mental patient! I dreaded this, the presentation of myself to them as the disgraceful failure I knew I was. It was a constant and sickening thought.

The only small consolation I could allow myself in this regard was that I was the one who was so afflicted, not one of them. I was truly glad of this. The thought of seeing one of them in my condition, of knowing that this kind of agony was being visited upon one of my family, was unbearable. If any of us had to undergo such torment, it was best that I be the one chosen. Still, they would be suffering because of me.

Mother, aged and confined to a wheelchair because of several strokes. Could she stand this bitter news in her enfeebled condition? The horrible fact that her beloved priest-son was in a mental institution could easily bring on another, perhaps fatal shock.

Relatives, friends, and acquaintances eventually would know, also. They would be properly sorrowful, but also very much ashamed of me.

Fellow priests! I had let them down. I had failed them badly. Instead of being a profitable servant, a healthy, income-producing member, here I was, a drag on their valiant efforts in behalf of our Congregation, an object of pity, perhaps scorn, and a financial burden.

As treasurer for the Congregation, I had worked and worried over our financial situation, had counted pennies, weighed investments carefully, watched expenditures, and had often retired at night to do battle with the bulky opponent of indebtedness in the squared ring of sleeplessness. Now, instead of being a *plus* to the Congregation in its hour of need, I had become one huge, abject *minus!*

Would I ever recover sufficiently to begin to repay all I owed? The best and most productive years were behind me. Looking ahead from the bleakness of my ruminations, I could not guarantee the Congregation any sure return on its considerable investment in me. I was a zero! A *minus* zero!

These and many other despondent reflections ill-prepared me for the late afternoon session with Dr. Mack. However, I did believe that I had a rather significant victory-over-self to present him. I was more than a little bit proud of it. I was sure he would be, also. It had to do with my former pill-taking, a subject that he had reviewed thoroughly and about which he was more concerned than I thought necessary. As his interest in this area grew, my discomfiture increased proportionately. But today, I would deflate the balloon of his concern, and at the same time I would assure him and myself of significant progress.

Sleep had been a practical impossibility from the first night of my arrival, for now there were no pills to induce slumber. The brief occasions of restless dozing afforded during the first few nights of hospitalization had been denied me for over a week. Body and mind clamored for rest. But I would not ask for a sedative. I was proving something to myself. Had I wished for a sleeping pill I could have had one, quite simply, although not officially.

It happened this way. Upon arrival, I had been relieved of my small pharmacy and honestly was glad to be rid of it. It represented not only an unwanted dependency, but also contained the real threat of addiction. Later on that first day, when unpacking at White Hall, I discovered a small bottle of pills which, probably after purchase some time before, had been left in the pocket of a seldom-used suit coat. As I gazed at the seductive red capsules, I thought immediately of turning them in, but then began to reflect. Barbiturates were a problem for me, a potential danger. But, I reasoned, if I could not sleep in the days to come and yet would not take a handy pill, then this would be good proof that actually I could do without them and therefore need not fear addiction. If I could pass this test in the hospital, then I would not have to face this problem after leaving.

As I returned bottle to pocket and suit to closet, I thought, "Occasion instant, decision difficult, experiment perilous!" We'll see who wins out in this "experiment perilous!" I felt quite sure of myself.

Strangely enough, despite the growing strain and the proliferation of dismal events during the ensuing two weeks, even during those desolate, wide-awake nights when tormenting thoughts made me almost cry out for the blessed relief of sleep, I knew with certainty that I would not succumb to temptation. At these moments, when staring with burning eyes at the dark grayness of the ceiling, room and mind reverberating with the uneven crescendo of traffic outside the window, I would think deliberately, almost with a morose delight, of my lust for sleep and the strength of my determined denial of any artificial relief.

Mentally, I would go through the simple process of securing the serene slumber that those gelatin capsules temptingly offered. I had only to get up, select a pill, draw a glass of water, swallow, and presto! Sleep! Blessed, welcome, refreshing sleep! How desperately needed! How agonizing its absence!

Yet, despite this unhealthy self-torture, I did not feel even strongly tempted to go through with this simple and delightfully envisioned process. "Honesty and effort," Dr. Mack had said, if I wanted to cure this emotional malaise. I had promised. I would not break it. I would not cheat or deceive, cost what it may. Already there was a mountain of self-accusation laid to my account. I would not add to it.

Besides, I had set out to prove that I could say "No!" to any kind of pill. To fail in this important test of will-power would add considerably to my depression, guilt, and feeling of futility. Also, I needed quite urgently some sort of accolade for my badly battered self-esteem. This one conquest of self, to be sure, would not solve my multiple problems, but it was a tasty little victory, costly but very much worthwhile. In this afternoon's session with Dr. Mack, I would tell him of my triumph. With a little glow of satisfaction, I anticipated his welcome reaction. I was sure he would applaud.

He did not. At best, he was less than neutral. At this moment of great expectation, surrounded and threatened as it was by a constantly growing distress, neutrality was a rejection. Reading his face as I told him about the pills and my victorious self-testing, I sensed quite keenly his controlled disapproval. Gently but seriously, he said:

"Did you think of the great harm that could have been done if another patient found those pills? Some of them, you know, are in pretty bad shape, perhaps suicidal." Then he added: "Father, please don't try to be your own doctor here. Let us do the doctoring. You be the patient. Turn the bottle in to the nurse."

He was lecturing me, reminding me of important fundamentals. He was right. And I was wrong, again! I saw it, now. Presumptuous! Imprudent! Foolish! How stupid could I become!

Chagrined, ashamed, I sat silent. The sweet taste of a meaningful victory had turned salt-bitter as subtle pride betrayed me again. It was to become an all-too-familiar and humiliating experience.

This session continued, and ended, in a dismal fashion. The frail seed of hope, nourished so carefully in the arid soil of many depressive days and tormented nights had, indeed, fallen on rocky ground. I felt worse than ever, useless, hopeless.

Before finally leaving the office, like a chastised child hoping for parental indulgence, I lingered by the door, seeking vainly for some sort of encouragement, trying to formulate questions that would not invite a negative answer, not wishing to leave him, for I could not envision hope coming from any other source, yet guiltily conscious that I was trying his patience and disrupting his closely organized schedule.

He was trying to be kind and gentle, I could see that, but just as surely I felt that there was nothing he could do or say that would ward off that imminent *something* that lurked nearby. As I stepped over the threshold and closed the office door, a loneliness, more pervasive than ever, enveloped me.

Just what I did during the next few minutes, I could not recall. Awareness returned as I found myself walking along the macadam roadway between White Hall and the high brick wall that bordered noisy Washington Street.

Something strange and frightening was taking place. Suddenly, I became intensely conscious of my body. It was trembling all over! . . . legs tingled and shook! . . . heart pounded madly! . . . chest constricted! . . . sweat beaded my face and trickled down my back! . . . hands palsied! . . . weak, exhausted, then suddenly bursting with energy! . . . I wanted to run and crumble to the ground at the same time! . . . to shriek, to cry! . . .

This was sheer horror! A terrifying, animal panic!

What was happening? What should I do? Reason groped blindly for an answer. I knew I needed help immediately, yet I dreaded having anyone see me in this fearsome condition.

Arnold! Yes! He would understand. He was a doctor, a friend. This was something physical. He could explain it. Perhaps it was due to lack of food or sleep. (I knew it wasn't.) I must find him. I would try his room. The thought of help at hand allowed me to focus my thoughts and to control somewhat the outward signs of this terrifying agitation.

Still trembling, I hurried furtively to White Hall, grateful that I met no other patients on the way. Nor were the nurses in view as I slipped through the door and ran up the stairs to Arnold's room. And oh, thank God! he was in, sitting lazily in an easy chair, reading. His half-smile of welcome faded to one of alarm as he saw my face.

"Bill!" he exclaimed, as he rose hastily. "What in the world is wrong with you?"

"I don't know, Arnold," I answered, breathing hard. "All of a sudden I felt as though I were going to explode . . . and now I'm shaking all over!"

"Here, sit down," he ordered, indicating his chair. "I'll take your pulse."

With a handkerchief in my free hand, I wiped sweat from my face and throat and felt the pounding in my neck. Arnold's hand was cool and steady on my wrist. It felt reassuring. The trembling lessened. I breathed easier.

After a few moments, he observed: "Your heart is beating like mad. What happened? What scared you? What have you been thinking about?"

"I don't know what happened, Arnold. I just left Dr. Mack's office and was taking a walk. Suddenly, this hit me, whatever it is. I haven't been eating or sleeping well, you know. Perhaps that's it. And then, well . . . there are a lot of things on my mind."

He looked at me keenly for a moment, a professional gaze, but concerned, sympathetic, and then said:

"You've had quite a spasm. Something's bothering you. Don't you think you should tell your doctor about this?"

"Good Lord, no!" I protested vehemently. "If he hears about this, I'll be bounced down to BB-4! Then, for sure, I'd crack up completely. No, there's no need to tell him. Besides, I'm feeling better now."

The last statement was true. The trembling had ceased. The terror had subsided into that old familiar lump of anxiety. I felt much more relaxed, although still shaken by the fearsome experience, and damp with perspiration.

"I think I'll take a cold shower," I said, not wishing to probe further into the reasons for this ominous occurrence, and fearing still more the consequences if Dr. Mack should hear of this episode.

"Well, all right," Arnold finally conceded. "But if this happens again, you should see Dr. Mack and tell him about it. You owe it to yourself and to him."

Just what it was in Arnold's presence that helped so much to calm me after this harrowing event, I was not sure. Perhaps, subconsciously, I felt that I could be my worst self in front of him, since he had gone through much the same experience. Also, in revealing my terrible condition to him, I probably felt that I would not have to suffer the dire consequences if Dr. Mack had seen me. He would have to act, and it would be drastic action, I was certain.

But something else had taken place when Arnold's firm hand held my trembling wrist. Some sort of deep and quieting human contact had been made in this simple gesture. It had effectively reduced the wild disorderliness of my emotions. Somehow, the turbulent cause of this extreme agitation had been reached and had responded to the palliative of a touch of a human, sympathetic presence, at least temporarily.

Perhaps . . . yes, it well could be that, for the moment, I did not feel left out, alone, abandoned, unwanted . . . that I could be accepted and wanted in the worst of my travail.

At any rate, whatever the cause, I now felt better. Not cured. Far from it. But, thank God, considerably relieved. I stood and attempted a reassuring smile as I thanked Arnold.

"O.K.," I said, in answer to his advice. "I'll keep an eye on it. Right now I need a cold shower. Thanks again, Arnold."

The cold shower may have helped, but after it, I was so exhausted, mentally and physically, that I lay on my bed for the half hour before the evening meal. I felt completely spent, dull, numb. It was far from a good feeling, for I knew that my constant anxiety, now only a faintly shuddering sensation, was still hauntingly present. But this feeling was still so much better than the terror I had recently experienced. I shuddered at the thought of it, and wondered bleakly if it would reappear.

It would. I had experienced the first storm warnings of a personality disintegration. The storm, in all its fury, would soon be unleashed.

In my lonely bedroom that evening, a listless weariness overtook me. Anxiety, still doggedly present, was, for the moment, dull and somewhat distant. Perhaps sheer physical exhaustion had blunted its attack. It was a minor but welcome relief. How good if I could be only weary! Perhaps the plague of anxiety would lessen even more if I said a rosary.

But I could not concentrate on the words and forgot to count off the beads. Perhaps my poor nervous system, excessively battered by its recent violence, now was so numb that it would refuse to respond to the stimulus of disturbing nightthoughts. Perhaps . . . perhaps I could sleep. I lay down and closed my eyes.

It was a vain effort, as I knew it would be. Anxiety, like

a muffled drum, thudded loudly enough to keep my mind lethargically responsive. The noise of traffic, thundering, panting, whispering, flowed unevenly through the open window. The parade of images, endlessly marching across my mind, halted periodically, to give top billing to the event of the afternoon. It dominated all other thoughts. I tried to banish it, and then tried to face it openly, to fathom it. I could not. The causes, whatever they were, had retreated to subterranean caverns, or could not be found because of the dense layer of physical exhaustion.

Strangely, despite my anticipated fear of being alone this evening, the panic of the afternoon did not return. Its after-effects, however, were still felt in a ceaseless restlessness, a light sweat, and a wide-awake, sightless staring at the shadowy ceiling. Twice, I arose and asked the night aide for warm milk, sipping it slowly in the hallway near her desk, while smoking a cigarette and indulging in desultory conversation.

The remaining long hours were passed by a slow pacing of the narrow confines of my room, watching the unending flow of night traffic from the escape-proof window, and finally, a fitful, exhausted drowsiness as the first light of dawn appeared.

## FRIDAY

Daylight seemed to revive all the morbid grimness that night had obscured and fatigue had muted. A despondent apathy encompassed me. It rose from within, slowly, implacably. I felt its strong and subtle growth, like the first numbness of a paralysis, as I trudged to St. Augustine's. It smothered awareness, reduced perception, expanded isolation.

Its foreboding, alienating effect was more evident in church. Above the side altar, Our Lady seemed remote, unreal, impersonal. Her smile, a polite courtesy; her serenity, an accusation that said: "See, Father. This is what faith, hope, trust, and confidence can do. You have been remiss."

In the Mass, Christ was silent, unapproachable, and uncommunicative, despite the attempted fervor of my plea that He grant a faint whisper of hope, at least. The apostles, martyrs, and saints whom I had rallied to my support stood far off, muffled in stone. Thanksgiving after Mass was a tape-recording of jumbled words.

At the breakfast table, only one curate appeared. I did not attempt to conceal my depression. I admitted that I was feeling quite low. Could I look over his library for some sort of reading material that might give me a lift? He was concerned, sympathetic, obliging. I could borrow anything that I thought might help. Cigars on his desk. Have one? I refused.

It was a poverty-stricken little library sheltered by dusty glass doors. Its anemic contents offered no solid food for my deep, emotional hunger pains. Just what was I looking for, anyway? Hope! Hope was the only word that came to mind. A deep, existential conviction that would reach way down deep to the roots of my anxiety and that would dissolve the epidemic of fear that was rapidly sickening my whole organism. Or else a radiant theological comprehension that would suffuse my spirit with the penetrating warmth of superlative confidence.

As I fingered the outdated, dusty volumes, I realized that there was nothing here that could help. Genicot, Merkelbach, Noldin, Ligouri, Tanquerey, etc. Moralists, legalists, all of them. The letter of the law, not its spirit. What did they know about the disturbed mind, the anguished spirit? What did they know, really, of the faith, hope, and trust they wrote about, except to classify them, label offenses against them, and insist that these were virtues that every Christian *should* have? What would these analyzers of the law have to say about a priest-mental patient who had none of these virtues to any significant degree? If, after being fervently sought for and still desperately needed, how did one go about securing them? The question floated on the silent, cigar-laden air.

Modern authors, more knowledgeable of humanity's anguish, and more alert to its deeper needs, would have more encouraging words for the anguished mind. Guardini, Vann, Rahner, van Kaam, Mailloux, Gleason, Curran, Kennedy. These were the kind of men whose thought I wanted and needed. But I had read them in the past when looking for answers to my multiplying problems. If they had had the solutions I hoped for, I would not now be in a mental hospital.

Despairingly, I closed the glass doors of the bookcase. Doors! With pitiless regularity, every hopeful door I had opened, I had to close again on the emptiness, the nothingness it revealed. There was nothingness in this bookcase . . . nothingness in any book . . . nothingness at the hospital . . . nothing in Dr. Mack's office . . . nothing at the altar . . . nothing in prayer . . . nothing in my past . . . nothing in the present or future . . . nothing inside me—or outside!

Moribund anxiety, which had inaugurated this day for me, momentarily had been stung into throbbing activity by these bitter reflections. Now, mercifully, it subsided into a mood of despondent lassitude. This was the organism's best defense against the menacing thrust of despair.

This Friday, with its grim early hours as a somber beginning, ran its dismal course in an aura of melancholy, despite the ideal October weather. Arnold was away on a weekend visit. His absence made me a little more fearful of a repetition of the previous day's horror. If it happened again, what would I do? To whom could I go? Not to any other patient. None would understand and, for sure, they would not keep it quiet. Nor could I go to the nurses. They would have to report it, and that would mean incarceration in BB-4! I refused to admit that I was Group Four material.

But had I not promised Arnold to tell my doctor if the agitation took place again? Yes, and I would do so. The experience had been terrible enough in itself to prompt me to tell Dr. Mack, despite the consequences. Today, however, I had no appointment with him. Perhaps I would talk about it tomorrow when I saw him.

As the day dragged on, despite a disturbing confusion, I tried to weigh the issue at hand. Sitting on a campus bench, attempting to counteract the chill of depression with the warmth of the sun, I set about assessing the situation as calmly as I could.

Perhaps, I suggested encouragingly to myself, I could survive

these discordant after-effects of yesterday's storm. Give me a
little time to pick up the debris. I had weathered the storm
itself, and twenty-four hours had elapsed without a recurrence.
Yes, a little more time and some good old-fashioned common
sense. I was a rational being, was I not?

On the other hand, reason itself had been battered badly
by the pounding of powerful emotions. Perhaps I should take
no chances. That direful "thing," whose menacing presence I
felt quite strongly at times, might get out of hand. I knew
that, eventually, I would have to tell Dr. Mack about this.
If I asked to see him today, I knew he would oblige me,
even at some inconvenience. But, I cautioned myself, to him
yesterday's episode might be a sure sign that I was getting
worse, disturbed enough to be "sent down" to a locked unit,
to Group Four—to dread BB-4!

No! I would not ask to see him today. I would brave it
through and wait for my regular appointment on the morrow.

At this moment of uncertain decision, alone with so many
unhappy thoughts and depressive feelings, I realized how slowly
the dismal hours would inch along before I could relieve myself, to some extent at least, by talking with Dr. Mack. I missed
him now, terribly.

True, little or nothing had been accomplished so far. But
he did listen. He was patient, kind, receptive of my varied
moods, and unangered by my stupidities. He was also adroit
and disarmingly resilient.

At times, I was very impatient with my doctor, demanding,
silently critical, disappointed in him. But now, as I saw him
and his position more objectively, I felt sorry for him.

This was his first year of residency at the hospital. Without
a great deal of helpful experience, here he was, burdened
with a sad-sack priest-patient who had failed not only to make
any progress, but who had regressed considerably. A regression
that seemed to approach puerility, at times.

How very embarrassing for him to make his report on me
to the discerning staff members! Here he was, a priest-psychia-
trist, trying to represent and uphold the dignity of Church
and priesthood in this secular institution, in the scientific world.

And here was I, a supposedly intelligent person, a priest of that same Catholic Church, a student and preacher of the Providential ways of God, and yet a dismal, abject *failure!* Not only as a representative of that Church and its priesthood, but as a person!

The grim facts were before me. I was failing him, as I had failed so many others in life. Superiors, co-workers, family, friends, and God Himself! What an absolute zero I had become! I shuddered as a tremor of yesterday's panic started to arise.

This type of thinking was bad, I warned myself, as I rose hurriedly from the warm bench. Keep it up, and for sure you will find yourself in BB-4, tied to a bed! Again, I felt that faint but definite premonition of an approaching disaster, the lurking presence of that "thing." I wiped my forehead. I must "walk off" these dangerous thoughts.

At a rapid pace, I set off to circle the campus.

Somehow, the day passed and melted into a warm night. Yesterday's terror had not returned, possibly because my apathy refused it entrance. But depression, in the form of a subdued anxiety, had been a constant, direful companion at every moment. It lay beside me now, as I reclined, sleepless and very lonely, on my bed. The warm milk, taken before retiring, had not helped to relax me. A constant stream of thought poured in and out of my mind.

All of these inner feelings, I noticed, had a common emotional denominator. Anxiety . . . fear . . . What did I fear? . . . everything nowadays . . . What a horror was yesterday's episode. . . . Would it happen again? . . . tonight? . . . tomorrow? . . . sure did louse up my life, my priesthood . . . damn, damn, damn fool! . . . just plain stupid . . . stomach pains again . . . lack of faith, of trust . . . But how do you get these things? . . . have prayed, intensely . . . no help . . . What else can I do? . . . This place hasn't helped. . . . Institute of the Dying! . . . I hate it . . . have become worse here . . . so many odd-looking people . . . like zombies . . . Will I be like them? . . . in a locked unit? . . . tied to a bed like Arnold? . . . stomach aching again . . . should have king-size ulcer before long . . . long! . . . "You are going to be here for a long time," Dr. Mack had said. . . . how long? . . . month? . . . four or more? . . . Mother will have to know I'm in a funny farm . . . family embarrassment . . . fellow priests . . . can't ever face them again . . . don't want to face anyone . . . just let me be alone . . . loneliness! . . . but I don't want to be lonely . . . That's what I hate about this place. . . . I'm alone . . . alone in a crowd . . . I don't belong here. . . . priest in a mental hospital . . . how awful! . . . like drowning . . . dying . . . dripping sweat now . . . a death sweat . . .

With this last thought, I shot up suddenly and sat on the edge of the bed, as wet as though I had just stepped out of the shower. I toweled myself off as best I could with trembling hands. God! this was awful, this line of thinking. All so negative, so damning of self, so fearsome.

"What are some of your night thoughts, Father?" Dr. Mack had asked when I told him of my continual sleeplessness. The implication was, I suppose, that these anxiety-producing preoccupations caused the tensions that made sleep impossible. If he wanted to know, then I'd let him know what they were. I couldn't stop them from coming, anyway. I slumped back into the bed. . . .

Dr. Mack . . . did I like him or hate him? . . . both, I guess . . . He must have talked to my Provincial. . . . What was decided? . . . Why didn't they tell me outright? . . . Time here cost money . . . dollars! . . . mounting up with every hour . . . those stupid questions the doctor asked . . . never any answers . . . no encouragement . . . just a "long time"! . . . Halifax! . . . Lord, what a mess that was. . . . I'll never get back to preaching . . . Mother will have another shock. . . . wish I had cancer . . . then no one would blame me . . . they'd all understand . . . Now, everyone scorns me . . . like Uriah Heep. . . . What a bastard that doctor in Halifax . . . and the lonely beach . . . How lonely I am now. . . . Damn that traffic noise . . . all night long. . . . Noise, so much of it, but nothing in it. . . . nothingness . . . trapped in nothingness . . . like those goldfish . . . but they were being cared for . . . they had a beauty that people loved . . . I had nothing, nothing but failure. . . . Yes, that was it . . . Father Failure, not Father Collins. . . . There goes Father FAILURE! . . . failure! failure! failure! FAILURE! . . .

Again I jerked myself upright and slid to the side of the bed. This was bad. I began to tremble. To hell with Dr. Mack and his night thoughts. Get doing something. Stop thinking and just do something. Get a smoke, a glass of warm milk, do some reading.

One o'clock, the alarm clock said. The warm air of my room vibrated with the uneven rush of night traffic, cars and trucks. I attempted to read a magazine but the print kept blurring and my eyes stung, so I walked around the room and then gazed out of the window. Watching the busyness of Washington Street was easier on my eyes, but they soon became sightless as despondent memory kept calling up a straggling and somber array of other demoralizing images.

Countless times I paced the limited area of my room, and then sat in the easy chair attempting to effect a mental boycott of all disturbing thoughts. It was useless. I decided to try the bed again. Futile. The abusive hit-and-run tactics of an ever-present anxiety prodded my tired body into almost ceaseless movement. I felt smothered.

Numbly, wearily, I sat on the side of the bed. The luminous hands of the alarm clock mutely indicated 3:00 A.M. Time! O Lord, if I could only turn back the clock about ten or twenty years and start all over again, do things differently, do them right! But this is a stupid wish. Typical of me. The past is what it is. Nothing can change it. My past is my history. It is me! The here-and-now me! Smeared all over with the tar of failure! Ignominy! Shame!

Hopeless and helpless, I stood before the wailing wall of a shattered life, eyes aching at the sight of it, a mind seered by the memory of it.

A wave of self-pity swept over me, but almost as quickly it subsided. Always, at these moments of incipient self-compassion, becoming more frequent of late, a hard, cold, vicious voice from deep within me would scornfully excoriate this dishonest emotion. Rapier-like, it would pierce to the heart of the matter and scathingly denounce this whining, whimpering indulgence as effeminate, childish, unmanly, a futile and fraudulent attempt to escape the responsibility that was mine and the fiasco that was me!

Unwilling, but unable to convince myself otherwise, I had come to abide by the harsh accusations of this dictatorial voice, and would smother almost automatically any temptation toward self-sympathy. But the determined and successful effort made to subdue this feeling only served to increase its unexpended energy, and that of other unrelieved emotions. There seemed to be no escape, no refuge for me in any direction. I was caught in a ghetto of depression. My stomach groaned in protest.

Thunderheads of that long-building storm were ominously close.

## SATURDAY

The room gradually lightened with the advent of another day. Numbly, I lay in the semitrance that had brought a sort of restless repose during the last hour or two of this long night.

The alarm clock clanged. I hated its raucous demand that I rise and face another dreary day. I thought briefly of staying in bed but knew I could not. Like Pavlov's dog, the organism that was me had been conditioned over the years to respond immediately to the call of duty. Besides, there was that strident, persecuting voice from deep within that would scornfully deride this type of infidelity, this shameful avoidance of what "should" be done.

Wearily, I sat on the edge of the bed and, with head in hands, tried to concentrate on the Morning Offering, on the Acts of Faith, Hope, and Charity, and attempted to recall something of David's plea in the 148th Psalm: "At dawn let me hear of your kindness, for in you I trust." Other words came, but they were without life, without meaning. They were dried up little husks, without savor or nourishment. Grimly,

I offered up whatever pain the day would bring, for my family, for the family of my Congregation.

Ah, yes! My Congregation. Its members, my "family in Christ," were out there working to pay my bills. Many, I was sure of it, were praying for me at this very moment. Perhaps I could repay their sacrifices for me by assuming some of their pain, or saving them from it. After all, as a religious family, we did form a miniature Mystical Body of Christ. We were, therefore, a vital organism subject to the ills and pains that affect every living body. If a hand could save a foot some pain, it would gladly do so, said St. Paul.

Really, it was not strange, then, that the small area of this Mystical Body that was me should suffer ill health, nor that, by the same token, I should be able to alleviate the sufferings of other members. Rather me, I agreed, than one of the other members. Perhaps I was better fitted for this ordeal. The thought was void of any joy. But spiritual training and personal conviction assured me of its validity. I forced my will to accept the thought. My feelings refused to do so. Mechanically, I prepared to go off to church.

Downstairs, the pleasant night aide warmed milk for me but did not indulge in the usual early-morning amenities. I was relieved. Perhaps she saw what I felt. I hoped not, but I knew that my silent moodiness did not go unnoticed, nor would it go unreported. But I was too tired to attempt to mask my feelings.

After finishing the milk in the sitting room, I lay on the sofa, gently massaging my burning eyes. I could do nothing about the tight knot in my stomach. Again, I felt the strong urge not to say Mass, to go back to bed. I knew I was not well, that some new mood was arising within me. It was an odd detachment, a feeling that was more strange than fearful. Perhaps, after all, I should go back to my room and try to let it wear off. But, no! This new condition was no excuse. I could walk, could I not? Then I was not sick. I could not absolve myself. I must say Holy Mass.

Besides, there might, there just might be a gleaning of hope to be derived from Mass today. There might be the answer to my fervent pleas for help. I could not risk losing that chance. With a determined effort, I rose and set off for church.

The strange feeling of alienation was still with me as I trudged along the noisy street. Except for the sloshing fear in my stomach, I was much more conscious of my feet than of traffic, people, and sunlight. My feet seemed leaden, and they ached with every step. I felt as though I were walking on tar. It must be the "drag of despair," I thought remotely, the dead weight of despondency. Head down, I wondered grimly if this pavement passing under my feet would ever, ever re-echo to the happy sounds of my footsteps. I could not believe it ever would.

During Mass, the feeling of remoteness became more pronounced. Like a Greek iconostasis, it effectively curtained me off from that hoped-for encounter with Christ and His Blessed Mother. The fervent thrust of my entreaties was not strong enough to pierce this curtain of isolation. My probings became weaker with the feeling that I had no right to any encouraging response from the sacred area beyond the screen because somehow or other I had failed. I had failed in faith, in trust, in courage. And so I deserved to be walled off from that Life behind the curtain.

Strangely, this silent rebuke, this rejection, did not greatly depress me. I felt almost resigned to my unworthiness. Perhaps the feeling of remoteness had dulled perception and numbed sensitivity. Words and actions had become strangely mechanical.

It was with this feeling that, at the conclusion of Mass with a less than faint hope, I raised my eyes to the Virgin above the altar. But she did not see me. She gazed far off into the world beyond and rewarded with a delightful smile those whose trust and love and courage were so laudable. They deserved her benignity. I did not.

Like some uninterested visitor viewing the ruins of an old cathedral, I felt myself to be alone and a stranger within the deserted sanctuary of my own soul.

It is difficult to describe the various moods that invaded the long hours of what was to be my last day at White

Hall. During the remainder of the morning I seemed, for the most part, to be in the protective custody of that strange apathy and remoteness that had started the day. Occasionally, however, there were spasmodic threats of agitation. But I managed to fend off these feelings with the encouraging thought that I would be seeing my doctor later on in the afternoon.

Saying the Breviary that morning took a supreme effort. I wanted to be really prayerful and hopeful, but could not. The God of the Psalms, alternating between absence and presence, punishment and peace, acceptance and rejection, confused and depressed me. Words would jumble, and at times my burning eyes would water. Finally, I put the Breviary aside and lay on the bed, asking the ceaseless and unanswerable question: "What is wrong with me?"

After the ordeal of eating was over, I walked alone—I seemed always to be alone, even when with others—around the campus, actually hoping for an increase of apathy because it seemed to be my only escape from depressing anxiety. Occupational therapy classes started at one-thirty. I did not want to attend, for I had come to fear and despise them as evidence of my failure. They reduced my status as a priest to a senseless dabbling in fruitless and childish activity. But I knew my failure to be present would be reported to Dr. Mack. He might easily spot the real reasons for my absence and would probably punish me by sending me down to dread BB-4. Reluctantly, I made my way to the leather class.

For a half hour or so, I worked listlessly at tooling a belt. A dull dread prevented any real work and produced only the faint sweat that was so symptomatic of my constant state of anxiety. Finally, the class instructor appeared at my side and informed me that I had visitors and that I was to return to White Hall. I could not guess who they might be, but any friends would be most welcome at this moment.

The visitors proved to be my Provincial and Father John, the two who knew me best, and for a while I felt almost normal in talking to them. Before long, however, I simply had to reveal my real feelings. I told them that I had apparently become much worse instead of better and that Dr. Mack had indicated that I would be hospitalized for a long time. Much of my agitation showed through. I could not hide it. Besides, I felt safer with them since they would not be reporting what was said. They tried to encourage me, but their words and logic did not register. I could only feel an additional guilt that their efforts were fruitless. I had burdened them with my failure and distressed them with the evidence of my agitation.

Time for my appointment with Dr. Mack was approaching. I could not bear the thought of having no one to talk to after the interview. Would they, please, I begged, wait around until after I saw the doctor? Perhaps something hopeful would take place in this session and I could tell them about it. Generously, they agreed to wait.

But this interview with the doctor seemed worse than any other. I desperately wanted some kind of encouragement, of hope, a word or thought that would quell the uprising of anxiety and enable me somehow to adjust to hospital life. Nothing he said, however, could dispel the dread and near panic that I strove to conceal from him. Confused and very much depressed, I returned to my visitors. I could not hide my extreme distress from them. Indeed, I made no attempt to do so. I was conscious only of a desperate need for hope in face of the increased foreboding as to what the near future would bring.

Finally, prodded by guilt for having selfishly detained and disturbed them, I suggested that they had other things to do and gave them the pathetic assurance that somehow or other things would turn out all right. I escorted them to the car and then, as it was about to move away, I was seized with an almost overwhelming urge to jump into the back seat and to scream at them to take me out of this hell-hole! In another impulsive instant, I would have done so, but they must have sensed this wild temptation, for they waved hastily and pulled sharply out of the parking space.

The sudden surge of energy that had accompanied the thought of escape was just as quickly drained out of me as the car passed through the gates. I stood there, exhausted, beaten, hopeless. A profound sense of bewildered loneliness rose up around me and within me.

Somehow, I made my way back to my room and lay on the bed in a state of apathy and dread. It was then that the terror returned.

This seizure had all the violent elements of Thursday's chaotic experience but was far more intense and uncontrollable. It was almost epileptic.

A severe trembling seized my body, and I grasped the sides of the mattress to control the wild spasms . . . leg, thigh, stomach, and chest muscles pulled and tugged until I felt they would tear apart. My heart was a huge fist hammering away against the rib cage . . . sweat poured down my cheeks and soaked my shirt . . . a dark void seemed to open below me but I grasped clutches of bed clothing and held on. I seemed to be rising and falling great distances . . . at one moment I was spinning around in vast confusion and then I saw the curtained windows and wanted to hurl myself through them. Again I felt myself sliding toward that bottomless pit. I gritted my teeth and held on . . . O God! don't let me fall over the edge! Tons of energy threatened to burst through me . . . I felt sure that I could run straight up the walls of my room. Run! Yes! that's what I wanted to do . . . to run! run! run! run! run! run! . . . to run without ever stopping . . . to run until utter exhaustion came to my relief. I wanted to run far out into the countryside and there crawl under a pile of leaves where no one could see me or find me . . .

Just how long this violence lasted, I do not know. Perhaps only a few minutes, perhaps much longer. I had lost track of time. Gradually, the spasms subsided and I lay there sweating and panting in exhaustion. Slowly, I began to think. This, then, this horrible panic was the "thing," the "animal," the lurking terror concerning which I had had so many forebodings. It had seized me and I was frightened, really frightened, but it was a fright that somehow shocked me back into some sort of rational self-control.

Reason, I said to myself, the God-given gift of reason, was my salvation and the only solution to what had taken place. Reason was my sure defense against the savagery of animal instincts that I had foolishly allowed to attack me. Let me think, now, let me think calmly and rationally. Orderly thought can control the emotions and solve their conflicts.

This horrible experience, I said firmly, was what happened when one allowed groundless and exaggerated fears to take over the whole personality. Depressive imaginings are a lie and, as such, they have no right to exist. Only the truth has a right to be and to guide one's life activities. Then, this being so, what is the truth about my situation right now?

Let's total up all the truthful facts about me, the "here and now" me. I am sane, I am sure of that, although I know I am badly shaken by this experience and I do have unsolved emotional conflicts. But I can think logically, as I am now doing, and therefore I can control my thought processes and refuse to surrender them to blind emotional upheavals. Good! Really, then, there is "nothing to fear but fear itself," as a wise man assured an anxious people. Since my fears are really groundless and a lie, I have always at hand the saving, reasoning power simply to shrug them off whenever they appear. Good! Very good!

What else can my reason assure me of at this moment? Yes, of course. There is the truth of theology. It tells me without qualification that God is present to me, closer to me than I am to myself. And this God is a God of love. Wonderful! How simple and yet how powerful a cure this thought could be in the face of deceitful fears. Let me delve into this thought and resolve to make it a constant attitude. All I had to do was to believe, really believe, in His presence and in His love. If fear rose again, I would simply believe more strongly in this magnificent truth.

The trembling and panting had now ceased altogether. A transformation was surely taking place, but I was still uncertain as to its nature and dependability. It pointed in the direction of hopefulness, but hope had been so long deferred that I wondered uneasily about this strange but welcome quietude. Why had it appeared so soon after and in contrast to the extreme terror that had so violently assaulted mind and body? I did not know, but I would, I must, try to expand and build upon this newfound hope.

Sitting on the bedside and with head in hands, I allowed the energizing implications of God's loving presence to permeate my whole being. My mind savored this rehabilitating truth with growing confidence. I knew clearly that I did not have the answers to my many emotional conflicts. And I was still puzzled and confused at what had taken place. But with an increasing assurance, I welcomed the unexpected armistice that had brought about a semblance of peace to my distraught emotions. Right now, I decided, my task was to keep thinking on the rational and theological truths that had been temporarily obscured but that now appeared as beacons of hope. These were the truths, after all, upon which I had built my whole life's work. They would keep me orientated whenever any other storm threats appeared.

Yes, that was it! I would grow in trust by a deepening of faith, a faith in the fact of God's presence, His indwelling, His abiding love. Think deeply on these truths, and more deeply still.

Anxiety, now, was but a very faint palpitation. Though weak and exhausted, I stood and took a deep breath of relief.

The dinner bell rang as I finished washing. Still shaken by my recent ordeal, but supported by its welcome aftermath of strange new hope, I pleasantly surprised myself by being able to swallow some food despite the faint uncertainty of my stomach.

At evening recreation, my billiards game was more controlled, but small waves of uneasiness kept disturbing me. Despite firmly directed attempts to recall convincingly the presence and love of God, I kept wondering if this newfound hope would sustain me through the long hours of the night. It did not.

Apprehension began to rise before retiring. It mounted steadily after I had reached my room despite intense efforts to recall with conviction the fact of God's knowledge of me and nearness to me. The emotions had renewed their conflict. The armistice had failed. I could feel the muffled-drum throbbings of fear. In a narrow triangle of activities, I paced the floor, tossed restlessly on the bed, and stared unseeingly out the window. Helplessly, I felt myself crumbling from within.

Aside from the major event of the night, which must have taken place hours later, I can only dimly recall some other happenings. On two occasions, I asked the night aide for warm milk and can remember sitting in the hall, near the large ashtray, smoking a cigarette and sipping the hot, sweet, liquid. I alternated between extreme depression and barely controlled agitation. I paced up and down the hall, numbly. Perhaps I was muttering to myself.

Finally, the kindly and concerned night aide, who must have been watching me closely, approached and asked if I would like to see Dr. Mack, if he was available, or a night supervisor. I hesitated. Such a request was unusual. It would be thoroughly reported on and discussed by staff doctors at their early-morning meeting. It would look bad for me, I knew, but by now I was too confused and depressed to care very much. Besides, I knew I needed help, and needed it badly.

As I nodded agreement, she led me down the hall and sat me across from her cubicle in a large easy chair that she pulled from Arnold's room. If he could see me now, I groaned. My condition was bad, very bad, and I knew it was going to get worse.

The night supervisor, stout, starched, and efficient, confirmed this feeling with a few probing questions. I hardly knew what she was saying, nor do I recall my answers, but I could clearly read my condemnation in the gray, gimlet eyes that quickly analyzed my depression as being extreme, perhaps dangerous. She gave me a sleeping tablet and escorted me to my room, but I knew she had made a more drastic decision. BB-4! It was inevitable. I had known it would happen, and it did! Well, after all, I was the world's biggest failure, wasn't I? Here was proof.

A pleasant drowsiness arose. I didn't care about anything except the blessed sleep that softly embraced me.

# CHAPTER VII

# SUNDAY

## *Decline and Fall*

---

*"My harness piece by piece*
*Thou hast hewn from me,*
*And smitten me to my knee;*
*I am defenseless—utterly."*
—Francis Thompson, *The Hound of Heaven*

Events of this chaotic day are confused, but some of them stand out in memory as evidence of the coercive awareness that I still grimly maintained.

Somehow I rose in time for breakfast and managed to swallow some black coffee and a bit of toast. The soporific effects of the sedative enabled me, I suppose, to stave off the memory and the implications of the past evening and to appear not unduly disturbed to my breakfast companions. As soon as I could respectfully do so, I excused myself and hastened to my room. There I sat on the side of the bed and tried to put an encouraging interpretation on the events of the night.

A knock on the door, and Miss Amadon appeared. Her face was kindly as always, but her eyes were serious and concerned. I feared what she had to say and braced myself for it.

"Father," she said. "You had a rather rough night. We're going to send you over to North Two where you can receive special help."

Her words sapped me of what little strength I had left. I slumped over until my head almost touched my knees. "This is it," I groaned in despair. "I'm being sent down to Group Four." Again I had failed, failed, failed.

"But Father, they can help you more over there," she insisted. "They can give you more time and attention. You'll get better more quickly over there."

She was pleading with me now to believe her. But I could not. If I had failed as a patient here at White Hall, why would I not fail again on North Two? And what would that mean? Where would I go from there?

A sense of weary hopelessness engulfed me even as my conscious mind tried to listen to the nurse's words of encouragement. But the only mental response I could muster was the fact that, during this moment of utter loneliness, I was not entirely alone. Here was a sensitive, kindly, compassionate human being standing beside me, attempting to share, as best she could, the mysterious sufferings of another human being. Her words were meaningless, and I rejected their attempted optimism. But her human presence and human concern was something real, something tangible, something welcomed and needed. And it was stirring something deep and responsive far down within me. I reached out and held her hand for a moment, then rose abjectly, gathered a few necessary objects, and followed her dispiritedly and mechanically down the stairs and to the foyer, where a male aide would escort me to North Two.

A murmur of voices came from the nearby dining room. At least, I thought gratefully, none of them were around to add further embarrassment to my shameful exit. I hesitated for a moment, staring at the floor. Painful as White Hall had been, it was at least familiar. Now I had to leave it because I had failed, miserably. Failure! Again, failure was forcing me into dread North Two. My confusion and hopelessness were so great that I could not even say a "good-bye" and "thanks" to Miss Amadon. I could only glance at her briefly and nod my gratitude. Then I turned and followed the male aide out the door and along the cement pathway that lead to the menacing strangeness of North Two.

It was only a short walk to this Group Four unit, perhaps a minute or two, but each moment was laden with a feeling of strange unreality. This person walking to his doom could not be me, and yet I knew it was no dream. Then, think, man, think! But, no. Just the effort to separate the real from the unreal was too painful. I preferred the limbo of nonthought. Yes! That's what I had to do. To make a supreme effort not to think . . . not to think about anyone or anything.

We paused before a heavy steel door just behind the store that was called "Here It Is." That's what I felt I was, an "it." The "it" that was now me was motioned through the open door to North Two. Only when it was slammed shut, with an echoing finality, was I jolted from my state of nonthought. I began to tremble with panic and fear. The aide, squat and dark-visaged, looked at me keenly for a moment and then motioned me up the two flights of steel-treaded stairs. Again we paused before a locked door while the aide selected a key. Weak, bewildered, helpless, I watched him as he inserted the key. I wanted to turn and run down the stairs but, no; there was that other locked door below. Besides, the aide had taken me firmly by the arm and ushered me through the door and into the hallway beyond. Behind me I heard the heavy door thud to a close and a lock turn.

This was it! Imprisoned! Trapped! No escape! The goldfish all over again. Everything appeared unreal and threatening. On either side of the corridor were numbered doors with small, squared, peephole windows. At the far end of the corridor was a glass-enclosed nurses' cubicle before which several patients sat and watched idly as we approached. I dreaded meeting them, and was most grateful when I did not have to do so. A nurse appeared from their midst and introduced herself. I immediately forgot her name.

She indicated a room on the left that I entered quickly, hardly listening to her words of welcome and assurance that she would be around again shortly to see if there was anything I wanted or needed. I wanted only to be by myself and away from the prying eyes of the other patients and personnel.

For a few moments I paced the narrow area of the room, which had one small-paned, heavily leaded window, a bed, a bureau, a chair, and a wardrobe. I paused and looked around the room, and then felt a rising anger. I hated the room! I hated it with a growing intensity, just as I hated the hospital and what it had not done for me.

But what could I do about the whole situation? Finally, I sat on the only chair in the room and nursed the rebellious forces within me. I had tried to be a good patient. I had conformed to all the rules. I had not given any trouble. And look what happened! Thrown under lock and key like a common criminal. I seethed with the rank injustice of it all and cursed the day I had entered the hospital.

Someone knocked on the door. A young fellow about twenty, whose name I later learned was Fred, poked his head around the corner of the door and said with a friendly smile:

"Hi, Father Collins!" Already they knew my name and disgrace. I fumed in helpless shame. "Welcome to North Two! Are you going over to Mass? We leave in about twenty minutes."

The chapel! Of course! It was only a short distance from the entrance gate. I could easily escape! A short run—and out!

"Yes. Sure. I'll be ready. Thanks."

He closed the door and I was left to plan my escape in more detail. Escape! Freedom! The thought energized me with feverish planning. I would walk along with the group until we approached the chapel. The gate was about 150 feet away. Despite my years, I was still athletic and was more than confident that, with a sudden burst of speed, I could easily outrace any male attendant in that short distance. I trembled with the thought of escape. It was daring. It was not at all like me, the continually conforming and decorous me that I had always been.

What would everyone think? What would the doctors and patients be saying? The hospital would be buzzing with it for days.

Also, what would my Provincial say, and do? Momentarily, I hesitated. Could I really take this drastic action with so many foreseeable adverse reactions? I looked around the room again and thought of the dreadfulness of my two weeks in White Hall.

Again, fear and anger arose, strongly and decisively. I could escape—and I would! I hated the hospital with a rage I never thought I possessed. But then, even the mildest of animals could put up with only so much abuse. I would risk all the results of an escape. Nothing could be as detestable as this unjust imprisonment.

Hurriedly, I gathered together a few objects I might need. All I had to do was to make the gate—and freedom! Once through the gate, I was a private citizen again, and no one, even the aides if they caught up with me, could force me to return. It was against the law.

And once outside I would experience the relief that I had not known for these past two weeks of unrelieved misery. The desire for freedom became overwhelming. As chaplain at a state prison, I had often wondered how those poor inmates had felt over the loss of their freedom. I had tried to put myself in their position. Unfree! How awful! Untrusted, watched, suspicioned, regimented, caged! God! How horrible the loss of human freedom! Now I knew how they felt. They must have been bursting with a suppressed, pent-up hatred such as I now felt.

Well, shortly, I would know freedom and relief, come what may. I savored the thought with increasing excitement.

At a knock on the door I turned and froze. It was Dr. Mack, the last person in the world I wanted to see. He greeted me with his usual smile, closed the door, and sat casually on the room's lone chair. I stood looking at him with barely controlled anger. His coming at this particular moment had ruined my plans for escape because he would stay for an hour at least.

"Well, now, Father, why don't you sit down and tell me what happened last night?"

Confused at his calm intrusion into my escape plans, I obeyed and sat tensely on the edge of the bed.

"Nothing happened, really," I answered, defensively. "I just couldn't sleep and had to walk up and down the corridor. Finally, I needed a sleeping pill."

"The night supervisor thought you were extremely agitated," he observed. "Would you mind telling me about it?"

"I don't know," I answered heatedly. "Besides, it doesn't make any difference. I'm going to leave this place. I want to get out of here now!"

I had come to a sudden decision. Since I couldn't escape as planned, then I would sign myself out of the hospital. It would, at least, be more dignified and less turbulent.

"And why do you want to leave?" he persisted. "What makes you so afraid to stay here?"

Rage welled up and boiled over. I couldn't control it and didn't want to.

"Because!" I shouted. "I've become worse every day since I entered this hell-hole! This isn't the Institute of Living. It's the Institute of Dying! Well, it's not going to kill me! I hate the damn place! I want out! Now!"

"No, Father," he said with exasperating calmness. "To release you now would be the worst thing we could do for you. For your own good, you will have to stay."

With this decisive sentencing, I rose in fury and screamed at him: "You can't keep me here against my will! I have rights! I don't want to stay and you can't keep me here!"

"Oh, yes I can," he said, eyes narrowed with decision and certainty. "I can have you committed."

For a moment I stared at him, hating him, I am sure, while the stark reality of this truth worked its way into comprehension. He could! He could have me committed. And he was convinced and ready to take such drastic action. He saw me as a very sick individual. He had only to pick up the phone, recount the situation as he saw it psychiatrically and, I knew, receive committal permission from my Provincial. The latter, for sure, would not want me around in my present condition, which might grow even worse. He had enough problems. Besides, he would readily conclude that the hospital was the only place where I could receive the help I needed.

Escape now, by way of the chapel, or any other way, was out of the question. It was too late. Another door in my life had closed. A sense of utter futility overwhelmed me. By now, intense rage had given way to the despair of impotence. Trembling, I sat down heavily on the side of the bed, burying my face in my hands. I had lost again. Failed again! What was next? I did not care.

Dr. Mack must have stayed the usual hour or so, but whatever was discussed is lost to memory. I am sure that he must have tried to assure me that remaining in the hospital was the best possible thing for me. But my mind was blanked out to his words. I can only recall that after he left, I took off my shoes and rolled over on the bed, face to the blank wall. . . . I was completely exhausted by the hopeless struggle against the continual undertow of misery and defeat. Apathy was my only relief. I gave in to it—completely. I did not want to struggle—to think—to escape—or to live.

A throaty, male voice aroused me from what must have been a lengthy state of nonthinking torpor.

"Hi, Father," it said, strongly and cheerfully. "How ya' doin'?" The voice belonged to a black aide, about thirty-five, with a pleasant face and friendly smile, who stood by my bed. I had not heard him enter the room. He wore a name plate on his jacket, but my tired eyes could not focus on the lettering. He helped me.

"The name's 'Charlie,'" he grinned. "Forget the last name. Everybody else does. Been here fifteen years. Everybody knows good old 'Charlie.' We're gonna take a little walk downstairs, Father. Some nice guys down there. You'll like 'em. All my friends. You'll spend the rest of the day down there. O.K. Father?"

There was nothing I could do but nod agreement. I had no will to resist, to question, not even to wonder what was going on. Other people were now managing my life. Let them. Like a dumb animal, I was being led around by a tether, a lasso of someone else's decisions. Doctors, nurses, aides alternated in the leading. Now it was Charlie's turn. He led the way. I followed. Out the hallway and through the locked door and down the steel-treaded stairwell that had seen my sorry ascent such a short time before.

We stopped before a heavy oak door marked North I while he peered through the small, square, wired-glass window before inserting his key. To my right was the solid steel door through which I had entered earlier in the morning from the comparative freedom of the hospital grounds.

Doors! Locked! Impassable! Never hopeful openings, but always grim, desolate closings. Again, fleetingly, I recalled my pity for those locked-in human beings during my chaplaincy at the state prison. Many had given up hope. I could read it in their eyes, their lifeless gestures, their shuffling gait. This, then, was the feeling that they had, that they had to live with, somehow or other. And now, their condition was mine! Their hopelessness was mine! This was simply incredible! Unbelievable! What had happened? What? What?

# CHAPTER VIII

# NORTH I

## The Bottom of the Pit

---

*"Deep into the darkness peering,*
*Long I stood there, wondering, fearing,*
*Doubting, dreaming dreams no mortal ever*
*Dared to dream before."*
—Edgar Allan Poe, *The Raven*

CHARLIE's firm hand had taken me by the elbow and guided me over the threshold and into the hallway of North I. It looked much the same as North II, "T"-shaped, with the same kind of doors on either side of the corridor, numbered and peep-holed, open or at least slightly ajar. Just before the glassed-in nurses' office, however, the corridor widened sufficiently to become a sort of public dormitory containing three cots, green quilt-covered and separated by small three-drawer bureaus.

The patients, teen-agers and older men, lounging, walking, playing cards, stopped long enough to stare at me with emotionless curiosity. I tried to close my mind off to what they were thinking about me. They all seemed quieter, more subdued than the rather noisy group upstairs. But they were staring. I did not like it. But then, too, Charlie had said it would be only for the day. I did not know why they had brought me here; it seemed odd, but then, of course, everything that was happening to me this day was odd—and frightening.

Charlie had stopped and beckoned to two young men who

were, I guessed rightly, male attendants assigned to the unit. Charlie made the introductions. The first, Jim Byrne, was small and wiry, with rugged features and a firm grip. The other, Doug Thomas, must have carried about 275 pounds on his six-foot, three-inch frame. He was overly stout but powerful. He smiled easily, and his voice was pleasantly soft. For some reason or other, I immediately liked them both and wanted to say something appropriate, but words, the right words, simply would not come.

As I stood there, looking around uncertainly, perspiring slightly with awkwardness and self-consciousness, a nurse approached and rescued me from further embarrassment, at least for the moment. She was young and attractive, perhaps only two or three years out of training. In her neat, white uniform she was poised, calm, assured, and gently authoritative. As a professional in the service of people, she showed all the expected results of good training. I had not. There was no respectable remnant of my priestly training left to give to those who needed me as a professional helper in the service of God and His people. I was the exact opposite of this confidently purposeful young woman. Now it was her turn to take my tether from Charlie's hand and to lead me around. What a miserable failure I was! God, O God, help me! Somehow . . . soon!

"This will be your bed, Father. You might want to rest during the day. Your clothing will arrive later on. Is there anything I can do for you?"

She could not, of course, free me from this miasma of strangeness, I reflected grimly. But she was kindly solicitous and, again, as I looked at her and envied the certainty and composure of her whole bearing, she was, I realized more keenly than before, a reminder of all that I should have been and was not. Perhaps never would be.

"My name is Miss Trainor," she volunteered, "and if you want anything at all, just call on me or one of the aides." I shook my head, thanked her, and went to the indicated cot, the middle one.

As so often before in my anguish, I sat on the side of the bed, uncertain as to what I should do or how I should act.

I wanted to lie down and to close my burning eyes. They had been abused for so long. For over two weeks they had not been given a natural, healthy, reviving sleep.

But I dared not lay down. People were watching and expecting. Doug sat across the hall at a card table, eyeing me covertly, I knew. Other patients were also looking at the new arrival. And they, too, knew I was a priest. I must put on some sort of casual attitude, a pose of normalcy, but how to do it? How could I prevent these perceptive watchers and knowers from seeing through me, examining curiously my turmoil and confusion? My mouth was dry and a small form of panic kept rising to my throat, almost gagging me. I must do something, anything. But what?

Doug was idly riffling cards. There was an empty chair. Casually, I hoped, I rose and sauntered over to him. He smiled an invitation to sit down.

"Would you like to play cards, Father? Gin rummy? Casino? Anything?" Desperately grateful for both the invitation and the necessary distraction, I readily agreed athough, I confessed, I did not know any of the games he mentioned.

It was a listless game I played, gin rummy, I think it was, with Doug easily winning every hand. Conversation was at a minimum, since I could not think of anything appropriate to say. My confused mind kept wondering why I had been brought down to this unit for the day.

During the game, a couple of patients approached and introduced themselves. One was Melvin, a tall, gangling, dark-featured lad of about sixteen. He came from New York and had been at the hospital for about two months. His bed, I noticed, was to the right of mine in the dormitory section. He appeared morose, angry, and restless, and at times would argue vociferously with the male aides.

Later on, another patient, who had been sitting lethargically on the bed to the left of mine, slowly approached the table and stood silently, staring at us for several moments.

Suddenly, he said: "May I have a cigarette, Father?" At the word "Father" I again felt the pang of distress. It reminded me that by now everyone knew of my disgrace. I would be campus gossip for days to come.

"Sure," I answered, glad to be of some personal service to someone, and to begin to break down the barriers of remoteness and stolid unfriendliness that seemed so characteristic of this strange unit and its strange inhabitants.

"This is Bob Stockton," Doug volunteered. "And a real nice guy," he added with a smile at the solemn-faced lad. Doug had to light the cigarette for Bob, since no patients in this ward were allowed to have matches. My own had been taken from me upon my arrival. I noticed that Bob's fingers were yellow-stained and appeared very brownish in certain places. After he moved away from our table, Doug told me that they would have to watch him very closely while smoking because he would often forget he had a cigarette and severe burns would result. For a moment, and with deep pity, I watched Bob as he stood in the middle of the corridor, staring fixedly at the floor while the blue smoke curled through his fingers. Later on, I learned that he had been a top-notch basketball player and had been an all-scholastic selection in a large city. Again I felt a stirring of pity for him and wondered what had brought him to this place so shortly after starring as a high school celebrity.

After a while, with my stomach again aching with anxiety, I told Doug that I would like to take a walk around the rest of the unit. He smiled acquiescence and fell in beside me. I wondered why he felt obliged to accompany me but was rather glad of the companionship. Then, too, every now and then he would stop a patient and introduce us; I would promptly forget the name. My mind was on other things.

The so-called recreation area was directly in front of the nurses' office, which had a two-foot-high wall surmounted by heavy plate glass. I also noticed that the dormitory area was similarly constructed, allowing a clear view of its patients from the office area. To the right of the "rec" room was a TV set and several straight-backed chairs. To the left, in a small bay-windowed section of the corridor, were several card tables, a radio, and a record player. Several young patients sat around or lay on the floor, listening to the latest hit recordings. The blaring noisiness disturbed me.

The corridor to the right led eventually to another heavy door which, like the one I had first entered with Charlie, had a small, wire-glassed window. To the left and right were individual rooms, all with their peep-holed doors open or slightly ajar. It was then that I realized that there were no catches on the door-jambs, hence they could not be tightly closed. All rooms whose interiors I could see had the same type of furniture as did the room I briefly occupied on North II: a green, quilt-covered bed, wardrobe, desk, and chair. Also, I noticed, all windows in the rooms, at the bay end of the corridor, and those above the dormitory, were opaqued. I wondered why.

It seemed to me that some sort of cheerful sunshine and day-light should be allowed into this somber and depressing unit. The whole atmosphere was one of drabness, monotony, and melan-choly. Walls and ceilings were a dull gray; the floor was covered with a nondescript linoleum; no pictures or bright colors relieved the disheartening weariness of corridors or rec room. It seemed more like a punishment ward than a well-planned unit designed to relieve, to distract, to cheer, to encourage the afflicted patient in his depressive thinking.

We returned to the dormitory area, and again I wanted to lie down and to relapse into that nonthinking phase that seemed to offer some form of escape from the drag and dread of aware-ness; of time, present and past; of my own selfness—this utterly strange self that simply could not be the real Father Collins.

But I must appear normal, since *they* were watching; now, more closely than ever before. Doug was beside me always, smiling and affable. As an aide, and therefore as part of the establishment, he must be making notes for his report about me. Yes! I must appear normal; I must get a good report and con-vince *them*, especially Dr. Mack, that I was really okay; that I belonged in a unit with normal people.

So many patients on the unit apparently were "not with it." Some silently sat apart and stared into nothingness; some lay on their beds as though they had simply given up on life and hope; others acted erratically, spasmodically. One elderly fellow, about sixty and bald-headed, passed by, mumbling to himself, then would stop and mumble unintelligibly to someone else. Another huge fellow (I later learned that his name was Terry) paced endlessly along the sides of each corridor, touching every waist-high protuberance, especially door handles, as he passed. He looked at no one as his immense bulk (he must have weighed 300 pounds on a six-foot, four-inch frame) strode rapidly up one side of the corridor and down the other, repeating his compulsive touching ritual without fail. I wondered what caused this.

As I attempted to saunter leisurely by my "bed for the day," as Charlie called it, something bothered me. It was something Miss Trainor had said, but I could not recall it. Besides, I reminded myself, I was in this awful place only for the rest of the day; that soon Charlie, cheerful and talkative, would return and rescue me from this unit of zombies; that I would be returned to North II where, at least, I would have a room of my own and could retreat when I needed to from these frightening reminders of what could happen to a human being—to me!

Though I tried hard to appear normal to Doug and to converse intelligently with him, I knew that my uppermost emotions were those of confusion, shame, anxiety, and a frequent relapse into apathy. I did not know what was going to happen to me—and I *did* want to know . . . to know why I was in North I . . . to know what sort of promised helpful treatment I was going to receive on North II when I returned there. But then, a sort of mental numbness would seize me and I would recall, with an almost automatic defensive remoteness, my horrible failure at White Hall and the fact that I no longer seemed to be able to direct my own life or to make my own decisions . . . that while I had been given one fair chance to prove myself at White Hall with normal patients, I was now practically reduced not only to indirection from within and its resultant confusion, but faced with a threatened disorientation that was even more frightening than the White Hall episodes. I wanted desperately to think about this. My logic-trained intellect wanted the truth of the whole situation. But my be-

wildered and fatigued mind, in exhausted and apathetic surrender, simply gave up the struggle.

And yet, it did not . . . it would not . . . it could not. There
must be logical answers to this new situation! But . . . what
were they?

It was about noon or later when the male aides began shouting in loud voices: "Lunch time!" "Lunch time!" Slowly, from
various rooms and areas of the corridor and rec room, patients
began to assemble near the locked door next to the nurses'
cubicle. Eventually, when lined up, there appeared to be about
twenty-two patients in all, ranging in age from about sixteen to
sixty. A dozen or more were teen-agers. It surprised me. I lined
up with the others, not because of hunger but because it was
the dutiful thing to do. With folded arms (seminary training?)
I stood near the wall, silent, ill-at-ease and very much self-
conscious. Now all the patients were getting a good look at
"the priest who failed." I gazed only at the unresponsive, mottled, and worn linoleum. It, at least, was not a mind, and
therefore indifferent to my condition. It was not accusing. It was
a *thing* and merely serviceable. Indifferent to the shuffling feet
of the mentally afflicted. If it could only understand and talk,
what stories it would have to tell. My shameful tale would be
among them.

"How far the mighty have fallen," I quoted to myself. After
all, I was the only priest in this sad assemblage of humanity.
As the other patients crowded around the locked door, I kept
my eyes on the innocuous linoleum. "Down!" How expressive
our language is of our real emotional outlook on life. It would
be much, much later on in therapy when I would come to
realize how characteristic it is of depressed people, especially
mental patients, to look down, not up. Their looking *down* was
an expression of the "downness" of their mental viewpoint, a
revealing external symptom of their self-evaluation, their worthlessness, their extremely low self-image.

Finally, after head-counting by Doug and Jim, the door was
opened and we descended a flight of stairs to a small area where
we stood momentarily before two locked doors. The one directly ahead led into the dining room. After this was opened, I

stood uncertainly near the entrance, looking about, until Doug assured me that I could sit wherever I wished. I chose a table that had only one occupant, Bob Stockton. He would not, I thought, in his extremely silent conduct, offer much difficulty by way of conversation; and he did not.

The thought of food was still repellent, of course, and my stomach rebelled at the smell and sight of it. I took but very little, toyed with that to kill time, but finally forced down some bread and black coffee. Now and then, Bob would look up at me with those curiously unblinking turquoise eyes which, despite his silence, gave me the distinct and sometimes uneasy sensation that his mind, though emotionally confused, was at times more than normally keen. The only observation he made, in response to my comments and observations, was a rather curious one, the full import of which I was not to realize until much later on that afternoon.

"You're on constant observation, too, Father," he said suddenly, but slowly and distinctly.

"Is that so, Bob? And what does that mean?" But he had fallen silent again, staring absently at the table while his yellowed fingers played with the silverware. The darker brown stains showed where he had been burned by smoldering cigarettes. Poor Bob, I thought, and wondered if his sickness included an insensitivity to pain. I wished, grimly, that my own affliction would have included an insensitivity to the twisting stomach pains that had been constantly with me almost from the day of my entrance.

The meal was finally over, much to my relief. Before leaving the dining room, I was introduced to another strange feature of this dreary unit. No one could leave until every piece of silverware was accounted for. This meant a careful counting by the nurses and aides and an impatient waiting by the patients. What a miserable place, I thought, and in spite of my empty, aching stomach and mental confusion, I consoled myself with the thought that before the day was over I would be back upstairs in North II where, I was sure, there would not be this extremely suspicious and regimented procedure. But why had they sent me down here, at all? It must be the worst unit in the hospital, I concluded, as I looked beyond "silent Bob" and at the room full of strangely assorted faces and listened to the sometimes senseless and/or violent conversations that were taking place around me.

Finally, the silverware count was okayed and we were returned upstairs again through the two locked doors. Again, I was faced with uncertainty as to what I should do. The bed was there and inviting me to those attractive few minutes of nonthinking. But, no! I *must* appear normal, and that meant being sociable, talking with others. Besides, I reasoned, it wouldn't be long before Charlie would come along to rescue me.

Listlessly, and though my eyes were seared with unrelieved sleeplessness, I agreed to Jim Byrne's invitation to play cards. Again it was gin rummy, and again I lost almost every hand. I realized that there was a certain skill to the game that I sadly lacked, but I was more concerned with the role of appearing personable and normal. For Jim must be reporting on me, also.

It was while I had been so occupied for an hour or so that I noticed, with a surge of sudden joy, that my friend "cheerful Charlie" was coming down the corridor. I hardly noticed that he was dragging along behind him a large blue canvas basket that slid along on a couple of wooden runners. He waved gaily to me as he stopped by my "bed for the day" and said:

"Here's your clothing, Father. Some of it. The rest has gone to the laundry room to be marked." Then he began to toss the clothing on the bed and other articles into the bureau drawers.

At first I did not comprehend what was taking place. Charlie should be taking me up to North II, not bringing down unneeded clothing. Then, with a rush of depressive understanding, I realized what it was that Miss Trainor meant when she said that my clothing would arrive later on. I was stunned!

Bob Stockton was right! "You're on constant observation, too, Father." I was to be a patient here in North II! Here in this hell-hole! And no room of my own . . . to live, day and night, in a public dormitory! . . . exposed helplessly to the curious and demeaning gaze of everyone who passed by . . . patients —aides—workers—doctors—nurses—personnel—and everyone else who might visit the unit. I was to be observed constantly, watched closely, escorted suspiciously by the male aides! So that's why Doug and Jim clung so tenaciously to me all during the morning and early afternoon! *"Constant observation!"*

Why? . . . Why? . . . Why?

Was I so emotionally dangerous that *they*—that mysterious, distant, impersonal clique of report-reading technicians—had decided arbitrarily that I could not be trusted to be alone? Did *they* really think that I was suicidal when the thought had never even occurred to me during the worst phases of depression? Or did they think I was dangerous—to others—barely controlling an unsuspected violence? What conclusions or strong suspicions had prompted Dr. Mack to make this horrible decision? Was I? . . . O God, help me! . . . was I really far, far worse than I knew or imagined?

In stunned, unbelieving silence my brain recorded the dreadful facts as presented by my senses. The whole scene, Charlie, the direct object of my vision . . . peripherally, the walls, ceiling, and opaqued windows . . . the other patients and Jim watching me closely . . . all . . . all became unreal with an unreality that precluded speech and almost paralyzed thought . . . except for the numbing realization that there was, after all, a bottom to the abyss of failure . . . and that I had reached this depth . . . and was hopelessly ensnared by it!

For a few stupefying moments this sensation of unreality was overwhelming, and I could not move or speak. Then, briefly, the generalized smog of numbness that had characterized most of the past three days left me, and I felt a chaotic panic arising from the depths of my being. I felt like jumping up and screaming wildly in protest at this injustice . . . at this unwarranted punishment . . . this shameful degradation. The urge, the energy, the caged-animal rage were all strongly there, ready and waiting for the word that would release their frenzied fury.

Strangely enough, however, another and a different deeply inbred attitude and habit took over and effectively displaced the imminent outburst of insensate violence. It was, oddly enough—and I realized it quite clearly at the time—my innate sense of neatness! Perhaps this was another feature of my home and seminary training. At any rate, it was automatically dominant at the moment.

Charlie had tossed my clothing haphazardly on the bed and bureau. This disarray offended my sense of orderliness —and I must rectify it. Though never finicky about neatness, I did demand of myself a certain tidiness, an expected decorum about my person and my living quarters.

Excusing myself automatically to Jim, I went over to my "bed for the day" and began to pack the few articles neatly into the three drawers of the small dresser and laid some other few items on the broad windowsill. All of this I did calmly, carefully, and methodically, but with a feeling of mechanical remoteness. It was, I suppose, a sort of automatic, defensive, reflex action . . . simply something practical to do at a moment of overwhelming crisis in order to maintain a threatened loss of control, much as a mother might start washing dishes after hearing the shocking news of the death of a loved one. In my case, this very practical something-to-do somehow allowed the rage and panic to pass. Somehow, too, it seemed to assure me that reason, responsibility, and adaptability were still in the ascendancy . . . that despite the unexpected assault of vicious events, I was still, to some extent, in control of myself and my immediate environment . . . that I was not an irresponsible zombie despite the dead weight of despondency and hopelessness that began once again to envelop me as I started to absorb the full meaning of this utter degradation.

With nothing else to occupy my hands, I stood for some long moments staring mutely at the stupid, opaqued window above my bed . . . the window that shut out the cheerful sunlight and azure blue sky . . . the green trees and the autumn amber leaves . . . the freely scampering squirrels . . . the soft October breeze . . . the refreshing smell of newly cut grass . . . and the sense of freedom that is so essential to human hope and human striving. Who did this? And why?

Why? Why this inhuman, unnatural, and complete cutting off from the beauty and reassurance of nature's loveliness, aliveness, bright promise, and cheerfulness? Why? Again, why were we, the poor, unwitting victims of emotional conflicts, why were we forbidden even to look at that God-given, refreshing, and blessed environment wherein man was intended to live, to grow, and to rejoice? Why? Why were we, who had not offended against society, we, the depressed, the anxious, the fearful, the despairing . . . why were we so senselessly punished? We who needed hope so desperately, why were we deprived deliberately of the sights and sounds of so much that would have been reassuring and hope-giving? It all seemed so wrong, so unjust, so inhuman, so contrary to the "living" this Institute was supposed to give.

There were no answers. There was so much I could not comprehend. Again, the apathy and numbness of mind returned. I sat on the edge of the bed in complete dejection. I did not care what *they*, the ever-vigilant watchers and recorders, might say or think or report. For these few moments I was going to be my real self, the self that now was a confused mixture of depression, anger, hopelessness, and isolation. I slipped off my shoes and lay face down on the bed.

No one bothered to approach me, or to share in my confusion and despair. More than ever, I felt the aloneness brought about by my abysmal failure. More than ever, I was alienated . . . alone and helpless . . . a failure to everyone and to everything . . . to priesthood and companions . . . to family and friends . . to God and grace . . . to life itself. All that I had loved and lived for, all that I trained myself to do in the service of God and others had come to nothing. . . . I really had become that "minus zero" with which I had labeled myself over a week ago.

And there was no one else to blame. . . . I was the sole cause of my present despicable condition. God forgive me! I knew He did, but in a very remote way. The fault, the entire fault was mine. . . . I did not know how, but it was undeniable that I, and I alone, was entirely blameworthy for this, my present pathetic condition.

The single bare consolation left to me was that I could close my burning eyes. They needed the relief of sleep even more than my confused mind needed answers to the multiple complexities of a disorganized, fragmented life. I closed them gratefully and attempted to enter into that most desirable phase of nonthinking. I tried to give in to absolute nothingness . . . and I must have succeeded, for it was late afternoon before I realized that someone was gently shaking my shoulder.

"Your medication, Father," said a gently smiling student nurse whose name I recalled was Miss Baker. On the day before, Dr. Mack had finally prescribed a tranquilizer of some kind for me. So far, it had no effect except to make me dizzy when I would start a sudden action. Now, as I started to rise from the bed, I fell back and almost lost consciousness.

"Take it easy, Father," said the nurse. "Just roll over and then try to sit up slowly." I did so and managed to take the pills and the thimble-sized paper cupful of water.

"How are you feeling?" Miss Baker inquired with some concern. I simply shook my head and lay down again. I did not want to face the grim reality of North I and the shame of constant observation. The sleep of exhaustion had been so welcome that I wanted simply to return to it.

"Dinner will be served in about a half hour," she smiled assuringly. I answered with a bleak nod and stared up unseeingly at the amorphous gray-white ceiling. The nonthinking phase had passed. Turgid and depressing thoughts again began their ruthless parading. There simply was no way to escape their accusations and implications.

*Constant observation!* I was now officially *branded* with this mark of opprobrium. It was positively the lowest possible grade of mental patient. I was to be watched closely, suspiciously, and to be reported on constantly . . . not trusted anywhere, at any time. There would be no privacy, not for one single moment! No relaxed and enjoyable aloneness. I was even to distrust myself at all times! Why? Because *they*, officialdom, had decreed it. On what basis, I could not even guess. But *they* had seen something, or thought they did.

"Did you ever think about death?" asked Dr. Mack sometime during the second week at White Hall. "Your own death, I mean."

"Sure," I answered readily enough. I have often thought how

wonderful it would be to be with God, forever. I began to think about this after ordination when I started to delve into the mystics, St. John of God, St. Teresa of Avila, Cassian, and many others. Also, when studying the English mystical poets of the seventeenth century for my master's degree, I admired intensely Richard Crashaw, John Donne, and many others whose poetry reflected a great desire to see and experience the love of God. I checked with modern theologians as to the permissibility of desiring death, even immediate death, in order to enter into this love of God. All of them affirmed that this desire was a legitimate and virtuous one provided the petitioner resigned himself to the will of God, and allowed Him to decide the moment and manner of dying.

"Death, to me," I concluded, as the doctor listened intently, "is not the end of life, but the beginning of a love life with God. And so, I have never feared death, mentally, at least, although I suppose my poor old body will naturally protest strongly when the moment comes."

This was my philosophy of death, and had roots just as deep as any other belief I loved and preached.

But, I wondered, still ceiling-gazing, how a psychiatrist would look at such an attitude on the part of an emotionally disturbed person. Would he conclude that such a desire easily could become the so-called "death wish" that psychiatry so often discussed? Had Dr. Mack, knowing my deep depression, feared that this latent, but truly Christian desire, might suddenly erupt into an uncontrollable self-hate that would have tragic results? Was this the "reasonable basis" that prompted the decision that I should be put on constant observation?

*Constant observation!* How I hated the label! and the implications! No privacy . . . no dignity . . . no trustworthiness . . . no priesthood . . . no independence . . . no freedom . . . no friends . . . no encouragement . . . no priest companions to share the burden . . . no outlets for my deepest thoughts . . . no real understanding of my real self . . . no intimacy with God, for, after so much fruitless importuning, He seemed more remote and unconcerned than ever.

My existence, as I evaluated it now, was an all-encompassing nothingness. From the apogee of the highest human calling, the priesthood, I had fallen ignominiously to the abysmal depths of disgraceful uselessness. I was nothing more than a *thing*, human to a degree, but unpredictable, suspicioned, and alone . . . so very much alone!

# CHAPTER IX

# A NIGHT TO REMEMBER
## Howl of Hatred

---

*"Oh, I have passed a miserable night,*
*So full of fearful dreams, of ugly sights,*
*That I would not spend another such a night,*
*Though 'twere to buy a world of happy days,*
*So full of dismal terror was the time."*
— Shakespeare: *Richard III*

DINNER that grim Sunday evening, as every evening, was early, about five-thirty. It was more dismal than any I can recall. Again, I could eat nothing but a slice or two of bread washed down with black coffee. Miss Trainor and the two student nurses had left about 7:00 P.M., and we were then supervised by three male aides. I made no attempt to socialize or to play cards; the effort seemed too much for my tired mind.

Sometime much later, perhaps about 9:00 P.M., Melvin, the young lad to my right who also was on constant observation, got into an argument with one of the aides. He ran up and down the corridors, shouting accusations and screaming epithets. What was worse, much to my horrified ears, he continually stated his intention to commit suicide the first chance he got. The aides, almost as though they expected this outburst, tried to reason with Mel and stayed close to him as he almost raced through the hallways. Finally, he flung himself on his bed and began to curse his parents with vehement hatred for having sent him to this "nut house" and his doctor for having confined him to this unit. His cursing of them and many others was frequently interspersed with threats of suicide. No one, he said, could stop him from doing this. He'd get the chance, sooner or later.

The whole scene was unbelievable and frightening. I saw and heard it all in a sort of dumfounded amazement. This cannot be real, I kept saying; it's too much like a scene from a movie overdramatizing child-parent conflict. And yet it was real, I knew, and I was caught up in the horror of it all. Caught up in it . . . and helpless.

Eventually, Mel quieted down somewhat and lay on his bed, face to the wall, still muttering curses and threats . . . and finally sobbing quietly. I felt an urge to go over to him, sit on the bed, and say something by way of sympathy. But, no, I might only start him off again. He might take his anger out on me. Besides, the aides were at hand. This was their job and they knew best how to handle it.

During all of this turmoil, most of the patients looked on with a sort of remote curiosity; others seemed to accept it matter-of-factly, as though it had happened before, and perhaps it had. After all, this was a "nut house."

Bob Stockton, however, had taken his usual stance in the middle of the corridor near the rec room. Whether or not Mel's outburst had set him off, I do not know; but suddenly he too began to stride slowly, with his strange, stiff-legged gait, up and down the corridors, and, in a controlled but deeply vicious tone, he began to excoriate his mother. I could hardly believe that this customarily quiet and soft-spoken youngster possessed such a violently profane and vitriolic vocabulary. Now and then, he would pause and stare at the floor, but the vehement cursing of his mother never stopped.

It was almost nightmarish to see and hear him. His rage simply welled up from some unfathomable depth and poured out of his mouth in a steady stream of vituperation. Interspersed with his seething rage there were, as with Mel, frequent threats of suicide as the only way out. It was better, he said, than living in this hell-hole, which was worse than his own home.

Again, as with Mel, the aides tried to reason with Bob and to placate him, but he seemed not to hear. Even the offer of a cigarette was ignored. And again, the majority of patients went on with their games and TV watching. To them, I thought, scenes like this must be an unextraordinary part of life in North I. To me, however, in disbelief at what I had just seen and heard, it was the "snake pit" reality of a mental hospital, about which some recovered patient had written some years before.

And here I was, a priest, in the very depths of the "pit"!

Bob was silent now. He was staring fixedly at the floor with his peculiar spread-legged stance. His eyes glazed, and he seemed to be in a trance. How awful, I thought, to be as sick as he quite clearly was. With varying emotions I looked at him, at Mel, and at the other inmates. Again, the unreality of the whole unit and its totally fantastic inhabitants engulfed my mind. I could not give credence to what I had just seen and heard. A dream! A nightmare! A temporary delusion! A fantasy of my exhausted and confused mind! Such an abominable experience simply could not be real—a real part of my life!

True, I had heard and read about these things, but never in my wildest imaginations had it ever occurred to me that such horrible expressions of uncontrolled human hatred and vicious rage actually would become a part of my own life, even though I was only a spectator. Murderous fury and intended suicide! Hand in hand! Side by side! How many of these other patients felt the same way? It simply could not be true that I belonged here among all these odd and dangerous excerpts of humanity.

And yet, I *knew* I was part of all this fantastic strangeness. I really *was* present to it, to these patients, to this unit. I really was "one of these" in a certain sense. The fact was inescapable. My reason and intellect were still normal, still capable of depending on the data of sensory experience. And I knew that they were telling me the truth about what sight and sound had presented to them for acceptance. Staggering though it was, the honest fact of my situation had to be admitted by the will. I could not discount it, minimize it, or discard it.

"Honesty and effort!" Somehow, despite the unbelievability of the past two weeks, the depression and panic at White Hall, the disgrace and shame of constant observation, the grimness of North I, the sickening scenes of the evening, anxiety about the present and the future, somehow I would have to make the "effort" to come to terms with them all. And somehow, somehow, I would have to accept and absorb the fact that human nature can become sick, very sick, emotionally. That I, too, was sick. That I, too, was "one of these." "O God, come to my assistance! O Lord, make haste to help me!"

Another, more disturbing thought occurred to me. My bed was between two violent and suicidal patients. What might their vicious tendencies unconsciously prompt them to do during the long night hours? What sudden, murderous impulse might they attempt, in spite of the all-night vigil of the male aides across the hall?

All of these dire qualms were increased by a new apprehension that lurked in the background of my confused mind. Would I, could I, possibly become as ravingly wild as Mel and Bob? Detention room? Straitjacket? Would I, confined long enough to this melancholy unit, begin to contemplate their stated solutions? Such a horrendous escape had never even entered my mind prior to this evening's wild scenes; but now, because fear generates more fear, the ghastly thought began to haunt me, subtly and with pinpricks of disquietude, as to what might happen to me.

After all, why *had* they sent me to this unit? And why *had* they seen fit to put me on constant observation? Why? Why, if they did not suspect . . . ?

"Lights out!" was at 11:00 P.M., but I decided to prepare for bed shortly after ten o'clock. Despite the anxiety, confusion, and dread, my body and mind cried out loudly for rest and sleep . . . and more sleep. I undressed and slipped on a bathrobe in order to take a shower. A male aide dutifully followed me into the toilet area and, like a peeping Tom, kept looking around the corner of the shower stall periodically.

Back beside my bed, I thought of kneeling and saying customary night prayers, but simply could not do so. It was not because there were so many others around me and observing me, but because I felt that this action would only remind them of my disgrace and cause them to think ridiculing thoughts about "the priest who failed." Taking my beads from my trouser pocket, I hastily slipped into bed. I wanted to be as anonymous as possible and to sleep as soon as possible; but then, memory reminded me of the two suicidal maniacs between whom I must try to sleep. I fingered the beads, but my mind was on other things.

Prayer? Yes. I knew I would always pray, but while my words went up, my thoughts remained below. There was no encounter with the divinity . . . nor any expectancy of the same . . . nor any intense importuning. These were only dutiful, mechanical whisperings from the depths of apathy, disillusionment, and self-condemnation . . . an attempted disbelief that all this was real . . . that all this had happened to me. Worse still, a disbelief that there was any hope in the morrow, the days to come, the weeks . . . months . . . perhaps . . . never!

God . . . and hopelessness. Thesis . . . and antithesis. God? Yes, I believed in Him, of course. I knew I did. Psalm 115, I think, assured me of His mysterious presence in the midst of suffering: "I believed, even when I said I am greatly afflicted." Job and David and countless others, saints and mystics, martyrs and the persecuted, all, throughout the ages, were undaunted in their faith despite the agony of pain.

God. Yes, He was around . . . someplace . . . everyplace, in fact, as age-old theology attested. But—and I could not banish the strange feeling—I had the odd sensation that He was probably gazing at me with a sort of distant concern . . . silently waiting . . . waiting, perhaps, for me to come to my senses. Yes, He knew about me . . . all about me . . . at this very moment . . . about my distress and agony. But then, He apparently was just as distant to His own Son at Gethsemani:

"Father, if it be possible, let this agony pass from me!" . . . but it did not pass . . . and mine? . . . I could not help but feel as though He had given my situation an appraising, knowing, decision-making glance . . . and decided to look over my case again, sometime . . . after all, *I* was the failure, was I not?

The distance from Him grew . . . I could not help it . . . I felt as though I were a cold-storage item . . . wrapped and numbered and shelved indefinitely . . . until my case would be given a reconsideration . . . until He might possibly find a use for me again . . . meanwhile, I was something that would keep indefinitely in the semi-aliveness of this refrigerated distance from the warmth of His presence . . . and love. But even in this justified Siberian banishment, I had the duty of prayer . . . and I did pray, verbally, at least . . . mechanically, impersonally . . . and then a guilt arose because of having entertained such foolish thoughts about this God of love. How could I, a priest, have wandered so far astray in speaking to, and thinking of, the Lord of all creation!

How foolish of me to be trying to divine the ways of Him Whose existence and purposes defied human probings with mystery upon mystery? And yet, there was a purpose for everything and in everything, for He could not act otherwise than with a planned, mysterious Providence. And so, this imagined, chilled numbness of my distance from Him, The Unreachable, was, in reality, His way of reaching me. Perhaps He wanted me to think on other things . . . the emotional conflicts that I knew were there . . . hidden deeply in the subconscious and concerning which I had more than a few strong indications, deriving both from my Halifax experience and more incisively from Dr. Mack here at the Institute . . . perhaps there was a meaningful and fruitful reason for this seeming absence of God . . . perhaps the very feeling of His absence would, if I perseveringly used that "honesty and effort" prescribed by Dr. Mack, reveal the proof of His actual presence and His real love . . . yes, these were thoughts I must delve into . . . I would . . . I must, indeed, if I wanted to survive, to be the priest-person I wanted to be.

Someone had once written, and I had so often quoted it

in my sermons: "God writes straight with crooked lines." Crooked lines . . . there were so many of them . . . so entangled . . . so much to decipher and untie and translate into understanding. . . . I finally fell asleep.

It was an uneventful night, and none of the fearful things took place that I had thought of when Bob and Mel lay on either side of me after the eleven-o'clock curfew. The only interruption to seven or eight hours of solid sleep came at some unknown hour when I was awakened suddenly by the steady beam of a flashlight held close to my eyes. I jumped up with a startled cry, but was told by a voice: "Take it easy, Father. Just checking. Go back to sleep." I could see dimly a white-clad male attendant move away and flash the light into Bob Stockton's face.

This, I learned the next day, was a nightly occurrence at the Institute to make sure that each patient was alive and accounted for. Later on in therapy, when I was feeling much better and came to know the "flashlight man," a male nurse named Harry, it became a rather humorous thing to try to outwit him on his nightly rounds. If I was awake and heard him coming, I would close my eyes and hold my breath in deathlike stillness. But somehow or other he could always detect signs of life. At times, however, after a few moments of eye-closed stillness with the beam on my eyes, I would suddenly shout: "Boo!" Harry would chuckle and continue his rounds.

Tonight's crude awakening, however, had been frightening, and another reminder of being under continual surveillance and suspicion. I looked across the room and saw a new male aide sitting quietly, watching me. I knew I would never become accustomed to this continued distrust, but there was some small consolation in realizing that there were alert, responsible people on hand during the night hours of unconscious helplessness in this unit of unpredictable and perhaps dangerous patients.

# CHAPTER X

# TWO WEEKS IN EXILE

## *Alone in Gethsemani*

---

*"I am forgotten like the unremembered dead;*
*I am like a dish that is broken.*
*I hear the whispers of the crowd*
*That frighten me from every side."*
—Psalm 30, ii

Nᴏᴛ ᴇᴠᴇʀʏ night ends with the dawn," someone has sagely observed. I awoke about a half-hour before the regular rising time of 7:00 ᴀ.ᴍ. My eyes were no longer burning, I noticed with gratitude, but gradually I began to recall the events of the evening and the dread fact of my imprisonment, for that is what North I and constant observation really meant. I attempted a prayer, the regular Morning Offering, but found myself staring at the gray-white ceiling and, strangely, forming some thoughts about it despite its unresponsiveness. Undoubtedly, they reflected my own self-attitudes, and life as it seemed to me now.

Faintly seamed and vacantly insensitive, it was so dumb, so mute, so heedlessly uncaring about the afflicted humanity it presided over day and night. If only it had a spate of color, a diversity of happy scenes, or a few encouraging or humorous phrases to remind the depressed of happier, more hopeful days . . . and of a possibly more buoyant and promising future . . . to "lift up your hearts," as in the Preface of the Mass. But there was only a blank indifference reflected in its bland and vacuous face. Despite the return of the familiar dread, which always

seemed to start in my stomach, I could not help but recall and
almost grin to myself at a story and a scene which, for some
reason, flashed into memory as I stared at the innocuous
ceiling.

It had happened some years ago at a national retreat con-
vention in Cincinnati when I was most active in this type of
work. At the final function, an elegant dinner, several hundred
delegates from all over the country had gathered to hear the
keynote address by one of the country's outstanding episcopal
speakers. Several more of the hierarchy adorned the head table
as well as local dignitaries. The master of ceremonies was a
young, articulate Notre Dame graduate and a city councilman
who has risen to fame in national politics in recent years. His
introduction of the episcopal orator was a masterpiece of keen
observation and spontaneous wit, in the course of which he
recounted another bishop's observations as he took part in the
consecration ceremonies that raised an elderly and hard-working
parish priest to the unexpected dignity of the episcopacy.

"As the consecration ceremonies proceeded," the M.C. quoted
the observing bishop, "I noticed that all the wrinkles of worry
and the lines of pastoral concern gradually disappeared from
his face and were replaced with a benign and vacuous expression." The crowd howled with laughter, as did the prelate who
was being introduced; even more so, I suppose, because the
awaited orator, now recently raised to the highest dignity in the
Church, was anything but "vacuous" either in face or in his
multiple and progressive activities. In his subsequent talk, the
prelate very adroitly referred to and humorously used the
"benign and vacuous" phrase to his own advantage and to the
huge appreciation of the audience.

Just why the words and scene should occur to me now, I do
not know, but in a way they were somehow appropriate and
encouraging. The latter, I think, because they assured me
that I still had retained my sense of humor and that I was still
capable of laughter, "the saving grace" as it has been called. The
former, I suppose, because the ceiling, though certainly not
"benign," really was blind and bland and "vacuous" . . . as were
so many faces and things in the unit . . . in the hospital . . .

in its regime . . . in my present pathetic condition . . . in my future life as I tried to envision it from this prone position . . . "prone" meant "prostrate" . . . I was prostrate . . . and my stomach ached. I had survived the night. What would the day bring by way of adversity?

After breakfast, a comparatively quiet experience, since Bob Stockton had subsided to his customary blank staring at nothing, we returned to the upper unit, where I made my bed as I had habitually done for years, and tidied up my bureau. It was shortly after this that Miss Trainor approached and gave me a brief outline of what my schedule would be like while on C.O. I could not leave the unit when the other patients went to classes or to the social area; I would have to entertain myself with whatever the rec room offered, although the aides and student nurses would be available for games or conversation. And Dr. Mack would come to the unit to see me instead of my going to his office. Was there anything at all she could do for me?

Again, she was attentively kind and seemingly a bit more concerned than the day before. Perhaps she was wondering how I had reacted to last night's turmoil. I assured her that I needed nothing. But her very neatness, certainty, and attitude of calm control was again an accusation to me, and I felt ill-at-ease and guilty. She was a success in her profession and exercised it efficiently, while I was a pathetic failure in my profession. She must be wondering how I, as a priest (I presumed from her name that she was a Catholic) could ever have allowed such a shameful thing to happen to me.

During the long hours of morning and afternoon while awaiting Dr. Mack's arrival, hopefully praying for the happy words of release he might bring with him, I played a few card games with the student nurse, Miss Baker, who, besides being a most pleasant and obliging person, also acquainted me with many of the aspects of specialized treatment in North I. She kept reassuring me that, despite the appearances of the unit, it did have a definite curative element and that many patients had to go through this kind of treatment to find the answers to their problems. These, again, were words, nice words, and well-intended, but anxiety still lay like lead in my stomach.

No visitors were allowed in the unit. On exceptional occasions, when visiting was allowed, the patient was escorted to an upper unit by a male aide, who would stand vigil outside the door. All mail, incoming or outgoing, was sent to the R.P. (responsible party). As prudence or circumstances dictated, the mail would be forwarded. This meant, I realized, that all my mail, coming or going, was in the hands of my Provincial. I hoped I would be allowed to see him soon.

Also, I learned, each treating doctor was under the direct supervision of a qualified and experienced psychiatrist, to whom he regularly referred each case. Periodically, each patient's case was reported on to the hospital staff of psychiatrists, who would thereupon advise the treatment-doctor as to the proper therapeutic direction.

With all this information and much more that I learned from patients and other noticeable hospital procedures, I began to feel less free and more imprisoned, physically and mentally. It seemed as though I had become a helpless victim of an intellectual and emotional imperialism. I could not, would not be allowed to be myself. I was to be carefully analyzed, inside and out, an odd specimen to be viewed under several impersonal but all-powerful microscopes. My life, my *selfness* was not to be my own private domain. It was going to be supervised, revealed, controlled, and directed by many technicians in a variety of ways.

Ordinarily, I suppose, in view of such an array of inhibiting and prohibiting systems of personality control, I would have begun to seethe with rage and rebellion. But, instead, a gradually prevailing apathy returned, probably induced by the sheer dead weight of the many adverse elements that were being laid, tier on tier, with unremitting regularity, upon the declining strength of my will to resist. The dynamics of hostility were effectively smothered, and I became more or less resigned to the unreal reality of North I and all that it seemed to represent by way of hopelessness.

During these long hours, while awaiting the arrival of Dr. Mack, I noticed an odd change that seemed to be taking place in my voice. It had descended in tone to about an octave lower than normal when I spoke, and the sound of it did not ring in my ears, but rather seemed to come from some several feet away, as though I had suddenly become a ventriloquist. It puzzled me, but I tried to put it aside as being purely imaginary. Or, perhaps, a case of laryngitis. But why the distant sound of it? Why did it seem to be coming from the people to whom I was speaking? It was another strange phenomenon of this strange unit with its strange people. But it was to continue for most of my stay on constant observation.

Finally Dr. Mack came, in the late afternoon. Since there was no privacy around my dormitory bed, our interview took place in a room temporarily vacated by a patient who must have been attending a class.

Immediately, of course, I demanded to know why I had been put in this unit and when was I going to be returned to North II where there was privacy, at least. I did not belong in this ward with a bunch of zombies, some of them dangerous; that the language was filthy and obscene; that some other patients were not only dangerous but suicidal; that the whole atmosphere was depressing and jail-like; that I hated constant observation and the unreasonable and unnecessary invasion of my right to privacy in the washroom; that there was no chance to enjoy God's sunlight and the beauty of nature, not even a chance to view it through a window; that this whole procedure was punishment, not rehabilitation; that it reminded me of the prison where I was chaplain and where the men grew worse instead of better under the lock-and-key system, the suspicion, regimentation, the loss of human rights and dignity; that I had not offended against society in any way. Then, why this incarceration? How could he justify this type of inhuman treatment for a person who needed help, hope, encouragement?

The doctor listened calmly and interestedly, allowing me full breadth of expression, but with that sort of professional know-it-all-ism which, on so many occasions, would cause a seething but controlled resentment within me.

He answered my wrathful spasm of questions and accusations with an attempted reasonableness that, I felt, he knew I would reject but that had to be presented to the logic-trained mind for future consideration as well as a solid basis for this present type of treatment and necessary incarceration.

My steady decline in White Hall and increased depression after two weeks had led the staff, after a thorough review of my whole case history, to send me to a unit, North II, which would, of its very nature, force me to de-isolate myself from the dangerous alienation that the comparative freedom of White Hall had allowed me. His decision to put me on constant observation was the result of my uncontrolled rage exhibited yesterday when he visited me; it seemed to indicate that I might attempt to escape, a common reaction in a patient who was demanding immediate release and was not fit for it.

This present type of treatment was decided upon solely for my own benefit; it was not a punishment in any sense of the word, but merely a prudent protection for any patient who showed signs of extreme rage, depression, and agitation. In justice to me and to the rehabilitation that I said I wanted and needed when I first entered, he simply had to take this course of action.

It was not, he admitted, the very best of circumstances for depressed patients, but North I was the only unit in the hospital that could offer the kind of help and self-protection that the staff thought I needed for the time being. He granted that the surroundings, the "jail-like" atmosphere, the constant observation, the "odd" patients, the lack of sunshine and nature, were also among the various aspects that must be very difficult to bear for a person with my comparatively protected background, the customary respect, dignity, and privacy, but all of this is what I would have to recognize, accept, and make a necessary part of rehabilitation if I sincerely wanted to return to a functional priesthood and to enjoy a normal, anxiety-free life.

In the first place, he pointed out with patient logic, I would have to admit that, despite my priesthood, I was an ordinary human being, afflicted with one of those unfortunate illnesses to which humans are subjected, at times. There are, he reminded me, many worse forms of human affliction. Perhaps, he suggested, perhaps in the course of therapy, I could learn much about other similarly afflicted persons and later on be of considerable help to them when theology and philosophy would be of no assistance whatsoever, as, apparently, they had not been in my case. Otherwise, I would not be where I was today. Also, that despite the dignity of the priesthood, ordination had not guaranteed me exemption from any kind of human illness.

"How old were you when you were ordained?" he asked. "About twenty-seven or twenty-eight," I answered. "And what were you before ordination?" he persisted. I answered, but with a dawning realization as to the import of question and answer.

"Just an ordinary human being," I said. He smiled gently, knowing that I was beginning to realize that I had been and always would be *human* and therefore subject to its variety of illnesses.

The doctor continued inexorably. With regard to the "zombie-like" and the "odd" and generally disturbed patients to whom I had referred, were these not also God's creatures? And if they appeared to be much sicker than I, should I as a Christian, as a priest, despise or reject them? Or, on the other hand in a Christ-like way, should I not pity them and perhaps try to help them, at least by an attempted socializing with them, conversing with them? If I felt isolated, alienated, and desperately wanted someone to share my aloneness, could I not see that they also needed someone to enter into their feelings of rejection?

"Perhaps," he suggested, "this could be the very reason why you are here among them. To present to them your priestliness. Did they not need priestliness and all that it implied more than the undisturbed, the undepressed? Were you ordained only for the normal people whom you met so distantly from the pulpit or confessional? Were you not ordained and therefore sent to redeem human nature . . . human nature in all of its needs and sickness? Perhaps there are many here who desperately need you, who look up to you as someone who has dedicated his life to afflicted human nature . . . and who perhaps would take an interest in them. This could be done in ordinary conversation, in showing some sort of interest in them, by playing games with them. Any one of these socializing actions might offer them the ray of hope they so desperately need."

"But," I objected defensively, "I feel even stranger than ever.

My voice, for instance. It's dropped about an octave lower and yet the sound of it isn't in my ears. It seems to be coming from about where you are. I know I'm not a ventriloquist. What's happening? What's wrong with me?"

The doctor nodded knowingly. "Many odd phenomena happen to people who are trying to reject reality, that is, life as it appears to threaten them. Life here and now, as it appears to you, is a decided threat to the self you have idealized throughout the years, a self that is impossible of acquisition even though you have demanded it of yourself. Not having attained it, you have called yourself a failure. No one else has. Your only failure has been to recognize your human limitations and inabilities, and to live within them. Your 'ventriloquist' voice is a sort of shrinking away from the reality that is you, from the real-life situation that now confronts you. Don't be surprised at things like this. Just be sure to mention them whenever they occur. I'll see you again in a day or two." He smiled reassuringly and left.

In these and in subsequent observations Dr. Mack would make by way of attempting to answer my demands and accusations, I am sure that he realized, as I did not and would not for some time to come, that my hostility, anxiety, and fear had far deeper roots and implications than the immediate ones that confinement to North I and constant observation had aroused. My immediate reaction to this interview was that I lost an important battle, namely, to be relieved of the indignity of "C.O.," and to be returned to the comparative privacy of a room in North II. I had failed. I still could not see why I must remain in this degrading situation. The doctor evidently knew that I could not see the rationale of my remaining in North I.

But the seed of something positive had been planted in this session, and in the many others that were to follow. Much as the defeat of my immediate hopes and aims rankled and depressed me, some of the basic truths stated by the doctor and their evident implications had started a germination of thought which, though unexpected and unwelcome at the time, were gradually to grow into healthier, constructive, and more realistic self-attitudes. They would grow but slowly, and would need much of that "honesty and effort" that the doctor had predicated upon my entrance as being absolutely necessary for any hoped-for cure.

Meanwhile, there was the need for much painful weeding. This was the *reality* that I now had to face. I dreaded all the implications of "honesty and effort," but even more so the amount of time all this would involve. Even though remotely, I realized that I had a huge task before me. And the results were uncertain.

But there are, thank God, people who feel for and who anticipate the pain of others. My Provincial and Father John had permission to visit me during the days of constant observation. It was with a mixture of shame and joy that I met them in a visiting room in an upper unit while the male aide stood guard outside the door. It was a most painful meeting, at first, but gradually the thought of my disgrace at having been reduced to the worst unit in the hospital gave way to the encouraging realization that they saw in it nothing more than a treatment necessary for my eventual recovery. They had seen the doctor, and he implied that "some progress" had been made despite the need to put me on constant observation. He assured them that some patients had to get worse before getting better. They got worse simply because they had been removed from all that was familiar to them, and a period of readjustment often brought about a temporary depression which, just as often, enabled the patient to verbalize his real feelings and eventually to get to the core of his problems.

But, I protested, my family would have to know sooner or later, and with mother in such poor health, I feared for her. They had also taken care of this, they assured me. They had decided that the family should know and had been informed this past week. Although very much concerned, they were happy to know that now I was getting the rest and the treatment at the very best of hospitals. My mother, they said, was not at all upset; in fact, she was glad that I was "getting a good rest for a change." Furthermore, my brothers and sisters would be down for a visit in a week or two.

Truly, my relief at this happy solution to an agonizing concern was tremendous. Here was my religious family, truly concerned, coming to the aid and assistance of my own family. My gratitude almost expressed itself in tears.

Also, they informed me, all other members of the Congregation had been informed of my hospitalization by letter and that I most certainly would be included in their daily prayers for a speedy recovery. However, under doctor's orders, I would not be receiving any letters from community members until the doctor thought it beneficial to me. Even well-wishing writers might attempt the wrong advice at this time and interfere with the planned treatment. This, too, was a great relief. They would have had to know sometime. Now they knew. They, too, had been among the many disturbing day and night thoughts I had since entering the hospital. I kept saying to myself at these times: "If only I could explain things to them . . . if only they knew of my agony . . . if only they would understand . . . if only I could hear from them: 'It's O.K., Bill. Don't worry. We understand. Take your time and follow the doctor's orders.'" How great would have been my relief! They would have absolved me, and I would have felt at peace, at least on this account. Now they knew, and I did not have the worry or concern about how or when they would be informed, or their reactions to the information.

As I walked back to North I with the aide at my side, I began to realize how many and varied were the guilts and shames and anxieties my hospitalization had occasioned, and what a wonderful thing human absolution in the form of understanding, compassion, and kindness could be. I now felt better, relieved at least of some of the peripheral fears that had concerned me and that had added no small weight to the burden of depression. Now, I felt, there were others who really cared and who, somehow or other, were with me; that I was not totally alone or abandoned; that my poor old "selfness," much as I despised it for its weakness and for being the cause of so much effort, expense, care, and worry by so many others, was, nonetheless, still the object of human concern and sincere personal prayer. It was an encouraging thought despite the thud of locked doors as I was led back to the prison block of North I. I did not feel so lonely for the rest of the day. Somehow, those who are *for* you are also *with* you.

# CHAPTER XI

# MY FELLOW PATIENTS

## Leprosy of the Mind

---

"We have come to the place where I said that you would see the woeful people who have lost the good of the intellect."

—Dante: *Inferno*

Initially, in the newness and strangeness of my presence in North I, I saw the various other patients from the viewpoint of what I considered to be my own normalcy. And, at first, very few of them appeared to be normal. Eventually, in the course of therapy, I began to realize the difficulty of defining this term, and had to admit that there was something "abnormal" about me, otherwise I would not have needed hospitalization. We were all "emotionally disturbed," and this was our common bond. Some patients here, however, were very sick, with a combination of emotional and physical afflictions.

There was the "mumbler," as I first called him before I learned his full name. He was both pathetic and the cause of much humorous comment among the patients. About sixty, bald, and unable to talk intelligibly, he would roam up and down the corridors like a sick, lost old dog. Unfortunately, he seemed to have an aversion to the washroom facilities and had no control over his natural functions. Usually, he would seek out someone's bed for these occasions and, of course, with disastrous results. Hence, all patients would keep a watch out for "Joe

Pants," as they called him, and shout out warnings to the aides or other patients when Joe would disappear into someone's room. More than once I had to pull him off my dormitory bed.

Then there was Terry, the hulking, jut-jawed, ex-footballer, who so methodically made his mechanical rounds of the corridors, touching various waist-high objects religiously, green eyes downcast, silent and alone in his strange "must" world of systematized tactility. Later on, when I began to play solitaire as an escape from the lassitude of the unit, Terry would often stop his pacing and look over my shoulder. Frequently, he would spot a move and silently point it out to me. It seemed to be his mute attempt to communicate with someone, but even on these occasions, when I would try to draw him into conversation, he would move away and resume his steady pacing and touching. Finally, I devised a way in which to inveigle him into my presence at least, with the purpose of getting him to talk. I would call him over and pretend I was stuck unless I could make another move. He would, of course, readily point it out. I would thank him and tell him he had a pretty sharp eye. Did he ever play baseball? He must have been a pretty good hitter, a real slugger. What about football? No one made much yardage through your position. What did you play? Guard? Tackle? I noticed that he avidly read sports magazines. But even this maneuver failed of dialogue. He would listen to my comments but simply seemed incapable of trusting himself to talk.

However, I felt that I had made some sort of human contact with Terry, that for the time being, at least, he had come out of his strange world of silence; that he had been given the feeling of being helpful to me in the card game and that his athletic ability had been recognized, even though he could not talk about it.

Later on, during the second of my two weeks on "C.O.," after using the same ploy and with the same predictable results, I began to feel the dawning of an insight. By giving or attempting to give a worthwhileness to Terry, I had, at the same time, given myself the same feeling. I had gone "outside" myself and "inside" someone else, presenting the "other" with an interest, a kindness, a *worthiness*, a respect and dignity, all of which I, myself, so badly needed. Perhaps I was to others, without my realizing it, as the doctor had intimated, a small ray of hope; that they had seen and accepted the fact of my human illness, just as they accepted the fact of their own sickness. They were not accusing or demeaning me; I was the only one who was doing that. In a very real sense, they did need me, the better part of me; and I, just as certainly needed them, the better part of them that I might be able to evoke by the interest, concern, kindness, and understanding that I could indicate easily by a casual conversation and that might often lead to a deeper, more helpful, and mutually fruitful relationship.

These strange "others," it began to occur more strongly to me, were really an integral part of my life, my *selfness*, and must, of necessity, play an increasingly important part in the healthy rehabilitation of the *self* that I had so despised and demeaned. What was it John Donne has said so well? "No man is an island, sufficient unto itself . . . every man is a piece of the Continent . . . if a clod is washed away, the Continent is the lesser for it . . . every man's death diminishes me because I am part of Mankind. . . . do not ask for whom the bell tolls; it tolls for thee." Humanity, all of it, is God's creation . . . we are the result of the solidarity of His creation . . . in our goodness and evil . . . and in our sickness.

Another of the very silent and uncommunicative types that inhabited North I was Dave Billings. Unlike the huge and harmless Terry, however, I was warned by the patients to be on my guard in Dave's presence. An ex-paratrooper, slim, thin, much smaller than I physically, with sparse, sandy hair and continually downcast, slate-blue eyes, he would silently and quickly pace the hallways on crepe-sole shoes. He was, so the patients informed me, a karate expert and had, a few weeks previously, suddenly and viciously attacked a fellow patient without any provocation. On many occasions, a warning sixth sense, which took the form of a prickling sensation in my neck, would prompt me to turn suddenly, and there would be Dave, studiously gazing at the floor as he veered around me and continued his silent, leopard-like prowling of the corridors. Eventually, I came to trust and to communicate with most of the patients, but I kept a wary eye out for the presence of Dave Billings. It was always an eerie feeling to find him a few soundless feet behind me.

As an indication of my changing attitudes toward these sick patients, and toward myself, there was the case of Ted Sanders. At first, he really "bugged" me. He was a sullen, 220-pound lad, with heavy-lidded green eyes, who would lie on the floor near the phonograph and play over and over the currently popular hit songs. I had to make a supreme but unsuccessful effort not to listen to his particular selection of repeated recordings.

At night, especially during the dread melancholy of hopelessness when confined to the dormitory and when I had retired an hour or so before eleven o'clock, the dolefully repeated strains of his favorite record by Barbra Streisand, "People Who Need People," would echo and re-echo through my mind and seemed to intensify almost beyond endurance a feeling of utter depression that threatened to overwhelm and submerge me. To one struggling desperately for the benignity of hope, this dirge, with its long-sustained notes of lamentation, seemed like a Banshee wail of despair. Even today, so long after the occasion and with a complete knowledge of what was taking place in me at the time, I still cannot bear to listen to the dire despondency her every song seems to revive.

Another sad melody Ted often played and that would prompt me to bury my head under the pillow was a melancholy song entitled, oddly enough, "Tony Baloney"! At least, that was what the muted words seemed to be saying. It did not relieve my depression very much, although I did smile grimly to myself when, one day near my card table, Ted played the song. This time, I realized that the words suited the mood of the music; they were "Only the Lonely"! Still another of Ted's repeated favorites that I could hardly stand was a direful dirge by Joan Baez: "All My Sorrows." God! How I hated these songs and singers and the endless repetition of their despondent pessimism.

Good music, classical music, I had always loved. It never

failed to inspire, uplift, and sometimes enrapture me: Beethoven, Chopin, Liszt, Brahms, Tchaikovsky, Verdi. All of these and many others I could listen to and thoroughly enjoy, sometimes almost lifted out of myself with a deep longing for something, for Someone, above and beyond me, from Whom I had been separated and, with an inexpressible, abiding desire, wanted to regain, to re-experience, to possess. In these not-infrequent occasions of musical appreciation, I would feel estranged from the world I wanted. With this extreme contrast in tastes, it is understandable how much I came to dislike Ted's music and, I am sure, the dislike extended to Ted himself.

And yet, it was Ted who perhaps esteemed me most from a quiet, respectful distance. One day he approached me and said that because he admired my conduct in the unit so much he wanted to become a Catholic, and how would he go about it? I was not only speechless at his request but, understandably, felt quite guilty. I had so much projected my dislike for his repetitious and mournful record-playing that it had also included his person. From his viewpoint of me, however, he had seen something admirable. It was so incongruous! That I, who was the "minus zero," the "failure" in so many ways, had unconsciously exhibited some natural qualities that were respected, honored, and wanted, amazed me completely . . . and warmed me, also. I told him that the necessary instruction would have to be done by the hospital chaplain and that he should make an appointment to see him.

Ted's aggressive and depressive states were well known and often exhibited. On two occasions, I saw him smash his clenched fist into the plastered walls of the corridor. After his badly bruised hand had been bandaged by the nurse, I would sit with him and ask him why he did such things. He could think of no reason except that a huge anger would come over him at times and he couldn't control the impulse to smash something. Again, late one evening, as he sat alone at a table with his head in his hands, he began to pound the table with his huge fists, sobbing and repeating over and over: "There's no hope for me! No hope! No one can help me!" I left my own table and went over to him, gently massaging his neck and shoulders, saying: "Others have made it, Ted. Give yourself another chance. Don't give up."

He continued his sobbing, however, and I felt I could do no more. What else could I say to him, I asked myself hopelessly, in view of my own failure as a priest and despondency about the future? There was, however, a "sharing" here in my futile attempt to reassure Ted. Perhaps, too, it was such gestures on my part that had prompted Ted to want to become a Catholic. At this moment, however, helpless though I was to relieve the youngster of his depression and hopelessness, I was being really concerned about someone other than myself and my own feelings. Here was a definite "giving" of myself to someone in his moment of need. In future interviews, Dr. Mack would have much to say about this "sharing" and "giving" and its curative potential.

It would take many pages to describe appropriately the rest of the "odd" roster of patients with whom I lived during my two months of servitude on North One. There was another distinctive personality on the unit, however, whom I will never forget. Joe was short and sixty, with a very small head of close-cropped gray hair, sharp blue eyes, cherubic cheeks and a figure that almost defies description. He was like two turnips with their flat ends put together. His shoulders were thin, but then suddenly his hips and stomach billowed out enormously. He literally overflowed every chair he sat in. Then he narrowed just as suddenly with tiny legs and small, child-sized feet. He was usually mild-mannered and often would sit by himself in the hallway, just outside his door, painting a numbered picture or sewing buttons on shirts.

All the while, in a bell-clear, penetrating voice, he would be talking about the price of rice in India in 1939, or quoting from some nineteenth-century poet. He came, I was told, from a very wealthy Connecticut family, was a graduate of some Ivy League college, had several degrees, had visited most countries in the world, and knew several languages. He also knew English and it was certain that he knew every four-letter word the Anglo-Saxons had ever uttered. Frequently, and with little or no pretext, he would enter into a wild orgy of profanity which would leave the air a deep, dark blue for several minutes after the aides had escorted him to his room.

Much later on however, when I was off "C.O." and allowed to go to classes and to the social area, I witnessed another and amazing Joe. In this large and well-appointed social and recreational area, Joe would usually continue his solitary painting or sewing while muttering to himself. Suddenly, one day, he went over to the piano and tentatively sounded a few resonant chords. The group paused and watched curiously because Joe had never even approached the piano in the several years he had spent at the hospital. Flexing his fingers a bit he then launched into a brilliant piano concerto, or perhaps a combination of several, for the music was unfamiliar to me. But if I closed my eyes, I well could have imagined myself listening to one of the modern masters at the keyboard. It was really fantastic!

Perhaps there were a multitude of technical faults in Joe's performance because, although a lover of piano concertos in particular, I am far from being a discerning critic of style and accuracy. But for me, at this moment, Joe was a supreme artist, a lover and perceptive interpreter of all the human emotions that a piano alone can produce at the command of its master. The social area, with its little group of afflicted and imprisoned patients, seemed to resound with a sympathetic and discerning musical expression of a mental patient's inexpressible desires, aspirations, despairs, depressions—and hopes.

Almost mesmerized at the scene, patients and staff members sat around in amazed concentration as this grotesque little figure, ridiculous in size and shape, produced with his stubby fingers a fantastic series of thunderous chords, rolling arpeggios, soaring melodies, brilliant cadenzas, and somber yet almost heavenly toccatas. Throughout the whole spontaneous performance I seemed to sense a theme of psalmodic hopefulness and desire.

Joe ended his rendition with his head bent slightly over the keyboard. The immediate resultant hush from the almost stunned audience was, I think, the greatest tribute that could have been given to him. Recovering, however, they rose as one and roared approval at Joe, crowding around him and begging for more. Joe only smiled vacantly and said he must get back to his sewing. Never again, to my knowledge, did Joe return to the piano. Several months later on, when I had been advanced to a higher unit, I learned that Joe had deteriorated quite badly and had to be removed to another sanitarium.

Of the several other sad specimens of afflicted humanity who made up my neighbors on North One during and after my "C.O." period, one other pathetic individual remains in memory. All the more so, I suppose, because he had been a practicing psychiatrist. About fifty-five, with sparse hair and thick-lensed glasses, Dr. Cousins appeared to be the epitome of the typical TV comic psychiatrist, far more "out of it" than his patients. He was excessively shy and extremely hesitant about doing anything. He had a morbid fear of touching anything, especially doorknobs. He would stand for long moments in wretched indecision before a door, and then pitifully ask someone to open it for him. Also, he could not bear to be touched by anyone. I found this out one day when, as he hesitated to proceed down the stairway to the dining room, I gently poked a finger into his back. He turned quickly in near terror and begged apologetically that I never touch him again. He was almost in tears as he wordlessly implored me to try to understand that which, I am sure, he could not understand himself.

Depressed myself, I could not but feel a deep and compassionate sympathy for this badly disturbed person with his multiple and obvious phobias. He, too, was a "professional"; he, too, must feel the crushing weight of shame for having "failed." Thereafter, I tried to treat him with extreme kindness and frequently went out of my way to engage him in conversation or to induce him into a game of cards. Shortly before I left North One, Dr. Cousins disappeared from the unit. It was rumored that he was sent to another hospital. I felt keenly the agony and frustration that must have been his.

These were some of the unfortunate humans who made up the patient-personnel of North I during my two months in the unit. There were many others, the raucous, the extroverted, the silent, the moody, the profane and wrathful, the compulsive and aggressive, the estranged and confused. So often, as I my-self paced the linoleum treadmill of apathy, up and down the corridors, a great pity would well up for these unwitting victims of life's vagaries. So many of them seemed to be afloat in a sea of loneliness, wallowing helplessly, aimlessly, rising and falling amid the waves of fear and desire, trapped victims of the weary cadence of routinized days and empty nights and without the assurance of a compass-fix toward the sheltering harbor of hope. But then, was I not also "one of them"?

My own sometimes sleepless nights, as I reviewed the vacuous days, were a kaleidoscope of blurred images beyond human assessment. Laden as I was with the cargo of depression, any directions, conclusions, and decisions were impossible of attain-ment and were apathetically set adrift into the mist and fog of a vague tomorrow.

If that tomorrow, however, happened to be a day on which I would be seeing Dr. Mack, who was now interviewing me three times weekly, a ray of hope would begin with the morning light and grow brighter as the time for the appointment neared. Desperately I did so want to talk to someone who might under-stand; and despite the continuation of the endless questions about siblings, displacement, childhood experiences, father and mother relationships, schooldays, teachers, seminary, and so forth, there were, at least, opportunities to express my present feelings and to pour out what I thought were deeper and more important problems and questions.

What I did not realize, but was beginning to absorb, was that my *whole* life from early childhood on, with its varied and multitudinous experiences, positive and negative, was really a *oneness;* that the past—with all of its major and minor fears, anxieties, defenses, hostilities, desires, inhibitions, doubts, lone-liness, together with the various structures I had established to cope with the real or imagined life-threats as I saw them—was formative of the *self* I now was; that all of these were still truly present and dynamically operative to a greater or lesser degree in my feelings today; those of depression, failure, hostility, aliena-tion, defensiveness, and all the other negative attitudes that I so readily projected into the minds of others, and even into the inanimate things around me. It was as though the pliable, wet clay of my early and adolescent years had been placed on the potter's wheel of life and had been poorly formed by an inexperienced apprentice. Eventually, the inherent defects of malformation, under the stress and strain of an emerging perfectionism and a demanding profession, began to appear to an ever more alarming degree and which, apparently, threatened to shatter the whole existence and worthwhileness of an ill-formed personality.

Perhaps it was this ceaseless repetition of returning to the past by the doctor and the forcing of me to co-relate past and present that brought a sudden, small "breakthrough." It happened one morning when I awoke at about 6:00 A.M. and lay in my dormitory "C.O." bed. Instead of the mechanical Morning Offering, I found myself looking up at what had always been the *nothingness* of the ceiling. Unexplainably, but with real conviction, I began an extemporaneous prayer: "Lord, it is good for me to be here! I am a sick guy, very sick emotionally. Of all the places on earth where I could be now, this is the best place for me. Even though I have had to suffer the indignity of constant observation and many other things, these people are concerned about me . . . they really are not punishing, threatening, sadistic . . . they are professionals, trained to aid the emotionally afflicted . . . and they, too, are human . . . with probably deeply human feelings about their patients . . . they want to help us get better. Yes, of course! . . . of all the other places I could be in my condition, this is the best possible place for me . . . and my present confinement and treatment is but a necessary means to a hopefully cured end. I thank you, my God, for your mysteriously wonderful way of helping me . . . what was it Augustine said about looking for You 'without' when all the time You were 'within'? . . . this is where I will find You and Your will for me . . . within me . . . within my attitudes and feelings . . . within the contents of my past . . . by the 'honesty and effort' I must apply to examine my *withinness* . . . to know and admit what has taken place there and is now still enigmatically present, threatening, hostile, and anxiety-producing . . . yes, the *real self*, the sick self is *within!* . . . and that is where I must seek and search and find the causes . . . was it not Shakespeare who said: 'The fault, dear Brutus, may not be in the stars but within ourselves'? . . . *in*sight, *inter*view, *inner*view . . ."

It was, I think, this humbling but absolutely necessary admission of my illness and its inner residence that made the remainder of my stay on "C.O." and North I not only bearable but gradually enlightening and slowly constructive. The admission reminded me of the many times I had listened to ex-alcoholics make the humble but honest admission of the fact that they were sick, alcoholically sick, and that the "moment of truth," the moment when they could and did make this admission that they needed help, was the time-dimensional element in their eventual acquisition of sobriety, with its consequent self-respect and rehabilitation.

Somehow, as I gazed at the heedless, gray-white ceiling, this day was brighter and more promising than any of the several that had preceded it. Something had changed for the better: I had given up a defense, the subconscious insistence that I was not as sick as *they* thought; that I did not have to assume the pose, or try to, of one who was perfectly normal; that I need no longer attempt to lie to myself about my condition or to defend the deception; that I really did *belong* to this group of afflicted humanity. Just as Father Damien on Molokai, knowing his leprous condition, could on that day address his flock as "my fellow lepers," so now I too could address myself, mentally at least, to these emotional castoffs as "my fellow sufferers in Christ."

Now, I knew, and knew it with relief, that I could more comfortably and constructively enter into their company, perhaps even helpfully into their lives. Perhaps there was something I could give them and share with them. Perhaps, as Dr. Mack had suggested, I really did have an apostolate with them, one into which I was forced by circumstances, but one to which, nonetheless, I could bring my precious priesthood. Another seed of hope had begun to germinate. It would, however, have its difficulties in growth and in the bearing of fruit.

This change in attitude, this acceptance, was, I am sure, sensed by Dr. Mack, although I did not attempt to articulate it to him. It was as yet too nebulous. Besides, as he and I well knew, there were many negative feelings still dominating my attitudes and causing depression. At this stage of treatment there were obvious lapses from my resolve of "honesty and effort" that had to be admitted and discussed.

I also became aware of the almost automatic readiness of depression and despair to penetrate and permeate my whole personality, my self-image, in any situation wherein I felt myself to be a "failure" by not measuring up to what I thought I "should" be, or to what others thought I "should" be. Narcissism, I believe, would describe all my negative reactions in this and many other similar circumstances; a self-aggrandizement, a self-idealism that could not tolerate real or imagined imperfection. The doctor had indicated this tendency several times before, but the realistic implications of it had failed to enter the realm of realization and had remained in the periphery of knowledge as just another psychiatric term. I mentioned this to the doctor and also recalled several other long-forgotten, similar situations where the very same shameful feelings had overwhelmed me and had produced a long-lasting and self-demeaning criticism and dislike.

He nodded assent and said: "Perhaps you are beginning to realize that the past is still a powerful element in your present and could be in your future unless we can locate the origins and the various reinforcements of them throughout your life. Then you will have to 'unlearn' a lot of things you have learned the wrong way. I suggest you do more thinking along these lines and try to relive emotionally many of those past, anxiety-producing occasions in your life." It was going to be a long but eventually productive process. Again I reminded myself of my resolve: "honesty and effort."

The next few days on "C.O." were occupied with an attempted recollection of my distant past experiences and their emotional import at the time. Although very difficult at first, and fearful at various times, it eventually became an interesting and revealing exploration of the *child* I thought I had put aside as unimportant and forgotten when I assumed the mantle of adulthood and the dignity of the priesthood. This necessary process of research, reliving, re-evaluation, and humble admission of the presence of the inner-child-of-the-past was to be a painful and embarrassing experience. Just as difficult and, at times, threatening, was the unlearning procedures through which I would have to pass in order to find my real self. I still did not realize all that would be necessary, but now there was, at least, the faint glimmering of hope for the future. It was a weakly glowing spark which, at times, would seem to disappear altogether, and then, with gradual persistence as new insights occurred and old attitudes were clarified and readjusted, would grow stronger and remain more consistently dominant and increasingly enlightening.

As evidence of some slight growth in accepting the reality of my condition, there was the rather sudden disappearance of my "ventriloquist" voice during the last day or so of constant observation. It was a welcome feeling to be able to hear my own voice in my own ears.

Other evidence remained, however, of my deep-seated anxiety. The faint but persistent perspiration that had characterized my entrance into White Hall was still with me and would remain with obstinant endurance for many weeks to come. The body has a multiplicity of ways to indicate externally its interior apprehension.

# CHAPTER XII

# ROOM 19

## *Grief—and the Hand of Hope*

---

*"Whatever crazy sorrow saith,*
*No life that breathes with human breath*
*Has ever truly longed for death."*
  —Tennyson: *The Two Voices*

JUST what it was that prompted the doctor to inform me one day that I was to be removed from constant observation and given a room, I do not know. Undoubtedly, however, he had sensed the positive changes in me; the more constructive and pliable attitudes in addition to the extreme lessening of hostility in being confined to North I. I was almost speechless with joy at the good news. Although still confined to the unit, I would have the delectable privacy of my own room, No. 19, at the very end of the west wing and in the quietest area of the ward. It would be as far away as possible from Ted's doleful recordings! After this interview with the doctor, which seemed more positive and promising than any before, I said a silent prayer of thanks. I felt like a free man again, although locked doors were still surrounding me.

With words of congratulations from both patients and nurses, I gathered my few belongings and hurried to my new quarters. Before unpacking, I sat on the side of the bed for several moments and luxuriated in the privacy that now was mine. It was a step forward and meant several other things, besides.

Now, I felt, there had been returned to me something of the human dignity that was mine by right. Even the "failure" at White Hall, although still a rankling shame in memory, seemed much more remote and much less accusing. Constant observation, disgraceful though it might have been, was a thing of the past. It, too, I knew, would gradually diminish as a "failure."

Also, with this precious room of my own, I knew somehow that I could and would become more familiar with and more understanding of my fellow patients. Much of my aloofness began slipping away, an aloofness prompted by shame rather than by deliberate choice. There was also an even stronger admission that I was "one-of-these," but a concomitant conviction that I had much to give them, if only by way of dialogue, interest, concern.

Not all patients in North I were odd, isolated, or unpredictable. Some of my companions, especially new arrivals during my past six weeks in the unit, were very well educated; some were professionals in various fields of research and education. It was this group, perhaps as much as my new status, new privileges, and changed attitudes that caused my last several weeks in North I to become not merely bearable, but often quite enjoyable. Among these professionals were doctors, lawyers, and college professors. As often as possible, we would gather together, exchanging views and engaging in spirited and rewarding conversations.

Since I could now receive visitors, it was not long before members of the family appeared. Apparently, they had seen the doctor before seeing me and had received some sort of cautious professional assurance that things were improving. Meeting them was much easier than I thought it would be. Readily enough, I told them that for years I had been bothered by something or other and was finally getting the treatment that I needed but was ashamed to ask for. They seemed much relieved at my appearance and composure. In turn, they assured me that mother had taken the news very well and had sent a message that I was to take a good rest, that I had been working too hard. It was a great relief to hear from them that she was more than holding her own and not unduly disturbed by my hospital "vacation," as she termed it.

My self-attitude in the unit was now much more confident and rewarding. Often, I would go out of my way to listen to young Melvin and all about his home situation. He had a brilliant mind and had become something of an expert at bridge. I would frequently remind him that he had a great intellectual future before him if only he would try to cooperate with his doctor's advice; that this was the only way he would eventually get out of the hospital. In talking to him, I was reminded of the way Arnold had talked so convincingly, and yet ineffectually, to me while at White Hall. But Mel needed the interest of others, and it was this I tried to give him.

My friend Terry was still pacing the corridors, but he would frequently stop to supervise my game of solitaire. I would make conversation, chiefly about sports, and he would listen attentively, but he never had a word in reply. However, I knew that he felt welcome in my presence, and with this I had to be content. Many others, too, I was sure of it now, had come to accept me and to trust me. Or perhaps it might well be that I had come to accept them just as they really were, for like breeds like, just as giving prompts gratitude. Possibly they had accepted me as I was from the beginning, but my continually projected shame and self-estrangement had seemed to keep them at a distance.

Although I enormously enjoyed the privacy and quiet of my new quarters, I was still keenly aware, due to the many questions and implications of my sessions with Dr. Mack, that I had more intricate problems to find, accept, and work through than I had ever suspected. While still in White Hall, Dr. Braceland, the psychiatrist-in-chief at the hospital, had given us a lecture in which he said: "There are no magic cures. If a cure comes it is going to come through hard work." I knew now what he meant. Probing into the past, with its attendant dread, was a most difficult thing, and the meanings gleaned were elusive.

In obedience to the doctor's orders and because of an innate curiosity, I would often allow my mind to wander and to wonder

about possible causes of my sickness, their subsequent re-enforce-
ment by similar events, and their consequent solidification into
so many artificial defenses, such as compulsive work, unreasonable fears, phobic symptoms, isolation, and a continual self-
demeaning attitude that I so readily summed up in the con-
temptuous word "failure." What life situations had induced so
much rigidity, so many inhibiting and prohibiting feelings that
had reduced my freedom to be a normal, reasonably self-
contented person, a functioning and productive priest?

"Try to review your life," suggested the doctor on many
occasions. "Try to recall and emotionally relive all of the happy
and joyful occasions of your life, but especially the fearful,
anxious, hostile, and depressive experiences of the past. Try also
to trace the continuity, the repetition of these emotions and
feelings as you passed from early childhood, adolescence, high
school, seminary training and then the years of your priesthood."

"Somewhere along the line," he observed, "you began and have
continually absorbed the idea, the conviction, that 'I'm not much
good.' Through this series of similar events and feelings that
have grown in intensity throughout the years, this failure complex of yours, this attitude that 'I'm no damn good,' has become an uncontrollable conviction to you. Hence, the depression,
anxiety, and panic you've gone through. You've got a lot of
thinking to do. It might be very disturbing, at times, because
you've had a pretty good dose of depression over the years. Just
don't be surprised too much when and if this depression returns."

It was difficult work and seemingly fruitless, because nothing
I unearthed would dispel the recurrent anxiety that still invaded
a part of almost every day. Much of the past was too deeply
buried to be easily excavated; some of it was discarded as being
unimportant; a good deal of it, however, was probably too
frightening to be recalled from the subconscious mind which, of
its nature, tends to protect itself from terribly threatening revelations and from exposure to further imagined harm. I had to
learn not only of these latter somehow or other, but also I had
to become convinced that those long-ago, real-life emotional
experiences—fearful, hostile, shameful, and intimidating—had
formed a whole complexity of negative self-attitudes, and that

these depressive forces were still dynamically present and dominantly operative in my actions and self-image. Real-life hospital experiences would begin to teach me these things. There soon took place that "pretty good dose of depression" the doctor had mentioned.

It was a Sunday morning. For the first time in almost three weeks I would be attending Mass. On the way over to the hospital chapel through the subterranean passageways interspersed with a series of locked doors, anxiety began to grow and expand. Miss Baker, with whom I was walking at the time, noticed my silence and gently inquired about how I felt. I could only tell her that I was a bit depressed, but that I didn't know just why. By the time we reached the chapel, however, the fear of something, whatever it was, had increased greatly. It was more an agitation than a depression. I could not fathom it.

Prior to Mass, confessions were heard by the visiting chaplain. He was, I must say, one of the kindest and most understanding of confessors, especially for mental patients. I told him who I was and a few other things that were on my mind. I also mentioned my anxiety, which seemed to grow more fearful as I came to the chapel.

"Well, Father," he said gently, "I wish I could explain everything to you, but I'm not a psychiatrist, just a priest. I can only suggest that you try to make a simple act of trust and then relax as much as possible. I know it is easy for me to say this, but probably very hard for you to make this act of faith with all your emotional problems. But do, please do, try to say and believe in the fact that God knows you and your present suffering, just as He knew and loved His only-begotten Son, Christ, as He hung on the cross. But He also loves you, just as much as He loved His own Son. Yes, difficult as it may be, try to think about His love for you."

For a few moments it was somewhat heartening to hear these words and to be reminded of a divine love, but it did little to reduce the gnawing anxiety that kept pace with me as I made my way to a pew near the front of the rather dark but attractive little Victorian style chapel. I knelt and tried to make my act of trust, and to relax. But the fearfulness grew, and soon I began to perspire rather profusely. After wiping my face, I half sat on the bench.

It was then that I realized that Miss Baker was kneeling beside me. Perhaps it was only coincidental, but I rather suspected that she was more than a little concerned about my anxiety and the perspiration that was an external indication of it. I was glad of her presence because she knew me quite well as a result of our many friendly and serious conversations, and her continually encouraging themes presented when I was terribly depressed and felt shamefully debased while on constant observation. But now her presence and covert watchfulness somewhat increased my anxiety. I did not want her to think that I was suffering a relapse to my former pitiful state, that my progress had been only temporary, that I had "failed" again. I gripped the pew in front of me to control my growing agitation, but frequently had to wipe my streaming brow and face.

As Mass progressed, I felt an entirely new and unfamiliar sensation arising. Besides the panicky fear of collapsing or suddenly, convulsively running out of the chapel, an action that would be shamefully noticeable and forever disgracefully recalled, an odd and frightening chill began to expand from my stomach, through my chest, and even down into my legs. My dread of something terrible about to happen became almost uncontrollable. The "cold sweat of fear" had seized me! Miss Baker, I am sure, was most concerned now and glanced at me frequently, openly, almost as though she wanted to speak to me, to find out what was wrong and to help me.

Desperately, I tried to follow the Mass with my missal, but the words were a blur. I could only look at the calmly functioning priest at the altar and say repeatedly: "That's where you should be now . . . that's what you should be doing, out in some parish church, offering the Holy Sacrifice and giving the bread of life, both the word and the Eucharist to the needy 'people of God.' Instead, you are a shivering, shaking, frightened specimen of fragmented humanity . . . made up of bits and pieces of confusion . . . you are most certainly that 'failure' you have so well named yourself . . . you'll never get up on an altar again

. . . you'll never be able to face people and preach to them . . . you'll never be that *good* priest, that productive priest . . ."

Just how I made my way to the Communion rail, I will never know. If it was not through sheer, blindly automatic will-power, then it must have been prompted by a desperation fear of making a public and unbearably shameful spectacle of myself before patients and personnel in a place where a priest should be peacefully at home with his God and in communion with Him. Miss Baker, walking beside me up to the rail and standing faithfully at hand in case of need, was also perhaps a steadying influence.

The painfully exhausting ordeal of Mass over, I blindly made my way back through the catacombs with the group, isolated from them, silent, discouraged, and still badly shaken by the mystifying magnitude of the strain that the chapel and Mass had occasioned. Miss Baker kept pace with me but made only a few sporadic attempts at conversation, to which I could give only distracted responses. I wanted to be alone, to have time in which to think about all that had happened, the cold sweat, the agitation, the near exposure of my panic . . . and the reasons for all of this. Back in the unit, I hurried to my room, closed the door, and sat on the side of the bed with head in hands, my mind swirling in a vortex of confusion. Something . . . or things had produced this avalanche of anxiety. What was it . . . what were they? For long minutes I sat there, completely lost in a labyrinth of bewildered dismay and depression.

It was then that Miss Baker came to the door and gently asked if I would like to talk about what had happened in the chapel. She could not help but notice my agitation. I had barely lifted my head when she entered, but nodded her to the chair. Talk! What good would it do? How can you talk about a mystery . . . an enigma concealed in a puzzle? What good had all that talking with Dr. Mack accomplished?

And yet, I knew that I had to talk with someone. Suppressed depression only breeds more of the same. Yes, I had learned this much. And I knew I could not keep pent up within me the rising despair that threatened to overflow the control gates of reason and inundate my mind with a form of panic that might, in turn, cause me to be returned to constant observation. This fearsome thought quickly prompted me to want to talk, to talk to anyone, especially to someone who would try to understand, who warmly and kindly wanted to share in and perhaps help relieve me of some of the intolerable weight of despair. I looked at her wordlessly, not knowing what to say. She helped me.

What had happened this morning? What feelings did I have before and during Mass? There is always a cause for such agitation. Perhaps it would help just to reveal such feelings as I could describe. Then, too, I would be better able to discuss everything with the doctor.

As best I could, I tried to describe the beginnings of anxiety at approaching the chapel . . . about being in the house of God but not being of it, now . . . my shame and guilt at seeing a priest at the altar, where I should be . . . my self-accusation at being so fearful at merely watching a Mass take place . . . the contrast between my agitation and the calm performance of the chaplain . . . the fear of jumping up and running out of the chapel . . . the strange, cold sweat and chills that had seized my whole body . . . the thought of perhaps never being able to say Mass again because of uncontrollable anxiety . . . of not being able to preach again . . . of not being able to do the many other priestly functions that I had loved so much during my twenty years of service . . . of the horrible present . . . of the feeling of having "failed" again after having made some progress . . . of my constantly uttered prayer to be "a good priest, a holy priest, an effective priest" . . . that I was none of these . . . never would be . . . I was nothing but a priest who failed! . . .

All the while I had not looked at Miss Baker. I was too much ashamed to see her reactions. Talking them out was bad enough. Nor had she spoken during the woeful misery of my recitation, its wretched present and desolate future. The summation of it, as I stopped speaking, overwhelmed me. And then the tears came.

It was as though a dam had burst . . . I could not stop it,

nor the sobbing . . . nor did I try to. This was me. The real me. The whole sad summary was the real me. . . . Why not admit it? . . . Why try to conceal it? . . . To cry was a shameful, childish, unmanly thing to do . . . but then, I was a shameful specimen of humanity, of the priesthood . . . this morning had proved it . . . Miss Baker saw it all . . . she saw me now . . . through her report the personnel and staff would know all about it. . . . "O God, come to my assistance. O Lord, make haste to help me" . . . a tortured cry from the depths of despondency . . .

In complete abjection, I hung my head lower still, trying to escape into that state of apathy that at times, at least, had given partial relief to the unbearable weight of tormenting anxiety. But I had a guest, a kindly one. I must observe the amenities. Without raising my head, I wiped my eyes and thanked Miss Baker for her concern and for listening. She said nothing. I was only aware of her silent presence. With a deep sigh, I now looked up at her and, much to my surprise and consternation, I saw tears streaming down her cheeks beneath her glasses. I looked at her, speechless and confused.

"But . . . but Miss Baker," I exclaimed. "Why are you crying? I am so terribly sorry for upsetting you."

"I'm crying," she said, "because I cannot help you." The reply stunned and shamed me. I felt so guilty for having subjected this kindly, but inexperienced young girl, barely out of her teens, to my impossible problems and laying such a huge emotional burden upon her. It was so selfish of me. Here again, I was imposing on others, afflicting them with the insuperable task of attempting to solve the unsolvable mystery of my anguish, although this had not been my intention.

"Please don't cry," I begged her. "Besides," I half-laughed in order to relieve her, "there have been more than enough tears shed here already. I'll be all right. And I can talk over the whole thing with Dr. Mack."

Strangely enough, I did feel somewhat better. After she left I thought about it. Why this minor but unexpected relief? Talking it out had helped, yes, even as it often did with Arnold and Dr. Mack on other occasions. Then, too, there was the natural alleviation that tears can bring about, the allowing of a normal human emotion to be expressed as it demanded and needed to be expressed.

But there was something more in all this. Yes. Someone had cared enough about me to enter into my deepest distress . . . to share in it. Someone had cried for me . . . even as Christ Himself had cried for His friend, the dead Lazarus, and for his grieving family. "No man is an island . . . any man's death diminishes me, because I am involved in mankind."

The room was empty, but the loneliness of an hour ago had greatly diminished. A compassionate, supportive presence had been here, still was here, somehow.

When I next saw Dr. Mack I knew, of course, that he had had a full report of Sunday's events. After greeting me with his customary smile, he said: "Well, now, Father. Tell me all about what happened Sunday."

In proper sequence, I told him everything I had said to Miss Baker.

"But," the doctor wanted to know, "what were your actual thoughts during Mass, when you entered the chapel, when you knelt and looked at the altar? What were you thinking when you saw the priest on the altar? If you were making comparisons on these occasions, what do you suppose they were?"

These and similar questions had occurred to me since Sunday's event, and I had thought about them in more detail. The anxiety probably originated because I was about to return to a place that was most suggestive of my "failure"; the chapel increased it because it reminded me of my "place of business," where I used to work but had been found wanting; the unproductive act of trust was proof again of my lack of faith in God; the altar was that elevated position where I "should" be; the pew represented the shamefully passive and captive situation where my "failure" had placed me; the priest, especially, in his calm, poised procedure, unruffled demeanor, composure, and self-assurance before the congregation, was everything that I, the priest "should" be . . . and was not!

All of this, I realized, was a negative comparison. What I

really was saying to myself was that I had fallen from the position of a comparatively dignified and useful priest needed by people and by my Congregation, to the unutterably disgraceful status of being a mental patient . . . who had already failed the first phase of hospital treatment . . . who doubted the success of the present therapy . . . who could not envision a happy return and a confident duplication of the calm decorum that was taking place on the altar . . . who could see nothing but the accusation and blameworthiness for everything that had led up to this present state of deplorable futility.

The doctor listened intently and then began probing more deeply into my feelings, attempting to clarify, for both me and himself, the more profound and obscure layers of unrecognized attitudes and meanings in all that had taken place Sunday and in other allied areas. Then he began to ask a series of questions which, I felt with surprise, were inappropriate in view of my distress. The queries seemed to indicate a subtly ominous trend in his estimation of me and in the eventual direction and perhaps disposal of my case.

"What would you do for a living, Father, if you could no longer practice the priesthood?" Startled at this totally unsuspected question, I gave the only spontaneous answer that leaped to my mind.

"If I couldn't be a priest," I responded with energetic conviction, "I wouldn't want to live! I'd rather die than not be a priest!"

"But," he persisted, "there might develop circumstances where a priest could no longer function as a priest. What would you do in such a situation?"

His persistence in this course of questioning by now had filled me with consternation. What was he leading up to? What kind of thinking did he want me to pursue? These psychiatrists are so subtle. What sort of action was he intimating that I consider as a resolution to my difficulties?

Suddenly, there occurred to me the case of Father Albert. He had indicated to several patients and personnel that he probably would not return to the priesthood after leaving the hospital. He was the one who most disheartened me with his pessimism when, in my first days at White Hall, I had looked to my fellow priests for some sort of strength, consolation, and hope. After that first talk with Albert, I avoided him. Father Tom was different. Although he hated the hospital, his great desire was to get back to the active priesthood and to teaching at the university. He was, in this area, at least a great help to me, and I was grateful to him.

But, Albert! Was Dr. Mack likening me to him? Was he hinting that perhaps the priesthood was not for me? That I, like Albert, should begin to think of other means of livelihood after hospitalization? That my recurrent anxiety of several years' standing was really an unconscious protest against the demands of the priesthood and religious life? That such a real possibility was revived during Sunday's Mass? That the real truth about my depression and phobias was an unconscious and reluctant admission that I was emotionally unfit for the profession I had chosen? All of this was the *seeming* import of the doctor's questions. It frightened me, terribly. In silence, I considered all of these apparent implications. But then, a new feeling began to arise.

*If*—and I was not entirely certain—*if* this was the doctor's new thought concerning me and my profession, I *knew* he was wrong! *I knew it from the depths of my being!* I knew it from the honest essence of my lifelong desires and sincerest aspirations. It was simply and totally inconceivable to me that I would or could be anything but a priest, or perform any work except in the context of my priesthood. My whole dedication, no matter how painful or demanding it might be, was entirely directed to service in the priesthood, to which I was totally convinced God had called me. He did not give and retract. Such would be entirely against His nature, especially in view of the love-desire I had for Him and for His service. There simply was no other answer. And I knew it with a solid and pervasive conviction that automatically emanated from my mind and heart and soul and emotions . . . despite the present distress of these emotions. As further evidence of this conviction, I could point to the twenty years of comparative joy with which I had served faithfully this priesthood . . . had served with a love that only devotion-despite-pain can produce and thereby prove beyond human questioning the validity of this love.

As I considered all this, my anger grew at the *seeming* implication of the doctor's insistent theme. Coming from him, it seemed incongruous, incredible! He, a priest; I, a priest. "Thou art a priest *forever,* according to the order of Melchisedech!" Whatever else I might be emotionally, I still *was* and *forever* would be a priest! It was this doctor's professional duty to help me resolve my emotional problems, not to desert my beloved priesthood. With increased bitterness, I reflected that I had conscientiously tried his "honesty and effort" formula. Now, for some totally unfounded reason, he was using my emotional and intellectual "honesty" by trying to divert my "effort" into a horribly objectionable direction. There seemed to be no other conclusion.

With an eruption of wrath, I stormed at him: "I came here for help . . . for help to get back on my feet . . . to return to the priesthood! That is what I came for! That is what I want! And the *only* thing I want! If you cannot or will not help me, then I don't want you or need you!"

In helpless rage, I swept everything off the desk beside which I had been sitting, and then buried my flushed and burning face into my folded arms. Feelings of hate, bitterness, rejection, betrayal, and hopelessness seethed and boiled within me. Here was another stinker, another bastard whom I had trusted and who had deceived me. He, of all people! A priest, a psychiatrist, a person whom I had come to respect and depend on, even to revere. Well, now he knew how I felt about him. Let him take it from there!

"From there" came nothing but silence. He must be re-evaluating his line of thought, I considered remotely, or perhaps trying to find words to assuage my outraged feelings. But again, rage smothered any kindly sentiment about him. Let him stew in his own failure to understand, for *he* had been the failure this time. Not I.

Just how long I remained in this position and mood, I do not know. It must have been for several minutes. When finally I raised my head to meet his evaluating gaze—he was not there!

He had, without my hearing him, left the room . . . and had left me with my angry, confused, and unresolved feelings.

For a moment I was dumfounded. He had never done this before. Why now? Why had he left without some sort of final, thought-provoking advice to engage my mind between interviews? Why? Now, all I could conclude was that he must have meant what he seemed to have implied by those questions about employment outside the priesthood. I began wondering fearfully as I stared at his empty chair. Did he really mean what he implied?

The thought was repugnant beyond words! And yet he, as a psychiatrist, *seemed* to have been suggesting just this. Could he be . . . O God! . . . could he have been right? But, no! He was wrong! Absolutely wrong! Still, he had left me with nothing else to think about . . . no certain or plausible explanations of that distraught Sunday morning.

Bewildered again, as so often before, there was nothing left for me to do but to have recourse to bed, after dutifully removing my shoes, and to think perhaps hopeful thoughts that might arise from a reconsideration of all that had taken place during this visit. Thoughts came, and questions, and direful wonderings.

Wonderings . . . questions . . . doubts . . . so many, so confusing . . . and no one to commune with except the stupid, silent ceiling . . . the stolid, unresponsive wall, and the hateful, opaqued window, all of which said, "Don't-look-at-me-for-answers."

If he was right! How awful! Frightening! Aloneness closed in on me. I seemed to have been reduced to a "thing" again . . . a once-upon-a-time dignified person . . . now become like one of those frayed murals I had seen in books of the ancient masters of the canvas. Scenes and personages, once beautiful, alive, inspirational, attractive, but now time-flaked and moisture-damaged . . . "a thing of beauty" was not a joy forever! I could walk and talk but bore only meager evidence of the priestly beauty, dignity, joy that once I had, once was to myself and to others. Now I lay here bearing the ignominy of my many defeated yesterdays and the tattered, torn banner of my hopeless tomorrows . . . a motley disarray of priestly failure and pathetic despondency.

Ceiling, walls, window . . . you are so damned stupid! . . . so stolid! . . . yet so dependable in your designed and intended function of support, protection, warmth, privacy for the humanity you encompass. How well you serve the purpose of your existence . . . but I, endowed with life, intelligence, faith, and with the highest human calling, Holy Orders . . . how have I justified myself through all of these extraordinary gifts? . . . what was all my vaunted priestly dignity now but a long, bony, accusing finger of failure? You, wall! How many desolate others in the past have turned to you with similar abject feelings of hopelessness, rejection, alienation, and despair? . . . emotional orphans, subverted and abandoned by the adversities of life . . . how I envy you with your irresponsibility, unfeelingness, and bland indifference . . . never threatened with the disgrace of failure, and with the persecution and the prosecution of duty and accountability . . . free from demanding desire, the effort of hope, the struggle to serve humanity's needs and solve its problems.

And yet! I don't envy you! You are a comparative nothingness! Serviceable, but dumb! I will not be reduced to nonlife, or to half a life! I want the fullness of existence! No matter what that existence may bring in its wake. It is the lot of humanity to suffer, yes, to suffer defeat and disillusionment, and to feel the sting of rejection, the burden of pain in mind and body, the dread of loneliness . . . but it is only humanity that can conquer its environment, its afflictions, its injuries . . . only man can cope with the adversities of life. . . . "If a man cannot rise above himself," said Wordsworth, "how poor a thing is man." . . . O God! Help me, please do help me to rise above myself. . . . "I will not leave you orphans." . . . "O Lord! Make haste to help me!"

The room had darkened during my long and rambling reflections. But now, suddenly, it was flooded with light. An aide, whose key was necessary to turn the lights off and on, remained by the door and the nurse in charge, Miss Trainor, stood by my bed with a tray of medications in her hand.

"Time for your medicine, Father," she said with her always gentle smile and offered me the paper cup of pills and another little paper cup of water.

My mood of apathetic despondency changed suddenly into one of perverse rebellion. Here was a representative of that impersonal officialdom that had distantly decreed a cure for my deeply human emotional problems by proposing to change the chemistry that was the least important part of the selfness that was me, that was made up also of far superior things, such as hope, affection, aspiration, love, earnestness, as well as pity, sympathy, loneliness, and misunderstanding. Pills! I needed trust, confidence, comprehension, reassurance, and encouragement . . . a helping hand to lift me from this pit of despondency and uncertainty. And here I was, being offered three little pellets that were as useless and as uncommunicative, as mute and as inhuman as the stupid walls, ceiling, and window during my lengthy monologue with them. Three tiny pills and I would feel better, perhaps cured! How stupid! It was farcical! Ridiculous! Outrageous! I was a suffering human being—and *they* offered me the futile mixture of some powdered herbs that were just as uncaring as the bed I lay on.

Turning my head to the wall, I muttered that I did not need the pills and would not take them. To hell with them—and with him. Yes, I knew my rebellion was an act of hostility toward the doctor. I had seen other patients refuse medication and could readily recognize the overt hostility toward someone, usually the doctor, that prompted their rejection. This was one way the patient had of "getting back" at that impersonal, hateful, nonunderstanding officialdom of doctors, staff, personnel, or someone else. I knew why I was refusing the pills, but rejoiced that I had some sort of weapon with which to counterattack and punish the hostile forces that hurt so much simply by not understanding, or by not trying to understand.

Miss Trainor stood there patiently; the male aide filled the doorway, ready to protect the nurse or to manhandle the recalcitrant patient.

"Father," she said, reproachfully, "you've never done this before. You have always been a cooperative patient. You know
you have to take the pills, otherwise . . . well, otherwise we'll
have to force you to take them. I know you wouldn't want that
kind of a report on your record."

Still faced wallward, I considered the situation. I had seen
other patients forced to swallow pills, and it was not a pretty
sight. It was revolting. The struggling, fighting, cursing, screaming—and the defeat. Yes, it was below my dignity, my self-respect. I alone would be the loser.

But more than that, I knew my hostility was not directed at
this competent and gentle little nurse, nor at the personnel
whom I liked and who would be forced reluctantly to that violent struggle that they probably detested. My real rebellion
and rage was directed toward Dr. Mack because of the supposed
direction of his questions that afternoon, plus, of course, his
silent and disconcerting departure from my room, which had
left me in such a state of abject confusion and depression. My
real declaration of war was with him, not with these harried
personnel who, after a long day of tense watchfulness over
other patients, would have a wretched and disgusting encounter
with a priest-patient. No. It was not fair to them. They had
always been most respectful and kindly toward me. In view of
my knowledge of what was taking place in me, it would really
be sinful to put up a struggle, to cause them dismay and anger.
And it would be dishonest on my part. A lie. An attempt to
express hostility through a fallacy. "Honesty and effort" . . . yes,
I would be honest . . . "this above all, to thine own self be
true and it follows as the night the day, thou canst not then be
false to any man." How many times I had preached this and
quoted it. Well, all right. I would be honest in spite of the
bastard. The anger was still there, but it was, at least, properly
directed . . . and admitted.

Still reluctant, however, I turned and looked at Miss Trainor.
I did not know her very well. We never had any such talks as
I had with Miss Baker. Somehow, this nurse, so calmly efficient
in her profession, had intimidated me. I knew it was caused
by a shame at my own professional failure, and, of course, it

would be childish and unjust to her to be the cause of any more difficulty than the day had already visited upon her. I took the pills and the water in a weary gesture of defeat.

"Are you bothered about something?" she asked, in her always kindly manner. "Is there anything I can do for you?"

Bothered! O God, how I was bothered! And there was so much help I needed. But what could she do? She'd probably end up in the same tearfully impotent condition as Miss Baker. Who could help, really? But "no man is an island . . ." and I was so terribly alone.

"May I talk to you?" I asked. It was an impulsive request, almost a desperation plea for some kind of help, a sort of mental "conditioned reflex" whereby the mind, in its spontaneous attempt to survive, automatically seeks and clings to any apparently saving device, be it a person or thing or thought. I had not intended to ask, but could not prevent the words from forming and sounding the question.

"Of course," she smiled gently, courteously, and motioned the male aide out into the hallway. I held my head in my hands for a while and then lay back on the bed, looking at the ceiling. What to say? How to say it? Would she understand? There was so much I did not understand myself.

At first, I started slowly. You knew of my agitation last Sunday, of course, and of my conversation with Miss Baker the same day. You personnel make reports and compare notes and all is discussed with the doctor. You also know something about my recent interview with Dr. Mack. I don't know what he has told you. But . . .

The words came faster now, almost pouring out along with my angry bewilderment, as I attempted to describe the hopeless and horrible feelings prompted by the apparent direction of the doctor's questions and revolting implications. Perhaps I was mistaken in my interpretation of what he meant, but I was unable to come to any other conclusion except that he was hinting at the possibility of my leaving the priesthood . . . getting other employment . . . relieving myself of the strains of my profession . . . there was a similar case at the hospital now, Father Albert . . . he seemed to be taking this way

out . . . but I loved my priesthood and always had . . . I'd
rather die than not be a priest . . . the priesthood to me is
life itself . . . how could the doctor, a priest himself, dare suggest
such a thing? . . . *if* he did not mean what he *seemed* to imply,
then why did he not try to relieve my distress? . . . why did
he leave me in such a state of terrible worry and concern as to
his real intent? . . . why did he sneak out, knowing that this
would surely bring about more depressive thoughts? . . .

Now and then, in answer to my agonizing questions, Miss
Trainor would respond with: "I don't know, Father" . . . or,
"Perhaps you misunderstood" . . . or, "You can speak to him
about this the next time" . . . or "Yes, I know you have tried,
you have been a good patient" . . .

She had no answers. Not to the questions for which I wanted
answers. I knew she wouldn't, couldn't. It all seemed so implacably hopeless. I was still that "refrigerated item," now even
farther removed from the life-giving warmth of reassurance and
hope, human and divine. This room, yes, this silent, impassive,
uncaring room had become a morgue for the ashes of my life's
efforts, aspirations, and priestly ambitions. The frayed mural of
my existence had finally faded into nothingness . . . oblivion.

The tears came. I turned my face to the wall as I felt them
whelming up from the abyss of my desolation. And the sobbing . . . uncontrollable . . . uninhibited . . . despairful . . .
The meaningfulness of my existence seemed to have been rent
asunder. And the collapse of the spirit is much worse than the
cave-in of a steel-girded building.

Thoughts and feelings still flashed in and out of my mind
despite the tears . . . strangely enough, most were about the
theological girders and rafters that had structured my life for
so many years. From the various psalms came: "I am numbed
and severely crushed. . . . I am very near to falling and my
grief is always with me. . . . What glory can I give you if I go
down into the grave? . . . Within me my soul is downcast. . . .
As the hind longs for the running waters, so my soul longs for
you, O God. . . . Have pity on me, O Lord, for my body is languishing. . . . Why have you lifted me up, O Lord, only to cast

me down? . . . Why do you stand aloof and hide in the time of
my distress? . . . From the bottomless pit, deliver me. . . ."

There was a bottomless pit near at hand, somewhere between
the bed and the impassive wall, and I felt myself slipping into
it. I didn't care.

But before I allowed myself to slip over the edge into I do
not know what, perhaps into the escape-world of what is called
psychosis, the state of unreality and delusion, I felt Miss Trainor's hand take mine, wordlessly. It was a light touch, gentle with
sympathy, attempted understanding, encouragement, an assurance that I was not completely alone in my agony even though
this was beyond the comprehension of my kindly and concerned listener. Again, as with Miss Baker, someone was willing
to enter into the mystery of my misery, herself undoubtedly lost
in its depths and unable, verbally, to show the way out. But—
and this was the thought that turned my mind away from the
feeling of and the wanting to fall—there was someone *with*
me . . . and to be *with* someone means to be *for* him, even
though unable to bring forth causes and cures.

This touch. What did it mean, really? It had changed something in me. Yes, in a sense it had given me a form of hope.
Hope was something I could not give myself. No one can, really.
Hope comes from outside, from someone else. Hope is life, just
as hopelessness can lead to death, mental and physical. *Touch
—hope—life.* Wasn't this what Michelangelo tried to indicate in
his Creation scene on the ceiling of the Sistine Chapel? God,
the source of life, reaching out and "touching" Adam and thereby
giving him life, yes, and hope, too, for with the dawning realization of the real but mysterious goodness, power, love, and
presence of this tremendous God, Adam would always hope
for a full and complete reunion with Him Who was his first
beginning and his last end.

The touch. "If I can but touch his garment I shall be cured,"
said the woman with an issue of blood. "Virtue has gone out
from me," said Christ as He allowed Himself to be touched.
And hope had its reward. An encounter had taken place, a
person-to-person relationship had been established. Hope had
come from one to another.

This touch. It was deeply meaningful, somehow. Gradually, the violence of my grief subsided. I was no longer alone, alienated and isolated by the staring and uncaring walls, and ceiling and window. The touch of a human hand had given me a "virtue" of some kind, had restored me to a semblance of self-control and reasonableness. I thought of the touch of Arnold's hand in my panicky moments at White Hall . . . of Miss Baker's helplessness but helpfully concerned presence . . . and now the firmly gentle assurance of this hand whose face I dare not look at lest I see the pathos of grief there, and I the cause of it.

When comparative calm had returned, Miss Trainor asked: "Father, would you like to see Dr. Mack tonight if he is available? I think he would want to know of your feelings." From the controlled tone of her voice I realized gratefully that she was not overcome with grief. I did not have to feel guilty about that, at least. Wiping my eyes, I looked at her and thought how God-sent she was, what wonderful patience and consideration.

In answer to her question, I nodded, and then tried to thank her for listening. It had helped, somehow, I told her. And yes, I would very much like to see the doctor. She smiled and said she would do her best to contact him.

Anger against the doctor had given way to more important considerations. There were so many questions I had to ask, so many doubts to be resolved. Then too, perhaps, after all my castigation of him, I had badly misinterpreted the trend of his questions. Perhaps there were other and positive answers to the method and manner of his probings. I simply could not be left for two or three days in this state of uncertainty. I was resolved to face all issues now, and leave nothing to doubt.

A variety of other thoughts occurred to me. I sat on the side of the bed and reflected. Surely, in the six weeks of hospitalization, I had suffered . . . had gone through some very intense agony . . . but had somehow survived . . . someone had always appeared to assist in some manner or other . . . this little nurse . . . how well she knew mental patients . . . didn't try to reason them out of their depressions . . . just listened and by listening she shared . . . and by sharing she gave the impetus to badly needed hope, strength, courage . . . "I will not leave you orphans" . . . and He did not . . . someone in their concern and sympathy had adopted me and restored me to a feeling of "belonging to the continent of mankind," as Donne put it. Much relieved, I went down to dinner.

Over a year later, when leaving the hospital, I made it a point to look up Miss Trainor who, by that time, had been appointed to the nursing education faculty, in order to thank her. I recalled expressly the horrible time I had experienced in Room 19, and told her I had often marveled at the kindly, efficient way in which she handled my extreme depression. What she did not know, I informed her, was that just before she took my hand, I was about to slip over the precipice of neurosis into what could have become a deeply psychotic state, that the touch of her hand brought me back to hope, rationality, and sane thinking. Quite candidly, she confessed that she could not think of a blessed thing to say to me at the time that would be of any help; that she could only spontaneously reach out and hold my hand so that I would know that she was still there, and that she was a deeply concerned human being who wanted, but did not know how, to relieve my unbearable suffering.

The admission surprised me considerably, but then, I reflected, sometimes the touch of a human hand is more powerful and curative than all the wisdom the tongue can utter. Often, since that day, and during the years of reflecting back on the scene in Room 19, I cannot think of her presence without recalling a somewhat similar but far more meaningful scene; it is that of the angel of encouragement who appeared to Christ in the Garden of Olives.

Later on that evening, Dr. Mack appeared with his usual smiling greeting, but with a touch of concern to it, I thought.

"I hear you've had a rough time this afternoon. Did you want to talk about it?"

With an apology for interrupting his evening plans, I told him that much of what he had said that afternoon had upset me terribly. Perhaps, I said, I entirely missed the point of his questioning about what I would do for a living if I could not function as a priest. The only implications that I could draw were that perhaps I should start thinking along the lines of preparing for another type of work. I inquired directly of him just what he had in mind. Did he, perhaps, suspect that I was another Father Albert who, it was widely rumored, was not going to return to the priesthood after leaving the hospital? Or did he think that with his formula, "honesty and effort," I could function reasonably well after working through my emotional problems? And why had he left so quietly, leaving me in a very confused and depressed condition? Why had he not given me the customary suggestions to think about between interviews? Knowing my easily induced depressive states, why had he acted as he did?

He listened attentively while I spoke and then mused reflectively for a while, gazing up at the ceiling, assembling his thoughts; then he observed:

"Father, as a psychiatrist, there is much I know about you, but there is still a great deal that I do not know about you. At times, I have to question and to probe and to listen to what you do not say as well as to what you are actually saying. I have to examine and analyze your various reactions in order to be more certain as to just what is taking place. Basic attitudes and dynamics are intermixed and of varying power and dominance. I do not know completely and conclusively the depth of all of your negative attitudes, nor do I know all of the possible applications of your emotional disturbances, nor the different directions they might take in certain situations. These are things that cannot be measured. However, in many instances, I could give a pretty accurate forecast of what you probably would do, or would feel.

"For instance, now. You were in White Hall for two weeks with comparative freedom of grounds, saying Mass, and so forth. You gradually worsened and then finally fell apart. And so, we had to put you under constant observation because you were so extremely distressed. We couldn't take a chance on what you might do. Now from the time you entered White

Hall until you were taken to North I, some great change had taken place in you. What do you suppose happened?"

"I lost my identity," I answered promptly. There was no need to think out this solution. "Upon entrance I saw myself as a dignified human being, a priest, one whom people looked up to and respected. Gradually, I guess, I lost all of this self-esteem when I was reduced to the realization that I was a mental patient. Then, in this strange place, I had no identity that I could accept and respect. Finally, I really became lost and frightened and depressed."

"Precisely," he observed. "And while we're on the subject of identity, tell me this. Do you think that going out to say Mass was a good thing for you?"

Again I could answer with insight. "No, it wasn't. In fact, it probably made me worse. I kept comparing continually the two things, the church where I should be and the hospital where I should not be, plus the priest I should be and the mental patient I should not be."

He nodded acquiescence. "So, your self-image, your self-esteem was based on a *role* you *should* be playing in life. According to your own words on many occasions, you had become a 'failure' at playing this role. That was your own conclusion. It was not the conclusion of the many others who knew you and who were served by you. But you were projecting your own negative self-attitudes into the minds of others and accepting these as a valid estimation of what you really were. It was, indeed, a vicious circle.

"Also," he continued, "I notice that many times you have used the word 'audience' when you meant 'congregation.' Role and audience. Instead of being yourself, you had to play a role, that of the perfectly performing priest in all circumstances. And you had to please an audience. But the audience you felt you never could please was really your own continual self-criticism. How could you ever win?

"What I was trying to do this afternoon," he continued, "was to have you recognize that you had your own hard-earned and praiseworthy qualities and values so that you could begin to establish a solid interior self-evaluation. Although it is true that we need some sort of approval from others for our acceptable and approvable self-image, it is equally true that we must have a deep conviction of our own inherent self-worth that does not depend on what others think or say or do.

"I had this in mind today when I asked what you could do by way of earning a living if you could not be a priest. If you did not become a priest, I am sure that you would have found a means of livelihood. I was trying to have you see that you had many good qualities and abilities that you have completely neglected in evaluating yourself. You have, as the psychological testings show, a better-than-average I.Q. You do not seem to realize this or accept it as an inherent self-value. You have been too busy playing an impossibly idealistic role. One in which, sooner or later, you were bound to fail.

"Now, in the light of this, tell me: What could you do if this country were taken over by Communists and you wanted to survive and operate secretly as a priest?"

"Oh!" I exclaimed, with dawning realization and relief. "That's simple. I have a master's degree. I could easily make a living teaching college English and still serve as a priest somehow or other."

He nodded, but observed very directly, "Again, I must point out to you that you have a habitual tendency to project the worst image of yourself into the minds of others and to accept it as factual about yourself. Your whole history shows this, from childhood up. That's why," he said with an understanding grin, "we had to go through those hundreds of questions about your whole life. The pattern of self-condemnation appeared in every phase of your relationships with others. This pattern of negative self-evaluation is just what took place this afternoon. It took place last Sunday at Mass, and at White Hall, on constant observation, and on many other occasions while you have been here. This accounts for your perfectionism, your 'musts' and 'shoulds' and all the other demanding things and persons you have met in life. You can, perhaps, accept all this intellectually and understand the theory. But there is going to be a lot of hard work necessary to change your emotional attitudes. These are deeply imbedded habits and are not changed overnight."

The doctor had much more to say in this vein, insisting that a *healthy* self-esteem is absolutely necessary in order to function comfortably in life, in any chosen profession, that this self-esteem is based on a solid feeling of one's *intrinsic* self-worth, that my extremely low self-esteem had caused me to react by establishing an impossibly idealistic self-image and demanding that I live up to it.

"If I were like you," he said, "I would feel ashamed and intimidated every time I listened to a great orator like Bishop Sheen. But I am not Bishop Sheen. I am not a great orator. I am a human being with human limitations and human abilities. I know that I can, through experience and study, better myself in some areas and become a more serviceable person to others who may need me—people, priests, and religious like yourself.

"You, too, are a human being. Somewhere, early in life and along the way to adulthood, you have been pretty badly smashed emotionally. These are the events we will have to examine, relive, bring out into the open, and recognize the fundamental dynamics that were and are taking place in you. You are not the best, nor are you the worst. The truth is somewhere in between. That is what therapy is all about; having people recognize, accept, and act with their abilities and within their limitations. It is the grandiose, the unrealistically self-idealized person who finds so much difficulty in living."

With regard to my priesthood, he assured me that psychiatry was not intent on changing a person's chosen life-work, but to help them to see and understand their basic emotional attitudes toward their work, life, and the people who made up their lives.

Why had he left so silently and while I was in a depressed mood? Hostility. This was and would be one of my basic problems. It had developed early in life, along with other negative attitudes. Here it was, showing itself again, just as it must have occurred times without number in the many years of my life when I was denied, or seemingly denied, that which was due to me, that which people owed to me, that which was unjustly inflicted upon me.

He knew that the feeling of anger would grow after he left, that it would generate more hostility. But, at the same time, it would bring into recognition the fact of its existence and perhaps the memory of other similar occasions during the past. This recognition of a past history of hostility, deeply rooted and constantly reoccurring, would enable me to recognize that the past was truly present in the "here and now" situation.

The doctor continued: "The big question with regard to hostility is: How are you going to handle it? What are you going to do about anger and rage when they appear? How are you going to give them a healthy outlet? One that will not depress or interfere seriously with the course of life, with personal relationships, with work, with the basic self-contentment that every person needs and wants? As a case in point, how did you handle the rage you felt when you looked up and found me gone? Now, you know how you handled it, the wrong way as you perhaps realize, because of the depressive thoughts it brought about."

The doctor stayed with me a long time that evening. Perhaps because he realized that this was a ripe time for me to consider the multiplicity of dynamics that were at work within me and that would, through lifelong habit, begin to operate and dominate in certain adverse situations. More than ever, I began to understand the enormous amount of work that had to be done. There really was no "magic cure," no simple solution. I would have to work and reflect and delve as never before. But, I felt, now I would become less impatient with myself, with therapy, and with the bound-to-come adversities.

After the doctor's leaving, I felt that the day, agonizing as it had been, did represent a breakthrough, one of the many that would reoccur in the months to come. The great difference between the afternoon's conference and the evening's discussion was that now I was no longer so adversely intimidated by whatever lay before me. I could still reasonably and more strongly hope for a return to my precious priesthood; in what limited capacity I did not know. But it was there, in the future, somewhere. And it was well worth the pain that might be involved. I was not an "Albert." Inherently, by conviction and desire, I was still a priest and I knew I always would be. Just how operational would depend on the dissolution and resolution of my various emotional conflicts. As to the hard work and time this would necessitate, well, I would just have to trust in the discretion of the doctor and in the mysterious curative method of the God Who must be, in His own enigmatic but providential way, working in my life even as this life was subjected to the regime of a mental hospital.

My prayer reflections that evening were not circumscribed by the mechanics of habit. They were a real dialogue, a communion without an importuning or a demand. "Try to relax in your act of trust," said the priest on Sunday morning. Now I could. "I will not leave you orphans," Christ had said . . . and He did not. Despite my agony, my aloneness, the threatened abyss of nothingness, He had been present . . . present in the person of Miss Trainor, of the doctor. More convincingly than before, I could say: "I believed, even though I am greatly afflicted." I knew I loved and wanted Him above all things and persons: "Even as the hind longs for running waters, so my soul longs for You, O God." . . . Patience. Yes, be patient, Bill, "Father" Collins, and someday you will be saying with David's joy: "Hope in the Lord. For I shall again be thanking him, in the presence of my savior and my God."

Pain and suffering. Yes, it is the lot of man to be subjected to the "slings and arrows" of fate, life as it occurs. . . . It is also his nature to cry out in rebellion against them, even as did Job in his argumentations with his God. But it is also the lot of man to accept the ultimate answer of Job: "God, in His Providence, is mystery."

Sleep came easily that night.

Perhaps as further proof that something really fundamental had been resolved in a constructive and positive manner on that memorable day and night in Room 19, the following Sunday Mass was a comparatively calm and peaceful experience. In this, as on succeeding Sundays, I felt more at home at Mass, and with a somewhat more enjoyable relaxation I could accept the fact of my being a patient, a mental patient, a "priest-mental patient" who would have to learn how to unlearn the negative attitudes of his life, as well as one who would have to learn through experience the real self, the self-ness, that was the actual "Bill Collins," the *human* person who also happened to be a *priest;* that the two were not incompatible but merely out of focus; that adjustments would have to be made, sometimes radical, on the part of both aspects of my self-image, real and imagined. I knew that many readjustments would be painful, but I also knew that I could work through them with more courage and perseverance.

Finally, too, there came the day when I was informed that I was to be transferred to North II. Another confirmation from *them* that I had progressed, that I was now ready for a "step up" to a better unit. Frankly, though, I did not relish the idea and tried to object. I had come to like the patients on North I; I had developed many close friendships and did not want to leave those with whom I had become so familiar. But I was being forced into another challenging situation. *They* thought I had grown enough to accept the challenge.

Here again, when discussing my reluctance with the doctor, I had something more to learn through experience. He had me realize that my reluctance to leave was, in great part, due to a sense of insecurity. That from a feeling of belonging-ness, familiarity, and acceptance in this unit, I was now presented with the insecurity of a new unit, with the difficult chore of facing and adjusting to the strangeness of twenty-two new personalities. It was, as the doctor talked about it, and as I clearly realized, not unrelated to many other similar past experiences and similar insecurities of my life, insecurities that had prompted me to set up a Maginot Line of defenses, of rigid protection and anxiety-producing watchfulness, plus a whole series of *shoulds* and *should nots* that had seemed absolutely necessary to maintain the image of my "idealized" self and its consequent imperialistic demands.

There was so much to learn, I thought, and to unlearn, as

I prepared to leave North I. But, I reflected, despite the pain of this unit and the subsequent liking of the people in it, experiences had taken place that had taught me much about myself. From now on I would be dealing with the *known*, rather than with the ominous and continual threat of the terrible *unknown*. I noted, too, in passing, as I packed my belongings, that my stomach was much less queasy than before, that for the past two weeks I had looked forward to meals and had thoroughly enjoyed them.

Yes, times had changed. I had changed.

# CHAPTER XIII

# NORTH II
## *Tears—and Some Answers*

---

"*Return, O my soul, to your tranquillity,*
*for the Lord has been good to you.*
*For he has freed my soul from death,*
*my eyes from tears, my feet from stumbling.*"
—Psalm 114

NORTH II was laid out exactly as was North I, with but few exceptions. It contained no open constant observation ward and, joyfully, its windows were clear. Real sunshine poured in through them and made it brighter and much more cheerful. I noticed this almost immediately even though the unit was a locked ward and freedom was as limited as in North I. However, I felt a slight queasiness about this strange new ward with its strange new faces. After unpacking (by an odd coincidence I was assigned the very room from which I had planned an escape just about two months before) I sat on the edge of the bed and tried to figure out exactly why I felt as I did, and why perspiring had returned.

Yes, I reasoned, I was intimidated by the new faces that had stared at me passively, curiously, wonderingly as I had passed down the hall. I had left the comparative security and friendliness of North I for this challenging new ward and its patients. I felt insecure and therefore somewhat frightened. Those silent faces were examining me and asking what a priest was doing in a mental hospital. Yes, these were my feelings

—and what was I going to do about them? Something positive, I decided. I could stay in my room and hide from this new challenge for a while, but something prodded me to go out and meet the challenge, whatever it was. Accordingly, I opened the door and strolled as unconcernedly as possible down the corridor.

Whenever I met a patient or male aide I forced myself to stop and introduce myself as "Bill" Collins. Almost without exception, they acknowledged the introduction and gave their own names; some wanted to chat a bit, and a few referred to me as "Father." So they knew who I was. Mentally, I shrugged off the realization and was thereby pleasantly surprised when I began to feel more at ease. I wasn't hiding anything. I was just trying to be myself, a person who also happened to be a priest. And I had given them the freedom of choosing between "Bill" and "Father." Gradually there developed a sense of satisfaction, even security, in being my own self in this small way and in allowing others to respond to me as they chose.

The only disappointment experienced in my sojourn was the fact that, although the windows were letting in sunshine, there was nothing of nature to be seen, merely the tops of various other buildings. But it was good to see the sky and clouds, an occasional bird, and a far-distant treetop with a few brown leaves still clinging to its branches. Somehow, it held out a promise for the future.

After dinner that evening, I deliberately forced myself into asking to be allowed to play cards with some of the patients. Gradually, I began to learn something about them, even to joke with them and about my own "hangups." Oddly enough, it seemed to open them up to the extent that they began discussing their own experiences, fears, and depressions. It was a good evening and a good start. The "risk" had been well worth the effort.

These patients seemed to be more "with it" than most of those in North I. There was Fred, the lad who had invited me to go to Mass on the day I had planned to escape. He was talkative, often argumentative, and frequently irritating to some of the other patients. He even bugged me a bit, at first, until I learned he had suffered brain damage and had a plate of some kind grafted onto his skull. This, I am sure, accounted for much of his dissatisfaction with life and with the hospital, and for the epileptic-like seizures to which he was occasionally subjected. Eventually, we became very friendly and often served Mass together on Sundays. Some few weeks after our first meeting I had regressed somewhat and was vainly trying to conceal a depressive mood. It was Fred who approached me and volunteered an unexpected but most welcome observation about me and my presence in North II.

"You know, Father," he began, "a bunch of us fellows were talking about you the other day and we thought it would be a good idea to let you know how much we appreciate having you with us. It must be tough for you, a priest, to put up with us, the dirty talk and all. But your example of accepting everything so calmly, obeying rules and orders and everything else about the place has been a great help to us. You don't bitch about things all day long like the rest of us. You're always good company and mix in with everyone, even the worst of us. We want you to know that we are glad to have you with us, but very sorry for whatever it was that brought you to this nut house. I guess we'd all get along better and get out of here sooner if we acted like you. I'm a Catholic and have met a lot of priests, but you're one of the very best I've met."

More than a little confused and embarrassed, I thanked him while assuring him that I had a lot to learn about myself and the reasons why I had to be hospitalized, that I was most grateful to the other patients for putting up with me, and to be sure to tell them how much I appreciated their vote of confidence in me.

Depression lifted somewhat, but I had to go back to my room, lie down, and think over what *others* thought of me. It was good to get such a boost, I thought, but let's be honest. There was a good deal of hostility in me toward the hospital and to many of its regulations and restrictions. I sometimes hated these things, but said nothing. Perhaps I would be better off if I let myself, my real self, explode now and then. But, no, I could never give vent to any such emotions. Home, school, seminary, and priestly training had always emphasized the suppression of any signs of anger. On the contrary, we were always taught to obey without question, to be on time, to be polite and considerate, to be respectful and passively accepting of whatever we might dislike.

Some deeper thoughts occurred to me during this meditation on my various emotions. Dimly, and in retrospect, I began to realize that I had suppressed many healthy human feelings and reactions in the past. I could not verbalize them at the moment, but I knew that they were part of my history and therefore were still present with me in some form or another. Despite the pleasure aroused by Fred's candid observations, I was really disturbed by them because what he and the other patients saw was not the real me. I was still playing a role learned by training and rote. Deeper motivations and subconscious attitudes remained to be discovered, disentangled, and resolved. Quite a task faced me, I knew, and it would take more work, time, and pain than I thought.

Up until this phase of my incarceration, about the middle of December, I had not been allowed visitors except my immediate superiors and, occasionally, members of my family. I could write to anyone, but letters to and from these people were automatically sent to my "responsible party," my Provincial, and were subject to his scrutiny. None were passed on to me. It hurt deeply, this alienation from friends and confreres. Then—it must have been about the eighteenth or nineteenth of December—there was a change in policy due, possibly, to a noticeable improvement in my over-all attitudes. There on my desk was a bundle of mail, most of it from confreres. The Provincial, undoubtedly, had been advised by Dr. Mack that letters of encouragement were indicated at this stage of treatment. The Provincial, in turn, must have sent a form letter to confreres urging them to write.

The letters were a beautiful pre-Christmas gift. Nothing could have pleased me more. I read them all, several times over. All of them represented a warm, human concern from those whom, by projection, I had thought had forgotten me, or were not at all interested in my painful striving for good health. Tears came, and continued to come as I read their encouraging contents. I still had concerned friends, those who really cared and who sympathized, those who wished me well and wanted me back with them again. Clutching the letters, I bowed my head and let the tears flow. They were tears of joy. Someone, many in fact, really did care. It was so good to be wanted by others, so wonderful to feel that I was still a real part of my community.

Since I had been allowed the use of a typewriter in this unit, I began to answer the letters, with an occasional time out to wipe away the tears that insisted on coming.

Shortly afterward Dr. Mack, during one of his visits, said:

"You're going home for Christmas holidays." Speechless at first, because of this totally unexpected act of trust and freedom, my "anxiety reflexes" finally prompted me to refuse.

"No," I answered firmly. "I don't want to go home. Not for a while yet."

"O.K. Tell me why you don't want to go home for Christmas." The answer was difficult, but I had to be honest.

"Because I'm not ready. I'm not ready to face family, relatives, and friends. It will be most embarrassing meeting them. I don't know how they are going to react. I think it will do more harm than good."

"So," observed Dr. Mack. "You are still afraid of people, of what they might think of you. You say that you want to return to your work as a priest. This means meeting people, you know. You'll have to do it sometime. Why not now? Don't you think your family and relatives love you enough to have you home? Don't you think your improved condition will be of some consolation to them, to your mother? We are showing trust in you. Why will you not show some trust in those who love you?

"Nevertheless," he continued, "the matter is settled. You are going home for a few days. Call up your brother and make arrangements."

Confused and fearful, but buoyed up by this show of trust and a chance to get out of the hospital for a few days, I made the necessary arrangements, although I slept uneasily for the two nights preceding my temporary liberation.

The one-hundred-mile ride home was filled with ambivalent feelings of shame and fear, of desire and joy. Once home, however, all negative feelings disappeared and joy grew with every hour. I was greeted warmly by mother in her wheelchair, with firm handshakes by brothers and relatives, with embraces and kisses from nephews and nieces. The whole atmosphere was a wonderful expression of human love and sympathy. Above all, there was the conviction that no one had deserted me, that no one blamed me for my condition, that all, without exception, wanted, loved, and rejoiced in my visitation. How much agony, I thought, they had gone through during the past several months, and yet how joyful they were to have me with them. All of this I could consider without a sense of guilt. Somehow, I had *absolved* myself, and together with the absolution there had come that good feeling that I had sought so desperately in the hospital.

But, here and now, the *good feeling* was given to me by the simple, human expressions of love and affection. I felt, oh, so very much at home, at home with real, live, loving people. Then, too, while the visit home may have been a trial run, devised by Dr. Mack and the hospital staff, nonetheless, it also showed that *they* trusted me. And trust is a form of love.

The good feeling remained with me all during the day, but there was a definite, nagging challenge that constantly occurred. A mile away was our retreat house and its members, my priestly family. How would they accept me? I did not know. But then, memory presented me with Dr. Mack's words, "You are still afraid of people, of what they might think of you. . . ." Suddenly, I decided to accept the challenge, to take the risk, regardless of results.

Here again, as at home, I was greeted warmly by the community members. They all seemed genuinely happy to see me and to know that I had come this far "out of the depths." Without shame or apology, I told them about the hospital, some of the things that went on there, a few of my personal experiences, my resolve to stay as long as necessary, and my gratitude for their letters. The general response was one of interest, concern and, above all, "Hurry back, Bill. We need you. But take your time and be sure of our prayers."

The challenge had been met! I had taken the "risk"—and I had won! The good feeling remained with me for the rest of the holidays and even when I returned to the hospital. I was anxious to tell Dr. Mack how I had made out, how I had overcome some inhibitions, at least.

Dr. Mack listened intently to the recitation of my Christmas experiences, nodding from time to time. After musing awhile, he observed:

"Inhibitions, you say. Usually, they stem from some fearsome or threatening circumstances in childhood. As a child, you learn how to 'live around' these fears, or you try to repress them, that is, to forget them. But, of course, once recorded in memory they are never forgotten completely and effectively. They lie hidden just below the conscious mind, the 'subconscious' as it is called. Given the right set of circumstances, however, they may burst forth in any one of a variety of ways, or they may take the form of depression, hostility, fear of the unknown, phobias, anxiety phases, and so forth. From your own words and the various feelings you have shown here in the hospital, it would seem that you have experienced several fearsome things early in life. Can you recall any happenings in your childhood that you feared, or resented, or wanted and was refused it? Are there any memories that hurt when you think about them?"

Hurtful memories? Oh, yes! There were a multitude of them as I looked back to my childhood. I began to relate some of them and then suddenly burst into tears, tears I could not control. I hung my head and covered my face. It was quite some time before the emotional spasm passed. The doctor remained silent. I wished he would go away and not be a witness to my weakness. Tears! At my age, and in front of a man. How I despised myself! So stupid, womanly, child-ish, unmanly!

"Why did you cry, Father?" the doctor asked in a mild tone.

"I don't know. Just feeling sorry for myself as a child, I guess."

"But these memories still hurt now, do they not? Enough to make you cry."

"No . . . yes, I guess so . . . but why should they? They happened so long ago."

"Try to tell me what feelings you had, the really deep, hurtful feelings that were revived when you were telling me of these childhood experiences."

Gone now was the good feeling that I had brought home from the Christmas holidays. I would much rather talk about those several triumphs, but the doctor, evidently, had spotted something more significant and wanted to pursue it.

"I don't know, really," I answered slowly. "They seemed to be feelings of loneliness, I think, of being unwanted, inade-quate, unjustly treated . . . feelings of wanting something very badly and being denied it."

"Yes," mused Dr. Mack. "And these feelings were prevalent over a period of several years, I suppose, and became fixated. They became your particularized attitudes toward life and toward yourself. They have, in great part, made up the self-image of which we have spoken before.

"That's quite a load of negative feelings to carry around with you for forty or forty-five years, isn't it? Is it any wonder that your emotional frustrations finally expressed themselves in the form of tears?

"Emotions," he continued, "are a good thing. God gave them to us for a very good reason. Tears, especially, tell us psychia-trists much about your past and present. They tell us that repressed memories are still operating within you, sometimes very powerfully. Depression, anxiety, even hostility are a form of crying, a crying out for help and understanding.

"You are emotional, Father, which is just the way you should be, because you are human. We doctors can understand and help people who are emotional, who try to find out why they are depressed, angry, fearful, or sorrowful to the point of tears. Some patients seal over their emotions, or deny them so successfully that we cannot reveal to them the origins and the realities of their conflicts that make them depressed, lonely, fearful, hostile.

"Keep thinking over your past and all of those hurtful episodes in your life. No matter how painful, they are going to help you more than you realize at this moment. And remember what I told you that would be necessary for an eventual cure: 'honesty and effort.' O.K.?"

For the next three days I did think, recalling my past as far back as I could. One fearsome memory, occasion, or attitude would inevitably resurrect others. I was amazed, in reliving them, at the emotions they aroused, and I began to compare them with other similar feelings and occasions. In many respects, I began to realize, my present feelings and attitudes were not so very much different than those of my distant past. It was amazing, sometimes frightening, at what I was uncovering and discovering.

There was so much to review and relive. So much to undo! So many positive and constructive attitudes to develop. It seemed as though I would have to go to school again, this time in order to learn the basics and the fundamentals of emotional development; to undergo a rehabilitation, a lengthy one, which alone could release me from the prison of my past.

"Well, Father," said Dr. Mack, "how did you make out on your homework?" I seemed to pass into a reverie. I was no longer a fifty-year-old adult. I was a child again.

"It must have been when I was two or three years old . . . sitting in my father's lap while he rocked back and forth in the old Boston rocker near the hot-air register. . . . I was so content, comfortable, warm, secure, and so very much loved. He would be singing in a soft, resonant baritone songs and words that I still remember . . . "Old Black Joe" . . . "And Her Golden Hair Was Hanging Down Her Back" . . . "Sweet Alice, Ben Bolt" . . . the last one was my favorite, for some reason or other. The words have always remained with me."

"And do you remember them now?" asked the doctor. "I have never heard that particular song."

"Oh, yes. I could even sing it for you." But I knew I could not. A lump had arisen in my throat and it was with difficulty that I recited the first stanza.

> O don't you remember sweet Alice, Ben Bolt?
> Sweet Alice, with hair so brown;
> Who laughed with delight at the stories you told,
> And trembled so much at your frown.

The memory was too much. The tears came. Dammit! Oh, damn those tears! Again, I had to hang my head in shame and embarrassment. Why should such an age-old recollection reduce me to shameful tears? I hated myself.

Gently, after the rain of emotion had passed, the doctor observed:

"So, the past is still very much with you, isn't it, Father? Try to tell me what feelings you had when sitting in your father's lap as he sang to you."

"Well, as I said, feelings of being loved, sheltered, secure, happiness in being held by my father . . . and lots of other things, I guess."

"But you cried after you recited 'Ben Bolt.' What words or feelings, do you think, brought on the tears especially after so many years of being an adult?"

"Two or three words, I think. 'Laughed' and 'delight,' and the contrast between those and 'trembled' and 'frown.'"

"And would you think it probable, Father, that you had many other similar experiences, similar feelings around that time and in the few years that followed?"

"Oh, yes. Many. I know that I was what you would call a 'displaced' child because a new baby brother came along when I was two years old. At sometime thereabouts, I suppose I must have felt that I was no longer the apple of my father's eye, that I was left out, no longer really loved and wanted. I don't know exactly when this change in feelings took place. I do know that when I had his love, I could hardly wait until he came home from work. I remember asking Mother everyday when Dad was coming home. Then I would wait in the yard until I saw him turn the bend in the road two hundred yards away. Then I'd run up the street to greet him and rejoice when he clasped me and lifted me up above his head. This was the big moment of my day.

"The next strong memory I have is that I feared him, for some reason or other. When I sensed it was time for him to come home, I would crawl under the front porch and wait there, safe in my hiding place, until I saw him approach. When he entered the yard, I could see only his long, blue-clad legs—he was a postman—passing by. I remained there, silent with longing as the smell of his pipe was wafted through the latticework. I guess I was saying to myself: 'I want you, Dad, but you don't seem to want me.' I have thought a lot about this but simply cannot account for this change of attitude on my part."

"Well, now, Father," said Dr. Mack. "You have recalled this hurtful situation pretty well. Were there any other incidents around this time or later that may have reinforced these feelings of fear and alienation?"

". . . yes." I had forgotten the supper hour and was sitting on a curbstone with the corner gang. Suddenly, Dad appeared and scolded me for not coming home on time. Then he took me by the ear and led me up the street. The ear hurt plenty, but I was more hurt by being shamed before the gang. There was more than shame, too. There was an extreme hostility toward my father.

"And then, there was the stone and glass incident. I was still too young to play baseball with the older kids, so I would just sit and watch. During one game I began throwing stones into a nearby swamp. I chanced upon a piece of glass and wondered which would go farther if I threw both stone and glass at the same time. The stone landed in the swamp, but the glass sailed in the opposite direction and hit one of the players just above the eye. Almost frozen with guilt and fright, I stood there looking at the blood-covered face of the boy. Everyone knew I had thrown the glass. I could only try to apologize in a childish way.

"By the time I got home, the news had preceded me. I entered the kitchen and there was Dad, combing his sparse hair before a large mirror. It sure was the wrong time to show up. Without a word, Dad grabbed me, threw me over his knees, and walloped me unmercifully with the hair brush. I know now, as I relive the scene, that there was a far deeper scream of protest and anger. I can remember it quite clearly. I was shouting to myself: 'This is unjust! It was an accident! Why punish me for an accident? You are wrong! You are unjust!'"

Memory was alive now. It was engaged in specifying similar and more recent events and feelings. It was like looking at a totem pole and being able to understand the continuity and meaning of its various symbols. But the symbols, although differing from each other, were all carved into the same pole.

"There have been a lot of other times, doctor," I continued, "when I have experienced identical feelings. There was the time in high school when one of the brothers approached my desk and without reason or warning knocked me clear out of my chair and into the aisle. I can remember standing up and screaming at him but I don't know what I said. He took me into his office and threatened to expel me. Although still angry and bewildered, I could do nothing but apologize for whatever I said, and then I broke into tears. I know I still have a 'hangup' on what I consider an injustice. It arouses rage, I know, just as it did when you threatened to have me committed. Somehow, I have not learned how to express this anger, how to let it out without hurting anyone or making the situation worse. So I keep it in and I guess it just smolders. I think, too, that I fear the results of my anger, of what I might do if I gave in to it, or what others might do in return. I just don't know how to figure this out."

Through all of this recital, Dr. Mack had listened silently and patiently. "Intently" is perhaps a better word, for I am sure that he was seeing me from a far more advantageous viewpoint than I saw myself. The picture-puzzle that was me was becoming clearer to him. I did not try to analyze my stories. That was his job. But I did see something significant emerging from my past. It was a hostility, an anger, the depth and extent of which I had never suspected. There were no tears on this occasion, for which I was grateful, because another emotion was dominating my reactions, a deep-rooted anger at injustice. It left no room for tears.

Finally, after several moments of silence, Dr. Mack observed: "That's about all we have time for today. Keep on recalling incidents such as these. You are really beginning to understand how very active your past still is in your present life. You are also beginning to sense the origins of your various feelings, attitudes, and needs. You wanted love and its variety of expressions, such as approval, affection, praise, acceptance, and so forth. Thinking that you were being denied all of this unjustly, you naturally began to devise ways and means of getting this, and of not getting hurt in the process. So, you worked out gradually a pattern of both offense and defense.

"Years of so acting and reacting have created habits and attitudes that are not going to be dissolved by the mere fact of your knowing and recognizing them. This will take time and effort, a 'backing off,' so to speak, in order to figure out why you have done or said certain things. The person you have been for so many years is still you, even though you have made some very valuable discoveries.

"As I have said before, do not be surprised when forms of your previous behavior show up again here in the hospital. Just remember *what*, *why*, and *how* things happened here, and then talk them over with me. Meanwhile, keep on recalling the fearsome events of the past, no matter how insignificant they seem. To me, they may be of extreme importance. Do some more homework. See you soon."

Recollection, I knew, would be a bruising ordeal at times, and would be accompanied by another kind of anguish, the shame of becoming tearful. Why couldn't I steel myself to recall the past without tears? "The gift of tears," someone has called this external manifestation of an interior grief. Perhaps, somehow, they were a gift, as Dr. Mack had implied. But I could not see them as a gift, and hated myself for not being able to control and absorb them in some other way. It would be quite some time before I could accept them naturally, evaluate them realistically, and search out the emotions that caused them.

Unit group discussions took place every week under the supervision of a psychiatrist. One of the patients, Fred, at this time, would preside and invite comments on anything pertaining to the ward, its personnel, regulations, and so forth. I always remained silent during these sessions since, I told myself, it was a useless function and never accomplished anything worthwhile. But the real reason, I knew, was a fear of standing up before the group and stating my strongly hostile feelings on many things.

On one evening, however, I was put on the spot. I was forced to talk. Dr. Silversmythe, a very pleasant fellow patient, had lodged a complaint, in his polite but firm manner, against the type of vulgar and filthy language which, while he didn't mind hearing it among men, he thought should be avoided when nurses were present. He thought that it was offensive to them and that they deserved more respect. Then Fred methodically asked each patient what feelings he might have on the subject. Some outspoken teen-agers, knowing that they were the offenders in this regard, defended their language as normal expressions of the day and age, and that it was the language that their parents and many adults used. This argument incensed me and I wanted to excoriate them for such a stupid attitude, lack of respect for women, and for their bad manners in general.

When Fred finally asked me directly what I thought on the matter, I was seized with fear and trembling. Forehead and hands were wet with perspiration as I stood up and, as calmly as possible under the circumstances, defended and agreed with Dr. Silversmythe's observation. All the while, I was conscious of a growing tension within me, a rage that I knew I could not contain if I expressed one small portion of it. Hurriedly, I concluded my remarks and sat down, wiping my forehead and trying to conceal any semblance of trembling. Later on in my room, I tried to figure out what emotions were involved in this episode, what deeper feelings had caused this nervousness, this nearly explosive outburst of anger. Anger. Yes. There certainly was much of that present. But there was something more than that present. I did not know what, except that it probably had something to do with the past as well as the subject on which I was asked to comment. Tomorrow I would see Dr. Mack and discuss the event.

As always, Dr. Mack listened intently to my story, nodding in recognition of my anger and fear, and then he lapsed into a few moments of thoughtfulness.

"Well, Father," he said, "exactly what was going on within you at that time, I cannot say positively. But there are many possibilities that you might want to consider. I will use examples that you have given me during these past few months.

"You have been and still are quite angry at many of the teen-agers among whom you have to live. You're angry at their noisiness, filthy language, their domination of the unit, their disrespect, and so forth. Your sense of justice, in other words, is outraged again, as it was so often during your childhood. They not only disturb you in these areas, but they do not measure up to your own idea of what a teen-ager should be. On the other hand, you have been praised by them; you know they respect you, and many admire you for the good example you have set for the unit. As a result, you have that so-called 'priestly image' to maintain before them.

"Now, as you know, 'ambivalence' is a state of having two opposing emotions fighting for expression or domination. So, during last night's discussion group and the question it posed, you probably found yourself with a deep anger wanting to be expressed in violent language; but you were also conscious of a strong desire to maintain your reputation as a 'nice guy,' a 'good patient,' a 'polite priest.' This second emotion, this need of approval from others, won out over the angry desire to explode at the teen-agers. It won out probably because you felt you would be utterly destroyed if others saw the *real* Bill Collins, the angry, condemning, hostile Father Collins.

"Meanwhile, quite a battle was going on throughout your whole nervous system. This would account for the sweating, trembling, fear, and panicky feelings you had before, during, and after the incident. Does all of this seem probable to you?"
As I nodded in thoughtful assent, he continued:

"You seem to be terribly afraid of your own anger, whether real or imaginary. Afraid that anger is going to lose for you the acceptance, the approval of others and the self-respect that you have longed for over the years. You sound as though you have a very deep-seated fear of the punishment or loss of love that a show of anger on your part might bring on. This is an unbearable thought for you; and so, sometimes at great effort, you have built up a wall of defenses to protect you from being hurt, as well as a system for seeking the approval you think you need. Does this possibility make any sense to you?"

Again I nodded acquiescence because, in those moments when I could back off and view myself more objectively, I could see, dimly at least, these very dynamics at work. In particular, the idea of "being afraid of your own anger" took on more important and larger dimensions. A lot of thinking would have to be done on this aspect of my personality.

"Here are some examples of how you built up a life pattern in order to protect yourself," Dr. Mack went on. "I will use your own words and feelings as you have described them to me. Perhaps you will be able to see the continuity of this life pattern, one that began early in childhood, that was reinforced in adolescence, and that you carried on into adult life.

"As a child you were very much afraid of your father and you could not communicate with him even though you desperately wanted his approval. You were afraid of failing in school before the class and of being scolded by the nuns. You were very much depressed when the eighth-grade nun, quoting your priest-confessor, told you that you were not fit for that particular school. You were intimidated by the brothers who taught you in high school, by their sometimes harsh treatment of other students. Your anger burst forth when, without any just reason, you were knocked out of your chair by a brother. Yes, you stood up and shouted out your rage against him, but in his office, and with the threat of expulsion facing you, you had recourse to tears and apologies.

"Through the example of a good priest, one who showed understanding and confidence in you, and with many other good motivations being present, you chose to enter the seminary. But even in this so-called holy place, you seemed to find yourself being rejected by several father figures who should have represented the 'fatherliness' of God, but they did not. You were, in some instances, disillusioned by them. Meanwhile, you were being given a highly idealistic impression of what a priest should be. You were afraid of being reprimanded, scolded in public, of failing, as you have termed it.

"Then, after the ordeal of a breakdown prior to ordination, you suffered that which to you, assumed tragic and frightening proportions. You were publicly shamed by the old monsignor during your first sermon. Again, you were betrayed by a father figure. You became impotent with embarrassment and suppressed rage.

"Let's add something else to the picture, to this life pattern of yours. Fearing failure so much and wanting approval even more, you began to establish, after ordination, a set of humanly impossible ideals of what you as a *person* and as a *priest* should be. You were straining for goals far beyond your reach, beyond the reach of any human being. Again, an ambivalence set in, reinforcing those other forms of ambivalence that we have discussed.

"Is it any wonder, then, that such severe and impossible demands as you made on yourself, together with the fear of failure, the hidden hostility, and the guilt-complex that built up over the years should eventually result in another breakdown and hospitalization?"

The brief, pointed logic of Dr. Mack's summary was undeniable. But, while my rational mind could accept it all as being probably true, my feelings were still confused, protesting, and defensive.

"Do you mean, then," I asked, "that on this particular occasion, this group meeting, that my whole nervous system was being affected by past experiences? That I was scared stiff lest my hostile self be seen by others and that this exposure would mean more guilt, more failure, more depression?"

"You think about it," he smiled. "You are the one who will have to be convinced one way or the other. I cannot make conclusions for you. I can only suggest possibilities and leave you the freedom to come to your own solid convictions."

I did much thinking during the next few days. Things began to cohere, to make more sense than when first heard and, more importantly, I had the feeling that I was beginning to find that *selfness* that the doctor had mentioned, that I was now dealing with *known* conflicts and attitudes. Hope was growing slowly, but definitely.

Meanwhile, during these more than two months in North II, my participation in and enjoyment of social and other group activities had vastly improved. I felt a belongingness, a genuine friendliness with patients, aides, nurses, and class teachers. Occupational therapy became more interesting, pleasurable, and challenging. In the ceramics group, there was Patricia, with her constant kindliness and soft, southern drawl; in the leather group, Diane seemed to lift the spirits of all with her constant good humor; in the weekly "sing-a-longs" there was Pat who, somehow or other, could get us all, despite our "down" days, to sing the old and new favorites with gusto. I would find myself bellowing away at the most popular pieces from *My Fair Lady* and *The Sound of Music*, thinking occasionally of the change in me and how good, how very good it felt to be able to sing at all.

In the social area, I found myself not at all alone or lonely. The supervisors there, Julie, Ilene, and Frances, were ideally suited for the task of helping us patients to have fun together by sharing in a variety of activities. We were made to feel at home; we were real persons to them and were always treated as normal human beings. It was here, perhaps more than elsewhere in the hospital, that I felt accepted, wanted, sometimes even needed when another patient would ask to talk to me about his feelings and problems. I did not attempt to solve the latter, since I knew that I knew so little about the variety of human conflicts, but I could and did listen with understanding and sympathy. This role alone always seemed to give my morale a boost. Perhaps it was because of a growing hopefulness, a hope now founded on a more solid and fertile ground.

As the days passed, and although still in a locked unit, I knew that some sort of welcome change was taking place in me. A new person was emerging; undefined as yet, but a person whom I liked much better than the one who had walked through the gates of the Institute of Living over five months before. I knew that I was still somewhere in the grammar school of emotional development, but I also knew that I was learning some valuable lessons—and applying them.

Yes, during some sessions with the doctor, tears would flow and shame would return along with the pain of the past. But now it was not so tragic, so horrible, so exaggerated. There had developed a greater amount of freedom of expression; a growing belief that, while my past might still be motivating my present, it was much less forceful and intimidating in many areas.

Prayer life had become quite simple but, I feel, much more productive. It was informal, yet more trustful, and it enabled me to be actively resigned to my life situation. A typical prayer might go something like this: "Here I am, Lord. Do with me whatever You will and I will do whatever I think You want me to do."

The time element, once my biggest concern, became less and less important. The "knowing" of myself became the challenging and interesting aspect of my sessions with the doctor and during the hours of leisurely reflection.

Late one evening—it must have been about mid-March—I was told to pack up, that I was being transferred to Butler II. I received the good news with an ever-increasing joy and anticipation. Butler II meant that I would be in a unit where patients were allowed grounds privileges; that I could freely walk around the campus and meet patients from Group Nine during certain hours of the day. It also meant that I had improved. *They,* the establishment, had seen fit to trust me! I packed quickly, thinking almost frantically that *they* might change their mind.

An aide assisted me in packing and then led me through several locked doors into Butler II. I hardly noticed the lounging patients, so eager was I to be free of North II and in the safety of my own room in this new unit. North I and North II, I reflected. Hell . . . purgatory . . . and then a sort of limbo. But those were behind me, now. Forever! Some two years later, after leaving the hospital, I learned that the wing containing these two units had been replaced with a bright, new sunlit building and a totally different manner of dealing with severe depressives.

The aide led me to a room at the end of the corridor. It had two windows, which looked out over the campus, which I could but dimly see in the late evening darkness. I was so excited that I could hardly sleep that night, so anxious was I to see God's beautiful nature once again.

# CHAPTER XIV

# BUTLER II
## Some More Answers

---

*"I do not know what I may appear to the world, but to myself I seem to have been only a boy playing on the sea-shore, whilst the great ocean of truth lay all undiscovered before me."*

—Sir Isaac Newton

ALTHOUGH more than delighted with this move up to Butler II, I had no idea of the extent of my joy until, upon waking with the dawn, I leaped from my bed and rushed to the window just in time to see the sun beginning to rise above the horizon of trees that surrounded the campus. I breathed in deeply of the chill morning air and felt, really felt, that freedom was flowing through my veins. Mist still partially shrouded some of the distant trees, but shafts of sunlight were bursting through the haze and dissipating it as though it were freeing the stately elms, maples, and evergreens from the dark night of anonymity and allowing them to show forth their new spring life and to display their beauty. The grass was dew-wet but alive with a tender green freshness, and squirrels darted about in search of breakfast. I simply stared and stared, almost fascinated by the scene. Then memory stirred and found words to describe my feelings, words from James Russell Lowell's *The Vision of Sir Launfal* which, as students in the seventh or eighth grade, we had to learn by heart. The lines were not in proper order, I knew, but I had to let them stream through my mind as exultant feelings and memory prompted.

> *What is so rare as a day in June?*
> *Then, if ever, come perfect days;*
> *Then Heaven tries earth if it be in tune,*
> *And over it, softly, her warm ear lays. . . .*
>
> *And whether we look or whether we listen,*
> *We hear life murmur or see it glisten. . . .*
>
> *'Tis Heaven alone that is given away,*
> *'Tis only God may be had for the asking;*
> *No price is set on the lavish summer,*
> *And June may be had by the poorest comer.*

The "poorest comer." That was me, for I had just come up "out of the depths." "Oh Lord!" I whispered to myself. "Let this be my morning prayer to You. May this vision of beauty be a promise of mental health . . . a promise of freedom . . . freedom from the dark anxieties of the past . . . belief that the worst is over and will never return . . . hope, strong hope for a happier future. Let hope flow in me . . . and out from me into others . . . let the past, no matter how painful, be of usefulness to me . . . to others . . . to You. But always, always let me experience and transfer the delightful music of life to other lives . . . and may this life's music always contain, no matter what the circumstances, themes of courage . . . hope . . . confidence . . . love . . . and all the other beautiful gifts and truths that a fallen humanity needs. . . ."

Never will I forget that morning, nor the many like it that were to follow. Even a rainy morn could not dampen my enthusiasm when looking out over the campus each day because, once again, I had recaptured in a far more meaningful way that happy Easter antiphon, the "Haec Dies": "This is the day that the Lord has made. Let us be glad and rejoice in it." I knew that no matter what kind of weather, there would be something, someone during the day to whom I could give a value, and would be receiving in the giving.

Butler II was a locked unit, since some of the patients were on probation and not allowed out on the grounds. Dr. Mack assured me that my pass card would be issued shortly, as it was, but I still resented the semi-imprisonment represented by an aide locking and unlocking doors whenever I wanted to get in or go out. I wanted full freedom and the trust that an open door would represent.

But the general feeling now was that I had added several more feet to the lifeline of hope and optimism, that I was in a much more determined and confident mood as I continued the struggle to climb up "out of the depths."

Much to my surprise and joy, I found that one of my fellow patients in Butler II was Father Tom, still full of dry wit and humorous stories. I was sorry that he had been demoted from Group Nine to Butler II, a Group Four unit, but even his demotion had a comical aspect to it. He had a town pass but had broken the rules by "having a few" on his way back to the hospital. Afraid that his dereliction would be detected, as it was, he had buried a pint somewhere on the property before reporting to his unit. As he told the story, it wasn't the demotion that had hurt his pride, but the fact that he, with his phenomenal memory, could not remember where he had buried the jug of joy.

Our walks around the grounds were a sort of search party, with Tom stopping every now and then at a likely hiding place, heeling a bit of dirt, shaking his head, and going on to another possible site. All the while he would be regaling me with extremely funny stories. Sometimes, I would have to sit on the grass and laugh myself out until the tears came. He would stare at me with his cherubic brown eyes and dead-pan face until I recovered enough to continue the walk, or rather the search. He loved raw vegetables and gnawed away at them just as did the friendly squirrels with the peanuts we often fed them.

One day, Tom came into my room chewing away at a succulent raw onion. I was glad of the ten feet that separated us as he sat in the guest chair.

"Notice anything different about me?" he asked. I looked him over and could see no change and told him so. He gnawed away at the onion, told a few more stories, and asked the same question again. This time I looked more closely and told him that the only difference I noticed was that horrible raw onion he was chewing on and which threatened to asphyxiate me. He seemed reassured about something, and then, after finishing the onion, he began to talk about his ability at total recall. To prove it, he quoted yards of Greek and Latin from the classics, plus several verses from Shakespeare and the English Romantic poets.

Finally, he stood up, stretched his arms above his head in a most satisfied way, and then pointed to his head.

"The memory," he said. "One of the best in the country. Total recall. It returned this morning and I went right out to the place where I buried you know what. Just finished it off and no one even suspects."

With peacock pride, he strolled out of my room. I, in turn, went over to my bed and laughed until my sides hurt. But the onion-laden room caused me to think a bit more about Tom. The onion was a coverup for a symptom, a weakness which, in turn, was a coverup for something far deeper. Just what it was I never did know, but, where I had come to accept and appreciate the hospital help, Tom's antagonism against psychiatrists and the Institute was so pronounced and bitter, even more so, than when I first met him. I felt real sympathy for him and wondered if and how I could help him.

Some few weeks after my arrival in Butler II, a young French priest, Father Pierre, was admitted as a patient, and it was a pleasure to have him. Outgoing, talkative, and gifted with a keen sense of humor, he became very popular with the dozen or so teen-agers in the unit. He knew their language, played their games, sang their songs, and regaled them with a variety of funny quips and stories. I wondered why he was there, since there appeared to be nothing at all wrong with him. One day, however, in a very somber mood and trembling with some sort of anxiety, he appeared in my room and asked to talk to me. Once seated, the tears came. Between fits of uncontrollable sobbing, I managed to gather some idea of his domestic burdens and parochial problems. My stock answers and attitudes which, I had come to realize, were the right ones, consisted of a patient, sympathetic listening and a gentle urging that all of this be told to his doctor. It helped somewhat, I suppose, but on another day shortly thereafter, he appeared in my doorway in a state of extreme excitement and agitation. So disturbed and confused was he, that I suggested we take a walk up and down the corridor, thinking that some of the muscular tension, at least, could be relieved. When near his room, I gently urged his trembling body through the door and forced him to sit on the bed, which creaked and vibrated from the spasmodic tremors of his quivering body.

"Now listen, Pete," I said gently (he preferred Pete to Pierre). "I don't know what is wrong with you but perhaps I can help you to get over the worst of this physical agitation. Take off your shirt and lie face down on the bed. You're going to get a good massage, and I'm going to be the masseur. Ever hear of that word? It's an old Gaelic word, you know," I kidded him.

"No. It's French," he muttered as he slipped off his sopping wet T-shirt and obediently lay down on the bed. I knew nothing about massaging, but I did know that any words of mine at this time would be useless. Gently but firmly, I started to knead the muscles around the neck and shoulders, down the spine and up again, working thumbs, fingers, and muscles into and around the vertebrae, rubbing and slapping the biceps and forearms, and returning to the neck cords. Gradually, the trembling ceased, the sweaty body relaxed, the eyes closed; for a moment I thought he had actually gone to sleep. He had not but, at least, he had regained control of the muscular spasms.

"Thanks, Bill," he murmured. "Think I'm O.K., now. I'll just stay here and rest awhile."

Back in my room, I sat down and reflected. Poor Pete . . . he needed so much more than I had given him . . . but I had given him something helpful . . . if only a touch . . . "The touch of a human hand" one poet spoke of concerning an old violin that regained its real worth and beauty when played by a master . . . myself and the touch of a hand . . . Arnold . . . Miss Amadon . . . Miss Trainor . . . the other forms of touching, reaching the human spirit . . . kindness, interest, sympathy, listening . . . sometimes the worst of human problems are solved or alleviated by the simple holding of hands, of touching . . . it meant a sharing and a caring . . . people . . . how much they needed other people . . . how much *I* needed other people . . . in responding to their needs, I fulfilled my own needs so very often.

On another day, Dr. Mack observed: "You are beginning to grasp the fact that there is a definite continuity in the pattern of your life, in your self-image, in your actions and reactions, and in your projections of these into the minds of others. I want you to do some more thinking on this, but I also want you to do something else, something positive, constructive, enjoyable. Now that you are out on the grounds, I would like you to look at nature, its beauty, its variety, its attractiveness. Don't merely look at a tree; try to see something more in it and beyond it. Do you know Joyce Kilmer's *Trees?*" I nodded because I knew it by heart.

"Well, then, when you look at a tree, recite those verses and see how you feel. Don't look only into the shadows of your past life, although this is important, but do both things at various times. Look in and look out. Do you know what I mean?"

Again I nodded, because I knew what he was pointing out; that a healthy self-image comes from within and from without; from within by understanding and dissolving one's interior conflicts and hangups, and from without as well, by appreciating deeply the health-giving beauty and truth that exists above and beyond the neurotic's narrowed and distorted vision of life; instead, "a vision of delight," which comes from trees, grass, flowers, animals and, especially, from people. Still before me, in other words, I had the task, an ongoing task, of unlearning a mass of negative, destructive self-attitudes, the "pattern of your life," as Dr. Mack would say, and a learning of a new, a healthier, and a happier pattern of thinking and acting.

It was like a rebirth, this learning and unlearning, as I attempted to put it into practice. With freedom of the grounds, I went out of my way to meet and talk to people, to listen to and encourage the depressed and anxious, to recite *Trees* while looking at the massive elms and maples with their small, new green leaves and bursting buds. There was something wonderful here, something beautifully and attractively mysterious. I was at peace with myself on these occasions because I could forget, for the time being, the still-unresolved problems that were mine. There was a time for these, to be sure, but there was also a time to love life, all kinds of life.

Father Tom and I had an "office" on the campus, which we shared with many other patients. It was only a bench under the maple trees and near the cement walk that circled the campus. We'd feed peanuts to the squirrels and soon were inundated by them as they sat and consumed vast quantities of the salty nuts while they sat on our knees, shoulders, and heads. Sometimes we'd have to retire temporarily with wet pants legs when the fat little gourmets automatically responded to the urge of nature. On the whole, however, it was so much fun gradually to win over a reluctant and suspicious squirrel by peanut-baiting. To them, food meant friendship, trust, security, freedom from fear. These unintelligent little animals needed such food—and so did I. They could be taught—and so could I. Yes, I was learning something, something very valuable.

At our "office," Father Tom would usually preside when people showed up. The spot became a sort of mecca for patients, because Tom was never without a funny story or a comically dramatized selection from the classics. He was a sort of "Lucy-in-reverse" psychiatrist, with his straight-faced humor and droll comments. He made patients forget their depressiveness and enabled them to laugh away many of their anxieties. Furthermore, he didn't even charge five cents for his services.

Pigeons, I think, were his favorites. He'd stretch out his hands loaded with popcorn and within seconds he'd be covered with the wing-flapping birds.

"Look!" he'd say to the gathering of patients. "A twentieth-century St. Francis!" At times, of course, he would have to abandon his role of St. Francis and rush off to the unit to change his shirt.

The pot-bellied squirrels, with their thick gray fur, I realized one day, were no longer a reminder of the bleakness of my life, such as I had experienced at White Hall. They were fun-loving little rascals, and with their trust and friendliness, they taught me many valuable lessons, aside from the enjoyable diversion of feeding them as they sat on my knee or poked their heads into my pockets in search of more food. I still look back at them with great fondness and can easily forgive them the several bites I suffered, although each time required an antitetanus shot and a scolding by the head nurse. I loved these little creatures of God who peopled His sheltering trees. In so many ways they were just like human beings in their need for care, trust, and security, as well as in their exaggerated and frightened reactions to what they thought were the dangers of life when, in reality, there was nothing to fear.

When the ground had hardened sufficiently, we were allowed to play tennis and softball. I was surprised at my tennis game, not having played for over twenty years, but the timing and skill had remained through this period; it had lain latent and needed only the observation of the tennis instructor to correct faults and to bring out the potential within me. Habit, I remember thinking at the time, had remained in my memory, muscles, nerves, and reflexes. The instructor had acted as a doctor by correcting certain errors. This gave me a helpful insight. In a negative way, hurtful memories had remained within me and had distorted both my self-image and my attitudes toward life. These harmful habits, by a process of relearning, would have to be corrected and replaced by emotionally healthier attitudes. This was my task: to go on working under the direction of Dr. Mack. It was another one of those hopeful thoughts that so often made a sudden and unexpected appearance.

Softball was an exciting challenge to me. Despite my age, I retained a good batting eye and often slammed doubles and triples. Speed afoot, while much slower than the youngster of thirty years before, was still evident in chasing down fly balls and in making sure-handed catches of line drives and difficult popups. This was fun, real fun. It was also a challenge—and I was responding with confidence in taking a risk on errors and strikeouts. It was all part of the game, and I did not feel like a failure when I really did fail after making a good effort.

All of this type of recreation was most encouraging in a subtle kind of way, as was my developing skills in occupational therapy and in "being myself" in personal relationships with other patients. All the while, I knew that there was much more work to be done, work within myself. This became evident and convincing in a series of sessions with Dr. Mack.

While alone one day at my fresh-air office, dispensing peanuts to my hungry congregation, I noticed a scrawny little brown squirrel who would attempt to approach the peanut-vending machine, which I had become, only to be chased away savagely by the bigger gray squirrels. I watched this happen several times—and then my eyes grew moist.

"What made you feel like this?" Dr. Mack wanted to know. The answer was easy because I knew it and felt it every time the little brown squirrel was chased away.

"I identified with the little fellow, I am sure. All my past feelings of being unwanted, unloved, unapproved, a failure, and so on, were revived, I suppose, when I saw that hungry little animal being so unjustly treated, rejected, chased away. You warned me not to be surprised when such feelings erupted again. So, I know that much about the situation, anyway."

The doctor nodded and thought awhile before observing:

"You have cried here on many occasions when recalling events of the past. This is good, as I have told you, because it reveals your real and deeper feelings, feelings and attitudes that you have carried over into your adult life. Are there any other events in your youth when you cried, or should have cried, and that you have not as yet mentioned?"

There was one that I had not mentioned because of the shame and guilt that arose at the thought of it. But—"honesty and effort" Dr. Mack had drilled into me. I would tell it, no matter what the shame.

"Well," I began timidly, "I cried on the day my father died.

I was thirteen or fourteen . . . for over a year Dad had been dying slowly of Hodgkin's Disease, coughing his life away. . . . We knew the end was near because the doctor and the priest were downstairs where Dad had been lying on a couch for several days. . . . I was upstairs reading a novel. . . . Suddenly, Mother cried out, and I knew Dad had died. . . . I cried, too, when I saw him lying there . . . someone had gone out of my life . . . but I knew my grief wasn't as deep, sincere is the word, I guess, as it should be. . . . Then, because I wanted to get away from something, I don't know what, I went back upstairs and resumed my reading. What an awful thing to do! Every time I recall the incident, I experience a horrible guilt."

In extreme self-hate now because of this shameful self-revelation, I could do nothing but stare at shoes of that person who had been so terribly selfish and ungrateful. I loathed him.

"Did you feel any guilt then at the way you acted?"

"Not at the time. I just felt a sort of . . . of nothing, I guess. But afterward, after the funeral, and every time I have thought about it during these many years, I have accused myself of being ungrateful, selfish, unfeeling, disloyal. All guilt feelings. Just as I feel now. I still feel shame and the guilt of hypocrisy at my pretended grief. Look! I'm not even at the point of tears now, and I believe I should be."

Dr. Mack remained silent. I felt he was condemning me, too. But memory was reviving other events and feelings associated with my Dad's death. Still not daring to look at the doctor, I began to speak of these occasions.

"It's an odd thing, doctor. I know I loved my Dad in my own childish way. You see, I admired him tremendously for the beautiful dahlias he grew and which had won many blue ribbons at town and city fairs. But I admired him especially for his athletic ability, about which he would never talk. I used to pour through the family album periodically and stare at him dressed up in those old-fashioned football and baseball uniforms. I loved to hear my uncles talk about his great ability on the ball field and in other sports. I knew I wanted to be like him.

"Then, after the funeral, Mother gave me Dad's wedding ring, saying that she knew he would want me to have it. I wore it for four years, never taking it off even while playing baseball, football, hockey, and everything. I had to give it to Mother when I entered the seminary after high school.

"Oh, yes! I did part with it on one occasion. I gave it to a girl friend and she gave me something, I don't know what, in return. You know how it is in high school. Puppy-love and tokens exchanged and that kind of stuff. But I gave her the ring with great reluctance. I remember feeling somewhat guilty about it. In fact, the next day I knew that I wanted the ring much more than the girl's affection, and so I asked her to return it for something else. She refused. I'm afraid I became very angry and, as I recall it, I think I said something to the effect that I'd take the ring back even if I had to break her finger. So she gave it back. She was really frightened, I guess. It was a long time before we had another date. I don't blame her. I don't know what made me demand the ring. Love and loyalty to Dad, I guess, and a guilt at betraying him.

"And then I can remember, especially when playing baseball in high school, looking at the ring or rubbing it whenever I got a base hit or made a good catch in the outfield.

"I don't know what to make of all this," I added. "But something was going on deep within me when I gave the ring away and then demanded its return. I can spot, I think, that the ring was symbolic of my love and admiration for my Dad. And then a sense of disloyalty followed by guilt, which I could be relieved of only when I took back the ring. There's much more involved, I am sure."

Dr. Mack sat silent for a while, staring at the ceiling, and then said:

"Interesting, all of it. The ring could have been symbolic of your deep desire for an external expression of father love. And giving away this external representation of your father's love for you quite possibly could have produced guilt and a sense of disloyalty. Again, that ambivalence of which we have spoken so often.

"Father figures. You've had quite a few substitutes for your own father for many years: men, women, the crowd, your work, fellow priests, superiors, and so forth. I mean all those from whom you expected or wanted expressions of approval, love, acceptance. This particular life pattern has been proved by your own words and actions in the several months you have been in this hospital.

"Let's consider, for example, your first breakdown prior to ordination. You were going to give yourself entirely to God-the-Father. Unhappily, you also had a superior, a father figure whom you once loved and admired, but you were rejected by him, smashed emotionally. You joined in the celebration of his birthday and then went to chapel, into the presence of God-the-Father. Suddenly, you experience this horrible feeling of being alienated, depressed, perhaps unwanted by this God, Who, by transference, has become another father figure.

"You might want to think this over," he continued, "namely, that your suppressed rage at your father figure superior, and the enormous guilt it must have produced, were transferred to God-the-Father, Whom you proposed to serve with love. Love vs. rage produced a terrible turmoil within you. Anxiety became prevalent and produced, in turn, a doubt as to whether God-the-Father wanted you. From your spiritual directors you received no lasting relief because they could not reach the roots of your conflicts. So you had to leave the seminary to think it over.

"Guilt feelings are easily transferable, especially when their real origins are unknown. In the confessional, you have had this experience in dealing with the scrupulous person. This person has the *feeling* of guilt, depression, and anxiety, and has to hang this guilt on something, or someone. But absolution does not resolve the basic guilt because its emotional origins are still present.

"You will want to do more thinking on all of this, I know. But, in recalling your particular life pattern as you know it now, try to see if, during your first breakdown, you were really saying to God-the-Father: 'I love You, God, but do You want me?' Just as you must have been saying this to your own father for so many years. Just as you have been saying the same thing to so many other people in your life. And always coming up with the doubt, the anxiety, the guilt, the depression of being worthless, a failure. Such an attitude could easily create a compulsive need to work, to do a better job, to please others no matter what the cost to yourself.

"You have not received shock treatment here because we have recognized your ability to reason, to think through things, and to come up with valuable insights. This is what I would like you to do now. In a leisurely way, try to think through some of these things you have mentioned and that I have commented on, and let me know what conclusions you arrive at, what may be probable, possible, certain, or doubtful."

That night my pillow was wet with tears. The scrawny little brown squirrel kept running in and out of my mind. There were many other thoughts, too. "I want you, God, but do You want me?" . . . "I want you, Dad, but do you want me?" . . . father figures . . . transference . . . guilt . . . compulsive work . . . the birthday party . . . my own father and God-the-Father. This latter thought predominated, eventually. The possible transference of feelings from one father to another father seemed to make sense when viewed in the context of my whole life pattern. Gradually, it became a probability, and then almost a certainty, a real explanation of what had taken place so many years ago. In a few days of thinking about it, the probable explanation became a conviction. I knew it to be true, and I knew it to be true because of the relief that accompanied its acceptance. The digging and uprooting had paid off. A hidden conflict had been exposed to the light of truth. It was like reading the last chapter of a mystery story.

"All right," said Dr. Mack after listening to my thoughts, solution, and relief about the matter. "But there is something more I want you to work on steadily, even after you leave this hospital. Whenever you recall anyone who has, in reality or not, hurt you in the past, I would like you to try to forgive them, to forgive them emotionally as well as intellectually. Unless you do, there is a good chance that your latent hostility will flare up again, along with anxiety, guilt, and depression. To be free of the fearsome past, you will have to forgive, a deep-down forgiveness. In the 'Our Father,' we say, '. . . as we forgive those who trespass against us. . . .' Well, now, for an emotional guilt, there is an emotional forgiveness necessary. Try it out during the next few days."

The point was well made. It meant more work, but I knew I could do it.

"Now, Father," said Dr. Mack in a later session, "can you recall any other incidents in your youth when you felt like crying over something, and didn't?"

"'Dahlia night,'" I said, with sudden, sad reminiscence.

"And what was 'dahlia night'?"

"Well, Dad grew about a half acre of dahlias in order to supplement his meager income as a letter carrier. He had a hot-house where he would splice different dahlia tubes together during the winter, plant them in the sand benches, and then grow them in the spring and summer. Dahlias are large, beautiful flowers with a wide variety of colorings. To each one of these dahlias, as they began to show distinctive and unique colors, he would put a name tag on the supporting pole. These were his creations, and he took great pride in them. As I said, he always had a display at the biggest fairs in the area and often won first prize. I was very proud of him on these occasions and when expert flower-growers would compliment him.

"'Dahlia night' came when the first frost was expected because it would quickly kill off the flowers. Then, Dad would call us out in the chill evening and begin cutting the dahlias and making attractive bouquets of them. Our job was to bring the flowers to various neighbors. I remember those evenings because Mother had clipped out a piece of poetry from the Boston *Globe* that described such dahlia-cutting nights. I memorized it then and have never forgotten it."

"Let me hear it," said Dr. Mack. A lump began to arise in my throat, but I fought it back and managed to recite the first verse in a trembling voice.

> *Apple-green west and an orange bar,*
> *And the lonesome gleam of the evening star;*
> *And: "Child, take the shears and cut what you will.*
> *Frost tonight, so cold and dead still."*

The lump was ready to burst. Those stupid tears were coming again. How I hated them. Dammit! Dammit! Damn! Anger at myself spilled over at the doctor and I found myself shouting at him: "I'm going to cry! And I don't give a blankety-blank damn what you think!"

Eventually the downpour stopped, but the anger remained. I wiped my eyes, looked challengingly at the doctor, and said, most forcefully: "So! I cried again. And any time I feel like crying, I'm going to do so. And to hell with what you think!"

He did say something. Something that totally surprised me. With his hands behind his head and a gentle smile on his face, he said:

"Well, now, Father Collins. Welcome back to the human race."

Surprised, speechless, and still dabbing at my wet eyes, nonetheless, the implications of his kindly observation were crystal clear. I was, and always had been, ashamed of this particular normal human expression of grief, and I had hated myself for having it, for letting it be seen by anyone. But, at the same time, in my declaration of independence to cry when I felt like it, I had uncovered another unhealthy inhibition (I wondered about its origins) and was freed from its clutches, convincingly. I felt greatly relieved at this insight. It was another step in the right direction, perhaps a giant step. I looked at Dr. Mack and smiled with him at this shared revelation.

"O.K., Father. Now, let's take this painful recollection. Why do you think that the memory of 'dahlia night' and the verse you recited made you cry now, some forty years later?"

"Lots of things, I guess. The words 'lonesome' and 'cold,' perhaps. But mostly, I think, it was because I felt so proud of my Dad when the neighbors would glow with delight. . . . Gosh! that's the same word in *Ben Bolt* that made me cry, isn't it? . . . And the neighbors were sure to remind me to thank my Dad for the flowers and for his kindness. I can remember trudging back for another bunch of flowers with an odd, disturbed feeling. I guess I felt like a messenger boy, not a real child of my father . . . that he was giving these people something beautiful . . . that he was withholding something beautiful from me.

"Then, too," I added in sudden recollection, "I was afraid to go out at night because of the Ku Klux Klan."

"You mean the Ku Klux Klan were active in your neighborhood?" asked the doctor with some surprise. "That's interesting. I would like to know more about your feelings at that time. We'll take it up at the next session."

Yes, I pondered, what were my real feelings during those years of the KKK? I was young, sensitive, and eight-to-ten years old at the time. What fear of people had started to germinate then? Here was something to think about; something to recall that would help me to understand another aspect of my personality development.

"You have thought about your feelings toward the Ku Klux Klan, I am sure, Father, but let's recapitulate a bit. We have uncovered many of the origins of your negative feelings, such as loneliness, hostility, guilt, rejection, and so forth. We have also seen some of your rather futile defenses against them. Now, present in all of these feelings there was fear, to a greater or lesser degree. Tell me what feelings of fear you had concerning the KKK?"

Having had the opportunity to review this area of my life, I told the doctor quite simply what I felt about the KKK from about the eighth to the eleventh years of my childhood.

Al Smith was being mentioned as a strong candidate for nomination by the Democratic party to run for the Presidency, the first Catholic who had ever been considered for that high office. The Klan was militantly opposed to blacks, Jews, and Catholics, and was very active politically and socially. Much of its hate literature was around. Some of it, apparently at night, had been left on our doorstep. I remember Mother and Dad talking about it, somberly and seriously. The pamphlets I had seen were full of accusations and threats. They really scared me.

Then, late one night—I must have been nine or ten years old—Mother awakened us three boys and led us to the back window of our bedroom, which looked out over a huge, several-thousand-acre park that we considered to be our backyard, since we hiked through it and camped out in it so often. The park was topped by the craggy slopes of Prospect Hill, the highest point around metropolitan Boston. And there, on the hill, less than a mile away, was blazing a huge, fiery cross. The Klan was showing its strength and, to me, its hatred. A hatred that would kill by fire or some other means, I felt, in my childish way.

Wide-eyed and horror-struck, I shivered in fear as I stood there by the window in my nightgown. Some people hated us, I remember thinking. Some people hated me, and were threatening me. Fire! They could burn down our house any night just as they were burning a cross to show their evil intent. Fear, a terrible fear of people, unknown people, seized me. Trembling in dread, I ran back to bed and pulled the blankets over my head. But I could not shut out the vision of the blazing cross, nor the thought that on some dark night, hatred in the form of a person would leap out at me from the shadows.

Yes, I concluded the story to the doctor, I did fear the feeling of fear, not just from this event, but probably from many other similar happenings in life. Dr. Mack had listened intently, then observed: "It's strange but very true that various forms of culture, the super-ego it is often called, have an extremely strong bearing on the development of one's personality. Here is something to think about during the next few days. Knowing what you do about your own life pattern, a pattern that everyone adopts toward themselves, toward others, and toward life, try to tell me as best you can, the various fearful aspects of culture to which you were subjected, such as those deriving from home, neighborhood, schooling, seminary, and the various social events and pressures that seem to have brought about so much fear and rigidity, so many inhibitions and defenses. Try to find the origins and continuity of this pattern. Don't work too hard at this. Just line up the events as best you can."

It was really amazing how long the list, incomplete, I am sure, of the many real and imaginary fearful and threatening events, persons, occasions, atmospheres, and so forth, that I recalled and noted during the next few days. In reviewing the list, I said to myself: So, these were some of the things that have gone into making my particular pattern of life, a pattern that eventually brought me into this hospital. At our next session I poured them out rather haphazardly.

There was home life, with which the doctor was well acquainted by now . . . fear of older fellows in the corner gang who used to bully and ridicule me at times . . . the greater fear of the KKK and the subsequent fear of nights . . . fear of being late for school because it meant a public scolding before the class . . . fear of failing in any course because the supervisor read the report cards publicly and we had to stand up and accept his chiding remarks . . . fear of the nuns, except two or three whom I loved and admired from a distance . . . no sympathetic understanding from teachers in grammar and high school . . . intimidation by the brothers who, I was sure, had to take boxing lessons as part of their training . . . but there was love and understanding from my stepfather, whom Mother married about a year after Dad's death . . . he was just great, and made every effort to keep us all happy. . . . I excelled at sports but was always afraid of the crowd, of failing before the crowd . . . fear of the old thunder-and-lightning pastor, but admiring the young curate who encouraged my thoughts about the priesthood . . . completely convinced of a vocation by visiting Dominican preachers who conducted a mission at our parish and who spoke so warmly about the love of God in contrast to the fire-and-brimstone preachers we usually had . . . fear and anger toward the brother who knocked me out of my chair . . . on the whole, however, happy high school years . . . eagerly looking forward to the seminary . . . but then the beginnings or revival of negative feelings . . . the strictness and regimentation . . . frequent threats of dismissal for the slightest infraction of rules . . . dominating and rejecting father figures, in contrast to impossible ideals of what a good seminarian and priest should be . . . running scared most of the time . . . hiding problems and our real selves lest we be dismissed . . . deprived of a chance to open up to an understanding priest, to communicate on a deeper level . . . all of this frustration and fear bursting through in the form of that first breakdown under a scornfully rejecting father figure superior . . . the agony of waiting for and wanting ordination . . . kindly help of spiritual directors didn't reach the roots of the real conflicts, which were emotional, not spiritual . . . after ordination trying to *prove* myself as a worthy member . . . seeing my Congregation as a demanding "they" . . . trying to be a worthy subject by overwork . . . the emotionally smashing blow delivered by the old monsignor . . . after that, always trying to *prove* myself by accepting every work asked of me . . . the grueling task of acquiring a master's degree while putting in full time as a prison chaplain . . . running a boys' camp during summer months when I should have been resting . . . taking on preaching assignments . . . retreats to nuns and giving them my time in long, exhausting hours of counseling . . . the increasing anxiety . . . nine years as Provincial councilor while keeping up various other works . . . finally, depression and need of psychiatric help . . . the tragic recourse to pills . . . the horrible failure at Halifax. . . .

"There is much more, I know, doctor, but this review has given me a pretty good idea, a convincing idea of what my life pattern was and how I came to be a mental patient."

The doctor nodded as I finished and then spent some time in thought before he spoke. "That's a pretty good capsulized presentation of your pattern of life and the causes of it. But, as I have said before, merely knowing it does not necessarily and immediately relieve you of the emotional habits of years. You have, and probably always will have, a lot of unlearning and relearning to do. And, by the way, have you given much thought to the forgiving of those many persons who have hurt you in the past?"

"Some," I answered. "But I know I have more work to do. For the most part, right now, I simply pray for them whenever I recall their names and the occasions of being hurt. However, I think I have made a great deal of progess with regard to my father. I realize that he was the victim of his own particular temperament, education, or lack of it, his own home environment, and so forth. Then, too, I have recalled all of his good points, his hard work to support me and the rest of the family in very difficult times, his love for dahlias, which must have meant that he had a deep appreciation of beauty, his working at this arduous task in order to make a few more dollars to give us the things that we could not have had otherwise, his honesty and the great respect his old friends had for him, his prolonged and agonizing suffering, his bravery in the face of death . . . and how much unspoken concern and love he must have had for us when he knew the end was near."

At this point, I hung my head and broke into unashamed tears. They were not for me, but for my father. In speaking as I did about him, a deeper realization of his essential goodness had suddenly overwhelmed me, and I knew that I was experiencing that emotional forgiveness of which Dr. Mack had spoken, as distinct from a merely intellectual forgiveness. Strangely enough, with the tears, I felt an interior liberation. Guilt and shame, I think, had been replaced with understanding, pity, and sympathy. I tried to explain this to the doctor, and I am sure he understood.

"Well now, Father, I think you are headed in the right direction. Let's see what the next few days will bring. Meanwhile, keep working on that emotional forgiveness. To be able to forgive others is an act of forgiving yourself, you know." With his usual encouraging smile, he was gone.

Something good, something really good, had taken place in this session. It was something greater and more promising than my own particular conclusions. Besides these most helpful insights, namely, the deeper conviction of a definite continuity in my life pattern, a better recognition of my real self, and the ability to forgive emotionally, there was something else. Hope! Yes, there was much more hope, now. And absolution, too. I was able to absolve others—and myself. But even with these considerations, I knew that another change had taken place. Just what it was, puzzled me. But I knew I felt very good.

Before I was able to see the doctor again, I received the great news that I was being moved up to Fuller II. Joy! This was a Group Nine unit and it meant more freedom of the grounds and, eventually, if all went well, a town pass. But best of all, it meant that I would be able to say Mass again, perhaps quite soon.

Again, I went through the hurried packing of sparse belongings and followed the aide through a couple of locked doors. Locked doors! How I had hated them at one time, and for a long time. Now, they were all behind me, and there I was in Fuller II.

I had made it! I had climbed up several more yards on the lifeline of hope.

"Nothing can stop me now," I said as I looked down the long corridor. The task of working through some of my remaining conflicts was still before me, but I knew I could do it. The time it might take meant little to me at this moment of triumph.

# CHAPTER XV

# FULLER II

## *Of People, Play, and Work*

---

> *"It is in consoling that we are consoled;*
> *It is in pardoning that we are pardoned;*
> *It is in giving that we receive;*
> *It is in understanding that we are understood;*
> *It is in loving that we are loved."*
> —Francis of Assisi

F ULLER II, an all-male unit, was almost a straight corridor with a bend to the right about halfway down; then it continued on to an open door. *An open door!* "Oh Lord," I breathed, "how wonderful!" For most of the day I would be free to come and go as I pleased. There was only the mere formality of signing the day book to indicate where I might be located. How much that *open door* meant to me! I know I must have stared at it for some moments in utter delight, wordless but so happy that I felt like laughing and crying at the same time.

To the left of the bend was a sort of rec room with comfortable chairs and card tables; to the right was the nurses' office, where I reported my presence and was assigned an empty room. I didn't bother unpacking. That could wait. I wanted to see the rest of the corridor and to secure a grounds pass so that I could use that *open* door as soon as possible.

Past the nurses' office, there were more patients' doors—and without peepholes! Halfway down this part of the hallway and to my left, I was pleasantly surprised to see a large recreation room, complete with sofas, stuffed chairs, TV set, and a beautiful view of the campus. To the right of this was a large, airy dining room, more patients' rooms—and the open door! I stepped across the threshold and breathed in deeply of the freedom, the trust, and the many other happy emotions that were stirring within me. It was a luxury beyond expression.

But first I must introduce myself to fellow patients, most of whom I had hardly noticed in my haste to experience the pleasure of walking through that lovely, freedom-giving open door.

It was easy to meet the other patients. Now I was "Bill" Collins, although all knew me as a priest and many would continue to address me as "Father." I didn't mind. They were given a choice and were left free to accept me as they saw fit. It was my *personality*, such as it was, that I presented to them and not the *role* of priest that had been added to it. All the other professional mental patients, especially the doctors, preferred to be called by their first names. It made it much easier for me to be treated as the *person* I really was. And I'm sure it put the other patients more at ease in my presence.

After about two weeks in Fuller II, Dr. Mack surprised me one day by asking if I would like to say Mass again. I almost jumped out of the chair with joy. It meant that I was ready to undertake another phase of whatever recovery program he and the staff had planned for me. I had not asked previously because I had come to trust Dr. Mack's evaluation of me and was willing to await his direction in this matter.

Two days later I said Mass at St. Augustine's for the first time in almost eight months. There was no strain or tension during the Mass, which I said on a side altar. Rather, there was a sense of solid contentment, a very comfortable feeling of belonging, of doing freely and easily that which I wanted to do joyfully. Needless to say, it was a Mass of thanksgiving. I was home again.

On returning to the hospital after Mass, I listened to the sound of my footsteps on the cement sidewalk and recalled the grim, despairful days at White Hall when, with leaden feet, I wondered and doubted whether this pavement would ever re-echo the light-hearted stride of a content and comfortable Father Collins. But now, the seemingly impossible miracle had taken place. On that warm, sunny day in May there was, thank God, a joyful buoyancy in my walking and a solid contentment in my heart. Somehow, I knew I had come closer to Christ; I was more identified with Him than ever before. I had been in the Garden of Olives with Him and had experienced something of His terrible fear and anxiety. I had heard His cry of despair on the cross and had uttered it many times during the first several weeks of hospitalization. Now, as I relished the clear, blue skies and the keen, fresh air, I felt that a resurrection was taking place; a rebirth of mind and soul.

Alone in my room after this most meaningful encounter with Christ at Mass, I did some more reflecting on the newly emerging person who was "Bill" and/or "Father" Collins. After some twenty-two years of praying for relief from chronic fears, anxieties, and phobias, an answer had been given to me; not in the way I had wanted it or sought after it, but rather, in *His* way, by hospitalization and intensive therapy; by a "putting off of the old man," as St. Paul phrased it, and by a putting on of the "new man," a new and realistic personality, a different and welcome perspective of myself and toward my true vocation in life. Twenty-two years to get an answer, I thought, and then smiled to myself as I recalled that St. Monica had to pray for only twenty years for the conversion of her son, St. Augustine. I had surpassed her record! A somewhat foolish thought, perhaps, but very human, and one that had a humorous overtone to it. I was happy that I could smile at myself—and laugh at the past.

Other thoughts poured in haphazardly, but with helpful clues and unsuspected insights. The story of Job occurred to me for some reason or other . . . he, too, had been terribly afflicted . . . but he was a fighter . . . a fighter with an amazing faith in God . . . he had angrily banished those so-called wise men who had tried to explain God's purpose in allowing his sorry plight . . . angry, too, at God, but, with courage born of faith, to argue with Him . . . with the same faith he concluded that God's reasons were far above human understanding or explanation . . . that God, in His own mysterious ways, was still a God of

love . . . that no human misunderstandings could change that
fact. . . . I, too, had been angry with God on a subconscious
level . . . anger produces guilt . . . anxiety . . . depression
. . . self-hatred . . . and many other things. It was, on the
whole, an interesting conjecture, and I knew I would have to
do some more honest thinking on the matter.

Meanwhile, with my newfound peace of mind after saying
Mass again, I could consider the happy fact that I was closer,
much closer to Christ in His humanness. Seminary training,
retreats, meditations, and readings had always stressed the
*divinity* of Christ. His humanity, His oneness with every member
of the human race, had been neglected or mitigated. I, through
pain allowed by Christ, had become far more closely identified
with Him. St. Paul had much to say about this, so I began to read
his letters on pain and suffering. To Timothy (Tim. 2:8–10) he
said:

> *Now remember: all who want to live a life of piety*
> *will have to suffer persecution.*

Many other passages in the same vein were contained in Paul's
letters. In flicking the pages, I chanced upon another Pauline
observation that gave me cause to stop and think. In Co-
rinthians 1:17–20 I read and reread with deep reflection Paul's
insightful viewpoint on human strength and human weakness.

> *For a foolish thing of God is wiser than man;*
> *And a weak thing of God is more powerful than men.*

How often had I called myself "weak," "stupid," "failure,"
"dumb," and a variety of similar negative, demeaning names. No
matter how "weak" I had thought myself to be, no matter how
much of a "failure" I was or would be, God, in His own mysterious ways, could and would use me, not as a "thing" but as the
unique and dignified *person* whom He had purposefully created,
and to whom, mysteriously again, He had given the added
dignity of Holy Orders, a gift supreme that allowed me to approach the altar of sacrifice with some of His own power, love,
and authority.

The "altar of sacrifice," I mused. There is a multiplicity of sacrificial altars in churches throughout the world. But there is not only that particular kind of altar whereon Holy Mass is said. Very often and perhaps more effectively, at times, the "altar of sacrifice" is the heart, the mind, the emotions of the person who must first "die unto himself" before he can begin to live his real self, before he can become fully alive to live with and for Christ, with and for others. In therapy, one gradually learns how to "die to the old self," the distorted attitudes, the unhealthy inhibitions, the internal conflicts, and so on, before he can discover the "new self," the real and healthy self, the generous and productive self.

The process of becoming mentally healthy, I concluded, was very much the same as the process of becoming a fully alive follower of Christ. My theology and therapy were beginning to form a warm friendship.

May, June, and July were wonderful months in many ways. Sessions with Dr. Mack were productive as well as instructive, and they helped, by way of repetition, to reinforce the healthy attitudes and constructive insights which, months before, I had only begun to discover. New areas were investigated, discussed, and worked upon by both of us. Occasionally, Dr. Mack would have to remind me in his gentle, understanding way, that old habits of thinking and reacting were in evidence again. He would then have me try to link them up with the past and to spot the present circumstance that had brought about their reappearance. Such incidents called for some intensive research when I had the time to be alone, but this kind of homework was interesting because I would put myself in the role of a detective, searching out clues that eventually unmasked the hidden culprits, my "criminal" emotions. This type of research was also encouraging because I was learning more and more about myself and because, whatever the hidden conflict, usually I could work through it on my own. There were times, however, when I would need the doctor's help in solving a complex emotional problem correctly.

Sports, too, enabled me to loosen up, to become involved in competition, to relax and have fun, to make mistakes without unduly blaming myself, although in this latter area, I had much to learn. This learning came the hard way.

Since baseball (softball at the hospital) had always been my favorite sport, I played it daily in games between the various units. My batting eye was still sharp and my speed afoot rather amazed me. Driving long balls beyond the outfielders and zipping line drives through the infield gave me quite a thrill. But, then, how could anyone miss hitting a ball the size of a grapefuit?

In many games between other units, I was often asked to umpire, a job that I gladly accepted because I prided myself with what I thought was an exact knowledge of the strike zone. All went well until the manager of the Institute softball team asked me to umpire their games with the fast, semiprofessional teams in the greater Hartford area. I begged off, saying that I didn't really know all the rules of the game and that I'd have to have my doctor's O.K.

The manager, Jerry, a young physical education teacher at the Institute and with whom I had become very friendly during volleyball games, said he would approach Dr. Mack. He handed me a rule book to study, meanwhile. The worst, of course, happened.

"Some more homework for you, Father," said Dr. Mack at our next session. "I want you to take on this job as umpire for the Institute team."

"But, no, Doctor," I pleaded. "Please! I don't know all the rules and these teams are professionals. I'd be pulling boners every inning. I'm just not qualified."

My protests were in vain. I had the rule book, said Dr. Mack. Study it. The Institute team thought highly of me as an umpire and had been unanimous in asking for me.

"What are you really afraid of, Father?" asked the doctor.

"I guess . . . well, I guess I'm afraid of making mistakes in public." The doctor nodded and smiled.

"The past is still very much in the present, wouldn't you say, Father?"

He was right, of course, but at the moment I was mad as hell at him for saying that which I had already spotted. I was angry, too, at those who had brought about this seemingly disastrous and threatening situation. But there was nothing I could do about it except study the rule book, which I did, day and night. There were so many rules, rules I had never heard of in baseball. Softball had its own set of regulations, and so many of them, worded confusingly and with an almost endless list of perplexing qualifications.

About three times a week I would umpire. It was sheer torture, for the most part. No one ever seemed satisfied with a close call. Pitcher, batter, catcher, opposing benches and the fans, all seemed convinced that I had only one eye and that it was located in the back of my head. Many a time, an irate batter would stick his face close to mine and shout his unprintable opinion of my cockeyed decisions. Pitchers and catchers would keep up a running comment on my blindness. The only security I had was the mask I wore. "Keep it on all the time, Bill," I said to myself. "If they start swinging, it'll hurt them more than you." Never did I have more sympathy for those fellows in the blue coats who had to umpire major league baseball games.

After each game, I would slink away from the crowd as quickly as possible, convinced that I had missed many balls and strikes, that I had done a lousy job. Damn the doctor! Damn the manager! Damn the players! Damn me!

After about a month of this agony, saying nothing about it to the doctor, he brought it up one day.

"How goes the umpiring?" he inquired.

"Lousy," I answered, "and I wish you'd relieve me of the job."

"I could do that easily enough," he said. "But don't you think you would feel worse if you backed off and hid yourself safely up in the stands? You are learning something very valuable out there on the field behind the catcher. Sure, you are making mistakes and getting clobbered by many people. But remember this: No one can please everyone else all the time. You've been trying to do just that all your life, and your nervous system has paid for it. That's one of the reasons you had to be hospitalized. You are learning gradually, however, whether you like it or not, that trying to please everyone in life is terribly unrealistic.

It simply cannot be done. Even the saints couldn't please everyone.

"You are also learning that in certain life situations you can do nothing more than your best, despite what others may think or say. You are also learning that you cannot live a healthy and comfortable life if you have to depend on the opinions of others all the time. It is true that we do need some approval from the outside, from others, at various times in our endeavors, but fundamentally we need a basic certainty about ourselves, which comes from within.

"For you, in view of your past conditioning, this interior value will come with time and experience; the experience, for instance, of standing on your own two feet before a crowd and doing what you honestly believe is the right thing to do, and shrugging off the human mistakes that we all make. This is that reality of life to which you want to return. We are preparing you for that.

"So," he concluded, "stay in there and help yourself to grow, in spite of the crowd. Frankly, I wonder how many of the ballplayers themselves could do as good a job as you are doing. At any rate, you are going to stay in there. Just keep your eye on the strike zone," he chuckled softly as he ended the session.

His over-all comments were right, I knew, but at the time they didn't help very much. Yes, on a far broader scale than I realized, the past was still very active in my present. But knowledge alone was not enough. I wondered if even the experience of working through this distressing situation as an umpire was worth it. But, I resolved, I'm not going to be a quitter, even if someone does sock me with a baseball bat.

Subsequent umpiring experiences left me no better off. After each game I quit the field as soon as I could. I felt like the "Charlie Brown" of softball at the Institute of Living.

Other things, however, seemed to be going very well, so well, in fact, that I asked the doctor if I could get a job in the city, as did so many patients who were slowly, and by experience, working themselves back into the once-familiar workaday world from which they had come and to which they hoped to return.

I felt a sort of impatience with the hospital; it was too confining and too protective. I had outgrown its usefulness, to a certain extent, at least, although I was aware of the need for more therapy and for certain "home" aspects of the hospital.

To my surprise and pleasure, Dr. Mack agreed to my request, and within a week I had secured a Social Security card and a job at a department store warehouse. No one knew that I was either a mental patient or a priest, except for the head of the personnel department, a Mrs. Rundy. She was a most kindly and understanding person who seemed to make an apostolate out of helping others. One year after my release from the Institute of Living, I made it a point to visit her and to thank her for all that she had done for me and to assure her that it was not a wasted effort.

My particular job consisted of hauling, lifting, and opening huge cartons containing women's pocketbooks and gloves. These I would have to stamp with a price tag and repack them for various branch stores in the Hartford area. I never realized how many different pocketbooks women needed, or thought they needed for different occasions. Clutch purses, evening purses, beaded purses, cocktail purses, shopping purses, "grandmother" purses, shoulder purses, all changing with the seasons. I was overwhelmed with the variety, shapes, and styles. "Good Lord," I remember saying to myself, "why didn't they just put pockets in their dresses and be done with all this expense and nonsense?"

It was hard work but I liked it, just as I had always liked physical labor as a relief from teaching, study, deskwork, and preaching. Besides enjoying the work, I learned a great deal more than I expected. Some fifteen men and women worked in the warehouse. To them I was just plain "Bill Collins," but I was seeing them in a different light. From their conversation, I would learn much about their domestic difficulties, sicknesses, financial problems, emotional conflicts, and a variety of other human situations that I had never really understood in my priestly service to people.

Often, I do not know why, they would seek me out for a talk or for advice. Perhaps they just wanted, quite humanly, to have someone to listen to them, to share their burden, to get the relief of opening up. More and more I began to realize how little we sheltered priests knew about the harsher realities of life, of the troubles, pains, doubts, and conflicts of the ordinary workaday person. How badly we missed the point in many of our sermons, how misunderstood by us were the laity, how we failed to reach them in spite of our best efforts. We simply were not with them enough, not intimately acquainted with their real, deeper, human problems.

"Worker-priests?" Yes, there was a definite need for them, a need for them to learn from the very people whom they served. If only for a short time, there was a need for priests to see and experience at first hand the nitty-gritty of life as it really is for the vast majority of people.

Packing a lunchbox each morning, hurrying to catch a bus, punching a timeclock, working hard for four straight hours, the casual relaxation at lunchtime with these fellow workers who treated me as the person I really was, another four hours of hard work, trudging home after work amid traffic and people, and a myriad of other things that make up a working day, did something good for me. It was hard for me to explain then and it still is now, but it was something that made me feel that I was a real, living part of the people in the streets, in their working moods, in their various difficulties, in their joys and in their burdens. I felt, I think, that I had touched life, or at least a part of life that I would never have come to know and understand, were it not for my hospitalization and the circumstances that had necessitated extensive therapy. I was both learning and unlearning by this kind of work. I was growing up realistically and in a constructive, positive way.

Since work made day sessions with the doctor impossible, he arranged to see me at night. As always, he listened intently to my feelings about work, the people I met, the things I did, the experiences that impressed me. It was during one of these evening meetings that the thought occurred to me that the doctor might have had, or did have, some misgivings about leaving me on my own for so long a period each day, five days a week.

Because he had never told me his real reason for allowing me to take such a job, I said kiddingly:

"Dr. Mack. I'm away all day and earning money. How do you know that I won't find a pretty blonde and take off with her?"

He nodded as though he had anticipated such a question, eventually.

"I'm not Almighty God and so I do not know what you will do tomorrow or a week from now. But I do know a great deal about you; much more than you will ever suspect. I know that right now you are very deeply committed to your priesthood, that you really love it more than anything else. It is my judgment that you would never be happy, really happy, in any other kind of life. You could prove me wrong, of course, but I rather think that the odds are in my favor."

A wave of mixed emotions submerged and confused me for a few moments. I would have to sort them out later on; but suddenly I became certain of one thing. Someone, this doctor who knew me inside out, really trusted me and believed in me, and in my love for the priesthood. Better still, I trusted and believed in myself and in my commitment. But what a wonderful feeling to have his support, his willingness to allow me to take a risk on myself, and to realize that the risk had paid such rich dividends in emotional growth, in self-security, in spiritual security. This glow of happiness lasted for many days.

Meanwhile, back at the ball field! After returning from work and getting a quick bite to eat, I was expected to umpire the evening softball game. I did so with the usual feelings of having done a poor job. At the end of the season, however, there was a big game coming up, one for which the Institute of Living team was practicing every night and that had all the patients in a state of excitement. The visiting team, the Heublein Club, had made the headlines on the sports pages about a week before by beating the nationally known team called "The King and His Court." The "king" was a fabulous pitcher who threw fast balls, hooks, and sliders from a variety of positions and who was so effective in striking out batters that he played with only four men in his "court," a catcher, a first baseman, a shortstop, and one outfielder. In any one season, while traveling throughout the country, they would win about 250 games and lose only a handful. And I was to umpire a game involving one of those few teams to have beaten the "king" that season!

There would be a huge crowd on hand. I was more than intimidated. I was scared. On the night before the game and during work the next day, I read and reread the rule book. I could hardly concentrate on either the rule book or my work. Purposely, I walked home from the warehouse that afternoon, delaying as much as possible in the hope that they would start the game without me and get someone else to umpire. It worked! After eating, I was told that the game had already started. What a relief! And I had a good excuse at hand if needed. From a safe distance on the far side of the campus, I watched the first inning of play. Then I decided it was safe enough to go down to the stands in order to get a better look at this really good ball team, the city champions.

It was one of the worst mistakes I had made in the hospital. One of the Institute of Living players caught sight of me and shouted for a time out. The other players beckoned me on; the patient-umpire who had been forced into duty also spotted me. He dashed over and frantically handed me the mask and counter.

"For God's sake, Bill, take over this job. I can't last another minute!" Sweat poured down his face, and his hands trembled. I was caught! Damn it all! I should have stayed out of sight! Reluctantly, I took the mask and put it on. Actually, I wanted to run away as fast as I could, but the word "quitter" stared me in the face. I could feel it smirking at me. "Challenge" and "risk" were other words that kept stabbing at me. Worst of all was the terrible squirming in the pit of my stomach. I took my place behind the catcher and shouted faintly from behind the mask: "Play ball!"

All went fairly well for the first two innings. The Heublein Club had one run by way of a homer before I took over the job of umpiring. The pitchers on both teams were bullet fast, with well-controlled hooks and sliders. My calls on balls and strikes were greeted with only the ordinary grunts and grumbles. In the third inning, an Institute of Living batter slashed a long drive for a homer. Tie score. After that, tension built up among the hundreds of fans on both sides. Now, each strike, ball, or hit was greeted with a roar of approval or disapproval. The tension with which I started the game grew worse with every bit of action on the field.

In the fifth inning "it" happened. With one out and baserunners on first and second, their catcher came to bat. A hit could mean a go-ahead run perhaps two. The visiting team and crowd set up a rhythmic chant for a hit. The catcher, volatile and openly critical at some of my calls in previous innings, set himself to smash the ball into the distant tennis courts. He swung savagely at the first pitch, a sinker, and just managed to top it. It hit the ground in front of home plate and then began to dribble slowly toward the foul line. He had dropped his bat in front of the plate as he streaked toward first. The ball, meanwhile, had squibbled back and had hit the bat in fair territory. Our catcher had no play at first, and the other runners had advanced. The other Institute players, however, set up a hollering protest and began to crowd around me, as did the players from the other team. I knew there was a rule covering just such a situation, but I could not recall it even if my life depended on it. I could only hear the yammering ballplayers and the background shouting of the crowd. Confused and badgered, I could only stand there amid the uproar, wishing that I were sick in bed with pneumonia or something. I had enough sense, however, to keep my mask on.

Suddenly, amid the clamor, the ruling came to me. "A batter is out if his bat hits the ball a second time in fair territory." The rule book was in my back pocket but there was no time to look up the exact wording. Holding up my hands for silence, I shouted: "The batter is out! The play is dead! Runners will return to their bases!"

Pandemonium, now. The catcher, standing on first base with the certainty that he was safe, dashed down the base line toward me, shouting and screaming. I braced myself, glad that I had kept on the face mask. Beside himself with rage, he pushed his face against the mask and furiously uttered some very unkind words about me, my ancestors, my eyesight, my sanity, my stupidity, and many other faults that should have disqualified me from even watching a ball game on TV, let alone trying to umpire one.

Finally, his manager and teammates pulled him away and assured him that the ruling was correct, that they had seen the ball hit the bat a second time in fair territory. The manager then approached me and said:

"You were right, Ump. That's what the rule book says." Then he motioned the catcher to the bench and the runners to return to their original bases. Safe, for the time being at least, I removed the mask and wiped my dripping face with a handkerchief, but the tension and trepidation remained. It was not much reduced when the next batter grounded out to end the inning. From then until the end of the game, I received considerable flak, unprintable of course, from the still-irate catcher. Finally, because of the deepening twilight, I had to call the game, which remained deadlocked.

Completely exhausted, and with the ache of embarrassment in the calves of my legs and in the pit of my stomach, I melted into the crowd and returned to my room. There, I looked up the ruling and found I was right in every respect. It was some sort of consolation, but not much. The old familiar feeling of having failed, somehow, kept nagging at me as I relived the home-plate furor time and again. But, thank God, the season was over. No more umpiring! What a relief!

About a week later, while sitting in my outdoor office one evening, feeding the squirrels, Jerry, the team manager, hurried over to see me. "You're a hard man to find, Father," he said. "Here's a little something from the ball team by way of showing our thanks for the very good job of umpiring you did for us this season."

More than a little surprised, I unwrapped the large package he handed me. It was a recently published book on the history of baseball, complete with stories, pictures, and records of all the great players and teams from the turn of the century. Confused, but gratified at the gift, which must have cost about fifteen dollars, I flicked through the pages and tried to thank Jerry and the team.

"Look at the front page, Father," said Jerry. I did so and found an inscription that read: "With thanks for a good job well done." Below it were the signatures of all the Institute of Living players. I read each of them slowly and then tried to express my gratitude again. I couldn't say much because of the lump in my throat. Clutching the book, I excused myself and hurried away to the safety of my room, lest Jerry and the other patients see the tears that I knew would come in abundance in a very short time. I was confused, proud, happy, and a lot of other things, at the moment; but I had to be alone in order to let out the mixed emotions. The tears relieved me greatly. They were, I know, primarily joyful tears.

The next evening, I showed the book and signatures to Dr. Mack. He flicked through the pages, noting that it was an expensive book and that I would enjoy reading it. Then he asked how I felt about the gift and the expression of appreciation it represented.

"Well," I said, "I guess it has given me a different view of myself. Although the book represents that 'approval from others,' as you would say, it has, at the same time, given me an inner approval. I guess I was selling myself short all during the ball season. I know I wasn't the best of umpires, but those 'in the know,' the players themselves, thought I had done a pretty good job. I both overrated myself in wanting to do a perfect job, which is positively impossible for any umpire," I smiled, "but I guess I did a much better job than I thought, even when underrating myself."

Dr. Mack nodded, and then observed: "You have learned much more than that, you know. It is true that you regressed to previous self-attitudes during your umpiring duties throughout the season. However, you did take a risk on yourself, even though I sort of forced you into a difficult position. But you did stay in there. You stood up to the crowd, the critical, angry crowd, and did what you thought had to be done. This is life. Real life. In many future circumstances, this experience will be an invaluable help in making decisions in spite of the crowd. It will help you to be yourself, that real self of which we have spoken many times. You will be better able to take a risk on yourself and to accept without guilt the human failings that often take place in spite of our best efforts. In taking those risks on your real self, you are offering yourself a chance to grow in emotional maturity. Your umpiring experiences and this book should help you to become more of a realist and less of a perfectionist.

"Let's see how it works out during the rest of the time you spend here. Once again, though, I warn you not to be surprised if and when you realize that you have regressed to your old attitudes. When it happens, try to stand off and view yourself objectively. See if you can analyze just what has taken place."

It was good advice, and I knew that it needed repetition. It represented that working through process that is so very necessary for the emotionally disturbed person.

On several occasions, I did regress in certain areas, but I also had sufficient analytic knowledge of myself to figure out the reasons. For example, in seeing the movie, *The Sound of Music*, I found myself crying in sympathy for the several children of a militaristic father when he would summon them by a whistle, line them up for inspection, and issue orders in a stentorian voice. Childhood memories had revived, and I reacted as I did because these helpless children were scared, regimented, treated as mechanical things, not as loved persons. Almost at the same time, I recalled again the little brown squirrel that was continually chased away by the big, gray bully squirrels.

In relating this to the doctor, and the analysis of my reactions, I added that often I felt the same way during some sessions with him. I said that I wanted the warmth of his personality, but had the suspicion that I was only a thing to him at times, a thing under a microscope to be examined, analyzed, categorized, and pigeonholed.

"Good," said Dr. Mack. "This would seem to indicate that you still have a strong fear of being rejected by others, and you project your own thoughts into the minds of others. It's a good point to think about. Let me know when you feel this way again. You might also want to recall what we have said before, namely, that where there is fear there is also a certain amount, perhaps a great amount, of latent, unrecognized hostility and aggression. Merely knowing this is not enough. You will have to continue to work through these feelings until you come up with a satisfactory, a comfortable self-attitude and other-attitude. I think you have a lot of work to do in this respect. Just keep me informed."

He was right, of course, but still I had to learn through experience. A rather classic example of my still latent and exaggerated desire for approval, plus a hidden hostility, occurred at Christmastime. I wanted to give a gift to the doctor, which is par for the course when a patient has established a fairly good rapport with his therapist. In recalling the incident now, I can laugh at myself because it well could have been one of those typical "wishy-washy Charlie Brown" situations.

It took me some time to decide on whether or not to buy a present for the doctor, and more time on what to buy him. I finally decided to get him two pairs of knee-length stockings because his bare shanks were often exposed and I felt sorry that he wasn't better protected from the cold winter winds. Having bought and carefully wrapped the gift in my room, I was afflicted suddenly with the thought that he might resent my trying to "buy him off" or "win his favor." He might even reject the gift. Then, how would I feel? Half-resolved to go through with the gift-giving, I started toward his office and then suddenly turned and rushed back to my room. What if he should see me? What would he think or say? Was there too much risk of being rejected? Then, I thought, instead of facing him with the gift, I would wait until I was sure his office would be empty, and leave the gaily wrapped gift at his door.

Again I started off with the gift, and this time I got as far as the empty waiting room outside the various doctors' offices. Fear seized me again, and I had to sit in one of the chairs, carefully hiding the gift beneath it. What if some doctor saw me putting the gift at Dr. Mack's door? What would he think? What would he say to Dr. Mack?

Cautiously, I arose and peered down the silent corridor with its several doors. Empty. I sped down the hall and quickly laid the gift at No. 17, Dr. Mack's office. I was only a few steps away when I heard a door open. Some doctor had seen me! Without daring to look back, I hurried breathlessly out of the building and returned to my room. The deed was done, but I felt undone. Now I would have to face Dr. Mack and listen to his observations, for better or worse. Fortunately, my next appointment was three days after Christmas. By that time, he might simmer down under the influence of a Christmas "good will." He might even forget about the gift.

He did not. And, as usual, my fear and anxiety were groundless. Upon entering his office, the first thing I saw was my unwrapped gift on his desk. Dr. Mack smiled at me and nodded at the gift.

"Very thoughtful of you, Father, and many thanks. Knee-length stockings, too. I guess we doctors sometimes do not practice what we preach about good health. I sure will appreciate the stockings when these winter winds start blowing snow up my legs. Thanks again."

More than relieved, I nodded at his thanks, but inside I felt lit up like a Charlie Brown Christmas tree. Again I had taken a risk, despite the many comical but very real misgivings, and it had paid off. Sometimes, I reflected, risks would not pay off. Nonetheless, it was my job to accept challenges, to take risks, and to shrug off mistakes.

Since I was not working after Christmas, having expected to be discharged shortly thereafter, I was more than a little bit nettled when Dr. Mack, in answer to my direct question on the matter, suggested that there were a few more things in my emotional life that he would want me to investigate. For instance, he said, he would like to know how I would react to parish work and to preaching; also, there was the matter of my particular phobic fear to explore. Would I consider going to one of my Congregation's parishes for weekend work? I was more than delighted and made arrangements to assist at one of our parishes about sixty miles away. It meant a bus trip each Friday afternoon, various church work on Saturday and Sunday, and a bus trip back to the hospital on a Monday.

The experience was good for me. Very good. For over a year I had not lived in a religious community and had been absent from any type of preaching or parochial work. It would be a challenge—and a risk. It would also be a change of scenery, atmosphere, and of people, people among whom I could put to work, perhaps, some of the lessons learned at the hospital.

Preaching was, at first, difficult. Although my talks were well prepared, there was a certain amount of tension involved when I ascended the pulpit. It was good to know this and to discuss it with Dr. Mack upon my return. I would tell him what I thought was producing this tension: being "on the spot" again before a "demanding" crowd; trying to do a better-than-good job, which was another regression to the past; seeing the congregation as "critical observers" rather than as eager, or perhaps indifferent, listeners; straining to get some sort of approval, external approval, rather than being content with doing the best I could and leaving it at that. Old habits returning, I would tell him, but now I felt that I knew what I was dealing with and was certain that this knowledge and experience would gradually dissipate these former negative attitudes.

It did, and in the five subsequent months of this kind of experience, I had reacquired that "at ease" feeling in the pulpit and with people, even though they were strangers. I did not strain at my sermons. I tried to bring a simple, warm, human-interest tone and hope to them in my talks. In this regard, I am sure that my warehouse experiences played a great part. Even though vested as a priest, I knew that I was being simply "Bill Collins." Humor, a kindly but point-making humor, was also included. It was not only a relief to me emotionally, but, I am sure, the congregation welcomed with warmth this change from the too-often ecclesiastical grimness or authoritarian pronouncements that so many clergymen bring to the pulpit.

Meanwhile, back at the hospital and sessions with Dr. Mack. The regression, of which he had warned me on numerous occasions, occurred in a variety of ways, most of which I could work through on my own. But there was one occasion of severe, suppressed hostility that must be told. It happened, as I recall, about the middle of March. A slight depression had set in and I could not locate its cause for about two weeks. Slowly but surely, I finally came to the realization that I was angry at

Dr. Mack! Why? I pondered the question for some time before being able to spot the reasons.

For one thing, he was rather unusually silent during our interviews. He'd let me do the talking and, when I ran out of thoughts, he'd sit there saying nothing. This galled me, just as my father's silence had irritated and angered me in childhood, and the unresponsiveness of other people throughout life. But far worse than this, I felt, was his failure, during this period, to give any positive direction, any approval of my efforts. There are two sides to every coin, I reasoned angrily. I'm doing all the work, the hard work of self-revelation, of self-analysis, sometimes of self-condemnation. But he'd just sit there, sometimes with his eyes closed as though he didn't give a darn as to what I said or did. Surely, I argued, there must be something worthwhile in me, something that he could commend me for, some helpful directions he could give, some sort of congratulation for my difficult efforts. But there was not even the remotest semblance of any approval. Dammit! I exploded to myself.

For some two weeks I simmered and steamed about the matter, and the depression became deeper and more alarming. I had to talk to someone about the matter because I didn't dare shout out my angry accusations to the doctor. There was too much to lose in such an outburst.

Fortunately, there was another priest-patient to whom I could go. He was older than I, much more perceptive, and had made rapid strides in therapy. He had become a sort of father figure to many of us patients, dispensing sound advice and good common sense. His unfailing good humor had made him a popular figure on the campus and in the social area. It was here that I sought him out and stated my angry feelings without qualifications. After hearing me out, he said:

"Go tell it all to your doctor, Bill. After all, you're paying your way through this place and you have every right in the world to express your feelings. Now, go in there and tell him off."

It took me two days to screw up the courage to act on his advice, but I did so, finally. Once seated before Dr. Mack, I knew I was going to say a lot of things. With barely restrained calmness, I told him bluntly that I had lost my trust in him, that once again I felt like a bug under his microscope, like a bunch of junk because of my own self-revelations and his silence, his lack of concern, his failure to give any positive direction, his refusal to respond and to approve of my efforts. My tongue churned out a glossolalia of similar accusations.

Dr. Mack adopted his usual pose of silent nodding as I recited my long litany of complaints, accusations, and bitterness. Once finished, I sat back, ready for his defensive comments, or his silence. If it was the latter, I had determined to get up and walk out—in silence. To hell with him!

"Tell me, Father," he said with unexpected mildness. "How long have you felt this way?"

"About two or three weeks, I guess. Maybe longer."

"Now, during all this time, you probably were saying something to yourself about me. What was it?"

Half lifting myself from the chair in sudden rage, I shouted: "I was saying that you were a bastard!"

With that unexpected explosion of extreme rage, I slumped back into the chair and covered my face with my hands. "You stupid fool! . . . now you've torn it . . . he'll send you back to North I . . . constant observation . . . he'll keep you there for a couple of months . . . you'll have to work your way back up again . . . all that hard work gone to hell . . ."

Not daring to look at him, I sat limply in the chair for several minutes. Finally, unable to stand the damnable silence, I braced myself to meet the worst, and so I raised my eyes to read my sentence. A sentencing to the hell of North I.

To my complete amazement, I saw him, hands behind his head, a big grin on his face, and his body shaking with suppressed mirth. He wasn't angry at all! He saw something very funny in the whole situation—and, gradually, so did I. Slowly, I began to relax, and with the relaxation I began to chuckle. Suddenly, he broke out into a guffaw of laughter and, before I knew it, I was indulging in a good, old, belly laugh, one of relief and delight at the doctor's reaction, I suppose, but mostly because I saw quite clearly how comically ridiculous I had become in my angry accusations and hostile demands. How childish, and yet how humanly peculiar to me was this regression. Regression! Now, I was learning how subtle and crafty its ways and means of expression. Then, too, I had "let out" my anger and had found that there was nothing, really, to be angry about; that I could have reasoned out the whole matter beforehand and either resolved it or simply discussed it with the doctor and thereby could have liquidated the depressive emotion in a harmless and helpful manner.

"Well now, Father," said Dr. Mack, still smiling. "I think you have a much better realization of what regression is and how dynamically present a latent hostility can be. Also, I am sure, you have learned through this experience today how a very minor thing can reawaken all that emotional rage that you have suppressed or repressed in your past life. Your hostility, I think you realize, was not directed at me, alone, but at all those other persons in the dim past who hurt and rejected you, who were unjust to you, or who withheld the kind and the amount of approval you thought you deserved and needed.

"You can get along without the kind of approval you were demanding of me. If I gave it in the way you thought you needed it, I would be doing you a grave injustice because I would hinder your healthy, realistic emotional growth. I'd become an emotional crutch to you, and you would go through the rest of your life looking for the same kind of crutch. You'd never grow up, in other words. You'd always be looking for someone else to play that role.

"I'm sure that now you feel very much relieved that you allowed the anger in you to explode as it did. And, by the way, I've been called worse things than you've said. If only these walls could talk, your ears would be singed." He smiled, in recollection, and then continued:

"Anger, as we have said before, is not a bad thing at all. It becomes a problem only when you have not learned how to cope with it, how to 'let it out' in a harmless or healthy way. Anger comes with human nature and it is just as natural to humanity as is the desire for food, for happiness, for love, and so forth. The worst thing you can do is to let anger simmer and smolder and build up.

"What has been one of your biggest problems is the way you handled, or mishandled, your angry emotions. In hiding them continually, as you did all your life, naturally you began to feel the guilt, the anxiety, and the depression that are bound to appear in various ways when you do not admit and recognize anger, and then allow the resultant tension to escape in some sort of noninjurious way.

"Also, in this regard, I gave you some homework to do several months ago. I wonder if you have been working at it. I refer to the forgiving of all those whom you think have injured you in life. Certainly, during these past two or three weeks, when you thought I was hurting you, you were not doing your homework, were you?"

He smiled, in forgiveness of me; I could only blush with the recognition of my own unforgiving attitude.

"Again, as we have said so often before, it has to be more than an intellectual forgiveness; it has to come from a changed emotional attitude toward people; it has to be a sort of sympathy for them, a sympathy for their ignorance, their human frailty, their misunderstanding—as well as your own. If you do not forgive with your emotions, then some residue of anger is going to remain. And then comes guilt and the vicious circle of various negative emotions it produces. Do some more thinking on all of this. It needs repetition.

"For most of us, even those who make a profession of studying the human emotional scale, recognizing and controlling anger in a healthy way is a lifetime job. And I suspect that you know now that it will be a lifelong job for you." He smiled, a deep, understanding smile, as I rose and left.

It was more than just a good session. It was a reminder of so much that I thought I knew by heart, and which I had, very humanly, forgotten to apply. Secretly, however, I gloated somewhat over the fact that I had made him talk so long and so pointedly. This, aside from the necessary "reminders," was what I really had wanted from him—a dialogue, a communication, a "talk out."

As for the "forgiving" aspect of my therapeutic homework, I knew I had done much work. It seemed that more such work was indicated. I resolved to go on a daily schedule of recalling events and persons who had, in any way, hurt me in the past. I would absolve each and every one as they came to mind. I would also absolve myself for the anger I had entertained toward them. And, yes, there was the "absolving" of God. The thought sounded absurd, but I had to admit, as I did when thinking on the story of Job, that I had been unconsciously angry at Him, and unconsciously guilty about it.

The "Three Absolutions," I dubbed this resolution. How really necessary such absolutions were. And how "freedom-giving" was the power and desire to absolve.

At the end of May, Dr. Mack informed me that the hospital staff had decided to release me early in June. Strangely enough, it came as a shock because I didn't really want to leave the Institute. It had been my home for almost two years. I would miss the many friends I had made among the patients and the personnel. But I knew I had to leave. The hospital and its therapeutic treatment had served its purpose. It had healed me to the extent that I was now ready to return to life with the most important conflicts recognized and resolved, to return to the people who needed me and whom I wanted to serve, and to the Congregation that had stood by me and supported me.

The Institute of Living. Once I had termed it the "Institute of Dying" in my anger and fear of it. I grimaced rather shamefully at the recollection. True, it was not a perfect hospital, especially with its emotionally unhealthy North I and II units. But these were soon to be replaced with up-to-date, healthy, and hope-giving new buildings. Then, too, I reflected, what human institution is perfect? Even the Church, a divine institution given over to human direction, was far from what it wanted to be. Of the Institute of Living, with its staff and personnel and its forward-looking leadership, I could well say of them: "We try harder." I know now, even as I knew when preparing to leave the hospital, that my sojourn there was, next to Holy Orders, the greatest blessing of my life.

Dr. Mack's final few sessions with me were most constructive and hopeful, but tinged with sorrow because I knew how much I would miss him and the hospital.

"You will learn much more about yourself and people outside the hospital than you have learned in here," he said. "We have given you some fundamental lessons in healthy living and have helped you to understand yourself better. You know pretty well your emotional patterns and how to deal with them. But you need that kind of confidence in yourself that only can come by doing things on your own, by taking yourself in hand and by knowing what is going on in any given emotion. You can deepen and broaden this self-confidence only by actual experience away from the security of the hospital. The same thing applies to the mistakes you make and your reactions to them.

"You have limitations. You will have to learn them, and learn to live within them, and to be satisfied with whatever results your efforts produce. Sometimes you will have to be satisfied with no results at all, except for the courage to have made an effort.

"You will agree, I am sure, that you are a pretty lucky guy to have had this type of education. Think of the countless thousands of desperate people who will never be able to receive what has been given to you.

"But," he added, "you can, because of your own experiences here, give so much more to people than you could two years ago. If you have prayed, and I know you have, then look upon the time spent here and the help you have received as the good Lord's answer to your prayers of many years in search of help. You, in turn, will often be the answer to someone else's prayers."

In early June, I left the Institute of Living. I shook hands with Dr. Mack and was not ashamed at my silent tears, which said more to him than any words. With many "best wishes" ringing in my ears from a large group of patients, and with a long, last look around the grounds and familiar buildings, I was taxied through the gateway by my good friend of my Halifax days, Father John.

A new life awaited me. I wondered about it.

# CHAPTER XVI

# AFTERMATH
## Freedom to Be

---

*"Those who sow in tears*
*shall reap rejoicing."*
—Psalm 125

T HIS book is being completed some five years after my "gradu-
ation" from the Institute of Living. I am glad to have had these
years of experience and reflection before attempting to tell my
story because, with the passage of time, I have acquired, through
contact with many people and by a working through of several
emotional situations, an objectivity and a perceptiveness that
would have been lacking had I embarked on this project immediately upon release from the hospital. Then, too, Dr. Mack's
final observation had proven to be true: "You will learn much
more about yourself and people outside the hospital than you
have learned in here."

It is true, however, that I started to jot down notes shortly
after leaving the Institute of Living. This was done almost solely
because of the urging and encouragement of my father confessor, Father Thomas Heath, O.P., whose book *In Face of
Anguish* drew me toward him as a priest who would understand
my condition and background. Author, professor, lecturer, poet,
and friend, he, more than any other, in his compassionate concern for suffering humanity, has been responsible for the appearance of this autobiography.

An earlier publication was prevented by a variety of unexpected events. Assigned immediately after hospitalization to a busy parish in northern Virginia, I had little time to think and write. Then came a spinal fusion, which left me with a partially paralyzed leg and which necessitated crutches and a cane for several months. After that, two heart attacks severely limited any writing for over a year. Strangely enough, all of this physical pain and the frustrating ordeal of not being able to work or write did no bother me in the least. I could always say to myself: "Well, Bill, nothing could be as bad as North I and constant observation!"

In the various challenges of parish work, to which I have now returned on a full-time basis; in counseling people wherein I could so often see myself and help others better to see and understand the deeply hidden dynamics that were the real cause of their depressions and guilts; in the various courses that I continue to take in pastoral counseling; in reading and meditating on the many excellent publications in the fields of psychology and psychiatry, I know that I have grown immensely toward that emotional maturity that is so necessary for the living of a happy and comfortable life as a person and as a priest.

Mistakes and failures I have made, and I know I will continue to make them throughout life. But they do not bother me and never depress me. I have come to that stage of reality wherein I accept my failure-prone life and activities as normal to human nature, the "human state of affairs," so to speak. Whenever a so-called "defeat" occurs, I accept it without "defeatism." But I do *learn* from such events. I learn to accept myself, and others, as I am, as they are. When success comes, I accept it peacefully, while rejoicing that my endeavors have produced some good results, either for myself or for others.

People, especially in the counseling relationship, have taught me much about myself, even though they thought that I was doing the teaching or directing. Some simply needed a kindly, interested listener and were helped, somehow or other, by a patient, sympathetic hearing. Perhaps they came to a solution on their own by the mere fact of having a chance to speak out their problems without fear of rejection or accusation. Others needed help desperately. In many such cases, after establishing a trusting relationship, I could begin to offer considerable assistance to the suffering person by calling upon my own therapeutic experiences, counseling courses, and book knowledge. After acquiring a fairly good grasp of the client's history and self-attitudes, I would, by using their own words and experiences, lead them to an investigation of the various probable causes of their anxiety, depression, or despair. It was this method that Dr. Mack used on me.

Here again, while helping someone else, I was being helped because, I felt, I was being trusted enough by another person to be invited into the sacred precincts of their inner self, into the areas of guilt, secret sins, shames, embarrassments, hostilities, and confusion. There is something rewarding beyond words in being so trusted and so invited.

Other cases were beyond my limited understanding of the human psyche. These, of course, I would refer to competent professional assistance.

The priest-counselor—and he need not be trained extensively as a therapist—finds himself in a unique position with regard to guilt-ridden people. As a priest he represents Christ, and so he can relieve and absolve moral guilt. As a counselor, one who has a fairly good understanding of interior human conflicts, he can, within the limits of his training and knowledge, absolve and liquidate emotional guilt. In the past five years I have had several such cases and as priest-counselor have had singular success.

As proof of the fact that sound psychotherapy can and does work for the person who works at it, I have found, by learning and by unlearning, by taking risks on my real selfness, that my phobic fears have disappeared and have been replaced by a new and healthy self-image. I am at ease with myself and with others in a way that I never thought possible several years ago.

My previous perfectionism, which usually had its basis in an unconscious hostility, has almost entirely evaporated, although it does reappear occasionally. It is easy to spot, however, and

I enjoy thoroughly this spotting of my old self, knowing that I am in control of the situation, that it does not control me. I can grin at the failures of my human nature and even invite others to laugh with me at predicaments which, in times past, I would have tried desperately to hide. I am, in other words, enjoying myself, my limited self; I am enjoying life as it is, even while engaged in the sometimes arduous task of showing others how to live a healthy and rewarding life.

Besides the pastoral counseling courses and extensive readings on the subject of human emotions, I have engaged in several other ways and means of continuing and expanding upon my hospital experiences. I have followed the advice of the Institute which, upon leaving, suggested and arranged for me to see a local psychiatrist for follow-up therapy as a preventive measure in the event that I might feel the need of professional assistance in the various problems that would arise in real-life situations outside the hospital. For the most part, I have been able to spot negative emotions on my own and to track them down and, in the process, to eliminate fear and anxiety. On two or three occasions during these follow-up interviews, I have needed professional help in understanding and in dissolving certain perplexing problems.

Also, as an educational and supportive measure, I have joined Recovery, Inc. This is a nationwide organization with over seven hundred chapters, located chiefly in major cities. A chapter is made up of a small group, numbering from about twelve to twenty-five people who have been or are under psychiatric care. Observers, those who sense that they may have emotional problems, are also welcome. The meetings are well supervised by trained, unpaid leaders who have undergone therapy themselves and who are well versed in the proceedings and principles as laid down in Dr. Abraham Low's book *Mental Health Through Will Training*. I never cease being amazed at the emotional help that these weekly meetings afford individuals by way of group support and constructive spotting. Recovery, Inc. has been given high praise by the

National Institute of Mental Health. It is my opinion that everyone, disturbed or not, could benefit immeasurably by joining or observing the healthy and helpful dynamics, and the friendships that emerge from these "self-help" and "group-support" meetings. Therapists themselves should investigate the movement in order to be acquainted with the encouragement and enlightenment it might well offer to their individual clients.

Therapy, while giving me a feeling of freedom from the enslaving anxieties of the unconscious mind, enabled me also to form an effective philosophy toward the more threatening aspects of life. It became more or less crystallized in the hospital after reading some of Paul Tillich's and Father Eugene Kennedy's observations concerning mental health and religion. In substance, it would appear something like this: "Life is a challenge, a challenge to be faced. In the very act of determining to face such challenges, there is also the presence of an act of freedom. Freedom, especially for the emotionally disturbed, consists in being able to be that which one really is, while allowing room for further growth. Freedom 'to be' is not that which one would *like* to be, nor is it that which one might like others to think him to be. It is, more realistically, a freedom to choose, in spite of adversity. In effect, one is saying to himself: 'this is *my* life. I am free to refuse its built-in challenges and to run away from fears. But I am also free to face these challenges, win or lose. Nonetheless, in facing up to them, I always win no matter what the outcome because I can hold up my head and endorse myself for having had the courage to try.'"

Then, too, therapy has resolved whatever "identity crisis" I might have had and about which so much is written today. Certainly, this was a terrible, anxiety-producing element when I first entered the hospital and it remained with me for the two months and more that I spent in White Hall and in the North I and II units. But sometime after the Room 19 incident, I know that gradually I grew from this confused state into a new, wholesome, and realistic identity. Now I can write with absolute conviction of being most comfortable and content ("happy" would not be too strong a word) with the person *who* I am and with the knowledge of *what* I am, of my *purpose* and work in life and in the priesthood.

Of my past, present, and future I can say that I embrace it all. I love it all, failures included.

Such a positive attitude toward self and life, in fact a very realistic and happy posture toward my own existence and all that it entails, has resulted, I am sure, from a successful therapeutic treatment and, subsequently, from a continual "risk taking" on the emerging "real self."

For me, a rather extended therapy was not only a necessity but, as I have said before, it was a distinct blessing, the greatest blessing in life, after ordination. It resolved my emotional identity crisis and prepared me for a more realistic and willing recommitment to the demands and obligations of my spiritual life and of my vows.

In this respect, and from my own personal viewpoint as I look out at a changing world, a changing society, a changing church, I have a wonderment concerning those among the married, the clergy, and the religious who once made a willing and sincere commitment by which they dutifully lived for many years and who have now left that commitment with the frequently heard and apparently justifiable reasonings against "structures," "restrictions," "incompatibility," "establishments," "systems," "authoritarianism," and so forth, when perhaps the real, underlying, and unrecognized causes were unresolved emotional conflicts. I wonder if they could have been helped, before uncommitting themselves, by an intensive spiritual and emotional therapy. As I reflect on this, I cannot help but recall again what a married woman said to me in the hospital.

"You poor priests. If only you were allowed to marry you wouldn't be in a place like this."

"My good woman," I answered, not too kindly, I am afraid, "marriage didn't keep you out of this place."

How many, I keep on wondering, could have been helped if they had the good fortune—painful at times, to be sure—that was afforded me.

All the above is, as I say, only a wonderment. Valid answers eventually will come from sociologists, psychiatrists, and other professionals in the areas of human emotions after studying a sufficient number of case histories. Certainly I am no authority on the matter but, from the meager evidence I have assembled in talking to and in counseling those who have made solemn commitments, quite often there do appear definite signs of hidden and unresolved inner conflicts, exacerbated and perhaps precipitated by an unstable society and by a restless church.

Emotionally and spiritually, my love for and acceptance of life as it is has vastly improved. As a person, I am a far, far cry from the confused and anxiety-ridden individual of ten and five years ago. Therapy, in helping to resolve my inner conflicts, has led to a considerable growth in faith—faith in my selfness, faith in humanity, faith in the mystery that is God. This is not "triumphalism." It is, rather, a Christian-human realism. From this vantage point of several years later, I can look back on my travail, and despite the agony, I was, all the time, saying with the Psalmist: "I believed even when I said: 'I am greatly afflicted.'"

With this newfound faith in my own selfness, there has developed a concomitant faith in others, a belief in and an ability to see and recognize in mankind a huge potential for goodness and growth in maturity, in spite of mistakes, failures, unlikableness, and the many other common, negative human characteristics. Escorting this feeling of belief in others, there is a still-growing confidence in a knowledgeable and directing Providence, truly present in the turmoil of today and in the uncertainty of tomorrow. Dickens' observation in *A Tale of Two Cities* that "It was the best of times; it was the worst of times" will be valid always, somewhere, sometime throughout the world.

As individuals, it is only by expanding on the "best" in us that we can hope to reduce the "worst" in us—and in the world.

No man can live without some kind of hope. When the security-giving sense of hope is gone, so, for all practical purposes, life is gone and a happy, productive living of that life.

Hopelessness is a particular danger to the emotionally disturbed person because the vacuum, created by the departure of hope, is readily filled with anxiety and depression.

Hope, it should be noted, always comes from without, from another person who is willing to help, to share, to accept, to believe, to support, to understand, and to help rekindle the dormant spark of hopefulness. This is what takes place in any successful therapy. Gradually, the patient places his trust and confidence in the therapist. By the same token, the patient learns to trust himself, to have confidence in himself. Eventually, he begins to trust and confide in others, and in life as it is, without any fear of damage to his own now healthy and solid self-image.

Basically, as I see it, therapy is founded on a philosophy of giving "hope to the hopeless."

For the religiously orientated person, there may be a need for a greater-than-human hope. Having gone through therapy, he may find that he needs something more than a resolution of his inner conflicts and a "coming to terms" with them. Usually, the therapist is limited in this regard because he, as a professional in the area of human emotions, can give only a human hope and, quite possibly, the basis for another kind of hope.

The clergyman-counselor who has a strong hope in himself, as well as in others, can, with these qualities, prepare the client for the reception of an immanent and transcendent hope, a hope that is not a "thing," or an "it," but, rather, a Person.

This, I presume, is what St. Thomas had in mind when he said "grace supposes nature." But that particular human nature must be emotionally healthy before grace (the Person) can work effectively in and through the individual.

Paul Tillich says much the same thing when he observes that the Holy Spirit works not only in the conscious mind, but in the subconscious mind, which is the very area where the dynamics of hidden conflicts distort and depress the human personality.

The clergyman-counselor can greatly assist a client in the acquisition of this personalized "hope beyond hope," a hope of which St. Paul spoke when he said: ". . . hope was *the* lesson that you learned from that truth-giving message of the gospel." (I Col. 4–6.)

As faith and hope are revived in therapy, whether on the natural or supernatural level, there is brought forth the inherent and necessary ability to love and to be loved. I shall not attempt to define love because it is such a huge word in its implications and so elastic in its application. Besides, all the great minds of the world—poets, philosophers, psychiatrists, and saints—have been able to utter only a few vain words by way of clarifying it. It means so many different things for so many different people. Nonetheless, no matter how defined, it does include the *trust* of faith and the *freedom* of hope. When anyone, especially the neurotic, begins to *trust* in himself and in others; when he feels *free* of the shackles of anxiety and depression, automatically he wants to love, that is, to serve others in a spontaneous variety of ways, and to feel, in turn, that he is loved, worthwhile, serviceable, purposeful, needed.

Only when he feels and expresses these mature aspects of love is he really growing into his real self. Perhaps this is what cartoonist Schulz had in mind when he has Linus say to Charlie Brown, after all the gang has pitched in and beautifully decorated his emaciated Christmas tree: "Nothing grows unless you really love it."

Most certainly it was what St. John meant when he said: "In this is charity: not as though we had loved God, but because He has first loved us . . ." (I Jn. 4:9). And it surely is what Christ meant when He tells us: "As the Father has loved me, I also have loved you. Abide in my love." (Jn. 15:9.)

Love, therefore, even within the very limited comments I have made upon it, should appear to be a most necessary ingredient of any successful therapy. "Nothing grows unless you love it" can apply to many things and to many aspects of personality growth. For example, in order to fulfill the Second Great Commandment, which orders us to "Love thy neighbor as thyself," the guilt-ridden person must first be taught how to forgive and love himself, despite his mistakes, sins, failures, and every other imperfection. Only then can he be changed from an unconscious "self-centeredness" to a healthy and responsive "other-centeredness." Only then can he begin to accept the "unlikable" others and to embark on a search for something good, wholesome, and worthwhile in them, and to devise ways and means of bringing these into existence.

Much more could be said about the natural and supernatural aspects of faith, hope, and love that are involved in the therapeutic encounter. I do not feel qualified to go much farther except to observe that, at least in my own particular case, I had to go through that "Triple Absolution" several times since release from the hospital. But now, with the lessons learned from the Book of Job, it has become a "Double Absolution," the forgiveness of myself and others.

As far as memory serves me, I call to mind frequently all those persons, past and present who, unwittingly or not, have injured me emotionally. I call them into my presence, talk with them, forgive and absolve them, and then go on to a recollection of their good qualities. On many such occasions, it seems as though I can feel the virus of hostility drain out of me. Better still, after each absolution, I feel a growing sense of freedom, a freedom from the enslaving past, and a freedom to forgive any such persons in the future. "They," the "outer environment," as Dr. Low would say, no longer control my emotional life, although I am not without strong emotions. By absolving others, however, I find that I can absolve myself. It is a most encouraging feeling and thereby prompts repetition.

The "Third Absolution" may be necessary for people with a religious background and who are in therapy. Very often in counseling, I have uncovered an anger toward God in persons who were totally unaware of it, but who suffered from the unconscious guilt that accompanies this attitude. Sometimes it prevents them from attending church services. As a priest-counselor, it has been a joyful experience to help a person to realize this guilt and to relieve him of it. As a follow-up, however, I ask such a person to read the Book of Job carefully and discuss it in future sessions. Invariably, the person is greatly relieved of guilt in this area and is more ready to delve into other sources of anxiety.

To the surprise of many who have known of my painful experiences while at the Institute of Living, my several return visits have never revived any nightmarish memories or fears. On the contrary, these visits and recollections of what I once was, have served to strengthen and support me, because I can see that the hospital with its particularized treatment of me, gave me what I needed, rather than that which my childish emotions had demanded upon entrance.

For my own welfare, the hospital had to administer the sometimes horrible-tasting medicine of disillusionment—the disillusionment of childish needs, of adolescent ignorance, of neurotic escapes and defenses, of puerile hostility, of impossible idealism, and of the exaggerated demands of the super-ego. Literally, I had to go back to school, to the kindergarten and grammar school of the emotional life, in order to see myself honestly and realistically.

This basic reeducation is an ongoing process and still needs much study and continual application. But it has prepared me to face the varied and unsuspected challenges of life without undue fear, to accept mistakes and failures without anxiety and, perhaps best of all, this emotional education has enabled me to relax in laughter at myself and to rejoice in the multiplicity of rewards that come, almost automatically, to those who dedicate themselves to the service of others.

Psychotherapy and religion, I have concluded, should walk hand in hand. Each has so much to offer the other. Both have contributed in giving me an ever-expanding love for life.